Letters That Paul Did Not Write

The Epistle to the Hebrews
and the Pauline Pseudepigrapha

by
Raymond F. Collins

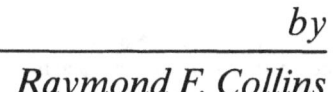

Wipf & Stock
PUBLISHERS
Eugene, Oregon

About the Author

Raymond F. Collins has been Professor of New Testament studies at the Catholic University of Leuven, Louvain, Belgium, since 1971. Among his most recent contributions to New Testament scholarship are: *Introduction to the New Testament* (Garden City, Doubleday, 1983); *Studies on the First Letter to the Thessalonians* (Louvain, University Press, 1984); and *Christian Morality: Biblical Foundations* (Notre Dame, University Press, 1986). A priest of the Providence, Rhode Island, diocese, Fr. Collins has served as a visiting professor at the Andover-Newton Theological School and at the University of Notre Dame. He has lectured in Europe, Asia and Africa, as well as in the United States and Canada.

Wipf and Stock Publishers
199 W 8th Ave, Suite 3
Eugene, OR 97401

Letters that Paul Did Not Write
The Epistle to the Hebrews and the Pauline Pseudepigrapha
By Collins, Raymond F.
Copyright©1988 by Collins, Raymond F.
ISBN: 1-59752-487-5
Publication date: 12/19/2005
Previously published by Michael Glazier, 1988

*"Whatever you do, in word or deed,
do everything in the name of the Lord Jesus,
giving thanks to God the Father through him."
(Col. 3:17)*

Table of Contents

Abbreviations 9

Foreword 15

    1. The Epistle to the Hebrews 19
    2. Ancient Writers 57
    3. The Pastoral Epistles 88
    4. To the Ephesians 132
    5. The Epistle to the Colossians 171
    6. The Second Epistle to the Thessalonians 209
    7. The Pauline Pseudepigrapha 242

Glossary of Terms 265

Bibliography 273

Index of Scripture References 311

Index of Names 323

Abbreviations

In addition to the standard abbreviations that are used for biblical references, the following abbreviations will occasionally be used:

ALGHJ	Arbeiten zur Literatur und Geschichte des hellenistichen Jüdentums
AnBib	Analecta Biblica
Asc. Isa.	Ascension of Isaiah
ASNU	Acta seminarii neotestamentici upsaliensis
ATR	*Anglican Theological Review*
AUSS	*Andrews University Seminary Studies*
AuV	Auslegung und Verkundigung
Barn.	Epistle of Barnabas
BeO	*Bibbia e oriente*
Bhr	Bibliothèque historique des réligions
BHT	Beiträge zur historischen Theologie
Bib	*Biblica*
BibS(F)	Biblische Studien (Freiburg)
BJRL	*Bulletin of the John Rylands University Library*
BLit	*Bibel und liturgie*
BTB	*Biblical Theology Bulletin*

BWANT	Beiträge zur Wissenschaft vom Alten und Neuen Testament
BZ	*Biblische Zeitschrift*
CBQ	*Catholic Biblical Quarterly*
CGNTC	Cambridge Greek New Testament Commentary
1 Clem.	1 Clement
CMCNEB	The Cambridge Bible Commentary on the New English Bible
CNT	Commentaire du Nouveau Testament
Did.	Didache
DS	*Enchiridion symbolorum definitionum et declarationum de rebus fidei et morum*, ed. by Henricus Denziger and Adolphus Schönmetzer (34th ed.: Barcelona, Herder, 1987).
DBSup	*Dictionaire de la Bible, Supplément*
EB	Etudes bibliques
EKK	Evangelisch-katholischer Kommentar zum Neuen Testament
Ep.	Epistola
EpR	*Epworth Review*
ET	English Translation
EvQ	*Evangelical Quarterly*
EvT	*Evangelische Theologie*
ExpTim	*Expository Times*
FRLANT	Forschungen zur Religion und Literatur des Alten und Neuen Testaments
FTS	Frankfürter theologische Studien
GBS	Guides to Biblical Scholarship
Gen. Rab.	Genesis Rabbah
GNC	A Good News Commentary
GNS	Good News Studies
GTJ	*Grace Theological Journal*
HibJ	*Hibbert Journal*

HKNT	Handkommentar zum Neuen Testament
HNT	Handbuch zum Neuen Testament
HNTC	Harper's New Testament Commentaries
HTKNT	Herders theologische Kommentar zum Neuen Testament
HUT	Hemeneutische Untersüchungen zur Theologie
IBS	Irish Biblical Studies
ICC	International Critical Commentary
IDBSup	Interpreter's Dictionary of the Bible, Supplementary volume
IlRev	Iliff Review
ITQ	Irish Theological Quarterly
JB	Jerusalem Bible
JBL	Journal of Biblical Literature
JSNT	Journal for the Study of the New Testament
JTS	Journal of Theological Studies
Jub.	Jubilees
KEK	Kritisch-exegetische Kommentar über das Neue Testament
LD	Lectio Divina
LTP	Laval théologique et philosophique
ModChurch	Modern Churchman
MaTS	Marburger theologische Studien
MuTS	Münchener theologische Studien
NAB	New American Bible
NCB	New Century Bible
NEB	New English Bible
NICNT	New International Commentary on the New Testament
NovT	Novum Testamentum
NovTSup	Novum Testamentum, Supplements
NTAbh	Neutestamentliche Abhandlungen

NTD	Das Neue Testament Deutsch
NTL	New Testament Library
NTM	New Testament Message
NTS	*New Testament Studies*
OBO	Orbis biblicus et orientalis
OTL	Old Testament Library
PG	Patrologia Graeca
Phil.	Polycarp, Letter to the Philippians
PL	Patrologia Latina
QD	Quaestiones disputatae
1QH	Thanksgiving Hymns from Qumran Cave 1
1QpHab	Commentary (*pesher*) on Habakkuk from Qumran Cave 1
1QS	Rule of the Community (*serek*) from Qumran Cave 1
11QMelch	Melchizedek text from Qumran Cave 11
RE	*Realencyclopädie für protestantische Theologie und Kirche*
ResQ	*Restoration Quarterly*
RevExp	*Review and Expositor*
RGG	*Religion in Geschichte und Gegenwart*
RHPR	*Révue d'histoire et de philosophie réligieuses*
RivB	*Rivista Biblica*
RNT	Regensburger Neues Testament
RoczTeolKan	*Roczniki Teologiczno-Kanoniczne*
RSV	Revised Standard Version
SB	Sources bibliques
SBL	Society of Biblical Literature
SBLDS	Society of Biblical Literature Dissertation Series
SBS	Stüttgarter Bibelstudien
SBT	Studies in Biblical Theology

SD	Studies and Documents
SNTS	Society for New Testament Studies
SNTSMS	Society for New Testament Studies, Monograph Series
STANT	Studien zum Alten und Neuen Testament
StTh	*Studia theologica*
SUNT	Studien zur Umwelt des Neuen Testaments
SWJT	*Southwestern Journal of Theology*
TBT	*The Bible Today*
TD	*Theology Digest*
ThEd	*Theological Education*
THKNT	Theologischer Handkommentar zum Neuen Testament
T.Jud.	Testament of Judah
T.Levi	Testament of Levi
TLZ	*Theologische Literaturzeitung*
TSK	*Theologische Studien und Kritiken*
TU	*Texte und Untersuchungen*
TZ	*Theologische Zeitschrift*
TZT	*Tübinger Zeitschrift für Theologie*
VE	*Vox Evangelica*
WBC	Word Biblical Commentary
WdF	Weg der Forschung
WUNT	Wissenschaftliche Untersuchungen zum Neuen Testament
ZAW	*Zeitschrift für die alttestamentliche Wissenschaft*
ZNW	*Zeitschrift für die neutestamentliche Wissenschaft*
ZTK	*Zeitschrift für Theologie und Kirche*

Foreword

In recent years an increasing number of single-volume commentaries on the epistles of Paul have commented upon only seven of the letters found in the New Testament, namely the epistle to the Romans, the two epistles to the Corinthians, the epistle to the Galatians, the epistle to the Philippians, the first epistle to the Thessalonians, and the epistle to Philemon. A tendency to restrict a commentary on Paul to these seven letters alone is also present in some of the more popular literature on the New Testament.

Those who have closely followed recent developments in New Testament scholarship are not surprised by the appearance of this new form of literature. They are well aware that, at various times during the past two centuries, different scholars have called into question the Pauline authorship of the remaining seven Pauline epistles in the New Testament, that is, the epistle to the Ephesians, the epistle to the Colossians, the second epistle to the Thessalonians, both the first and second epistles to Timothy, the epistle to Titus, and the epistle of Paul to the Hebrews.

Although the questioning first began in radical critical circles it has become, by the present time, rather common in all exegetical circles. Every serious interpreter of the New Testament text must at least deal with the possibility that these seven works were not written by Paul. As a result, virtually everyone who interprets the New Testament in a scholarly fashion at the present time groups Romans, 1-2 Corinthians, Galatians, Philippians, 1 Thessalonians, and Philemon together as the indisputably Pauline works. Scholars do this even when they might personally hold that 2 Thessalonians and Colossians, for example, were written by Paul the apostle. They have to recognize that not all scholars share their opinion on the matter.

It is these developments in biblical scholarship which have led to the publication of commentaries on Paul's epistles which, in fact, comment only on the indisputably Pauline letters. A person who is not an expert in the field of Pauline interpretation may well ask "what about the other letters?" "Are they of little importance or are they to be abandoned altogether?" I have written this book in an attempt to answer these questions. The book is not intended for scholars. It is intended for students of the New Testament who want to know what happened to the other letters, why this has happened, and what does all of this mean at the present time. The book presumes that the reader is generally familiar with Paul's letters. My suggestion is that each of the disputed epistles be reread before the reader of these pages turns to the chapter which deals with the respective epistle.

The sequence of chapters in this book might well strike the uninitiated reader as a bit strange. The rationale for the ordering of the chapters is relatively simple and reflects, moreover, my personal academic journey. The book treats the disputed epistles in an order of which reflects the weight of scholarly judgment denying or questioning of the Pauline authorship of each of these texts. Thus it deals with Hebrews before the pastorals, and with the pastorals before Ephesians, Colossians, and 2 Thessalonians.

In the five chapters devoted individually to these epistles, I am offering my readers a brief historical overview of the development of exegetical opinion on the issue of authorship. Having surveyed the field, I then present the most serious reasons cited by scholars in their determination that one or another epistle was not written by Paul. Hebrews stands in a category all by itself since it does not claim to have been written by Paul. Its christology is singularly important. Accordingly, I have begun this book with a study of the christology of Hebrews, an approach that subsequently allows me to dwell briefly upon the christology of the other disputed texts.

Despite its title, the subject of this book is really not the denial of the Pauline authorship of seven books in the New Testament. The subject of this book is the significance of these books in themselves. The second chapter briefly reviews the religious and cultural conditions within which these books were written, thereby elucidating their origins somewhat. The non-Pauline origin of these seven books raises a host of issues for believers, the churches, and exegetes themselves. The final chapter of this book addresses itself to some of these issues.

Brevity is a characteristic of this work. As I wrote it, I experienced no little frustration in limiting my words. Were I to have done justice to the various authors' thoughts on the Lord Jesus Christ and the life which develops because one believes in him, I should have written so much more. Yet I felt constrained to be brief in order that the entire issue of the Pauline pseudepigrapha be treated in a single volume. Concern for brevity has also led me to limit the bibliographies at the end of each chapter to a few titles written in English.

I can only hope that my brevity has not brought confusion to a consideration of topics that are admittedly highly complex. My real hope is that these reflections help the reader to better understand the sacred page. To the extent that my hope is realized, the true significance of Paul the apostle for the life of the church will be appreciated all the more.

1

The Epistle to the Hebrews

When, in 1546, the Council of Trent decreed that the list of sacred books included fourteen letters of the apostle Paul and that this list included the epistle to the Hebrews (DS 1503) the Council fathers were echoing a tradition which they thought needed to be reiterated in light of the fact that Martin Luther had relegated the epistle to the Hebrews, along with the letters of James and Jude and the book of Revelation, to an appendix in his recently published German translation of the Bible. The fact that tensions within the church during the sixteenth century led the Council fathers to echo earlier tradition is not at all surprising; what is surprising is that tradition included an epistle to the Hebrews among "the epistles of Paul the apostle."

At no place within the text of Hebrews does the epistle claim to have been written by Paul, and in no place does it say that it was written to Hebrews. The lack of this information is principally due to the fact that the epistle to the Hebrews does not begin in the same way as do the other letters of Paul the apostle. Each of these letters begins with a greeting which is reminiscent of the greetings typically found in the personal letters of ancient Hellenistic writers. Usually they begin with a mention of the person or persons who were sending the letter, an indication of those to whom the letter was being sent, and a standard greeting. The first words of ancient Hellenistic letters went something like "Thomas to James, greetings." Paul began the first of his letters in this fashion when he wrote "Paul, Silvanus and Timothy to the church of the Thessalonians, grace to you and peace." The epistle to the Hebrews, however, lacks the standard epistolary opening. In its place is to be found a rather formal prologue which speaks of the revelation of God through his son (Heb 1:1-4). In length, this prologue is comparable to the prologue of the Gospel according to Luke (Luke 1:1-4), but its content inevitably prompts comparison with the prologue of the Fourth Gospel (John 1:1-18). Both the prologue to the Fourth Gospel and the prologue to the Hebrews present a vision of the Pre-existent one who has come into the world as a Revealer beyond compare with earlier prophetic figures.

The absence of the standard epistolary greeting from the beginning of the epistle to the Hebrews means that this is the only one of the fourteen letters traditionally attributed to Paul which does not explicitly claim Pauline authorship. In fact, the name of the apostle is never mentioned in the epistle. One might easily assume that the mention of "our brother Timothy," recently released from prison (Heb 13:23), is a reference to the long-time companion of Paul and draw the conclusion that the epistle was written by Paul. Such an assumption might be easily made, but it might be made all too quickly. Timothy was not an uncommon name in antiquity. Christians commonly referred to one another as brother and sister (see 1 Cor 9:5, for example). Thus, it is not demonstrably certain that the Timothy of Heb 13:23 is the same individual as the companion of Paul whose name appears in 1 Thess 1:1. Even if both texts were making reference to the same person, one must remember that it is hardly likely that Paul would have been the only early Christian to refer to Timothy as "our brother." Paul was wont to call Timothy "our brother" (see 1 Thess 3:2), but the language was hardly restricted to Paul alone. Indeed in the opening of each of the letters to Timothy, Timothy is called "my child" rather than "our brother" (1 Tim 1:2; 2 Tim 1:2; cf. 1 Cor 4:17). So much for the familial metaphor.

The fact that the traditional letter formulary is absent from the beginning of the epistle to the Hebrews also means that those for whom the text was intended are not indicated at the beginning of the document, as is the case with all of the other letters in the Pauline corpus of the New Testament. "To the

Hebrews" was added as a superscription or title of the text at some time during the late second century when it had become customary for Christians to identify some of their significant texts by means of a reference to those for whom they had been originally intended. At that time Paul's letter to the Romans was given the title "To the Romans," but Paul's own words were "to all God's beloved in Rome, who are called to be saints" (Rom 1:6). The practice of providing titles for revered Christian writings proved to be very useful as the Christian scriptures came to be collected together and "published" in the form of scrolls and codices. By means of these titles one work could be easily distinguished from another.

Thus, the title "To the Hebrews" is a useful addition by a second-century indexer, but it offers no real clue as to the identity of those for whom the epistle was originally intended. As a matter of fact, the word "Hebrew" occurs only three times in the entire New Testament. Twice Paul uses it to express pride in his Hebrew heritage (Phil 3:5; 2 Cor 11:22); once Luke uses it to indicate a group of Christian Jews (Acts 6:1). This group of Jewish believers were in tension with another group of believing Jews, the "Hellenists," who complained that the former were not sufficiently sympathetic to their needs for social welfare, specifically the needs of their widows. Apparently the "Hellenists" were a group of Christian Jews who spoke Greek, while the "Hebrews" were Christian Jews who spoke Hebrew (perhaps Aramaic) and who remained fiercely loyal to the temple and its cult.

A Homily

Since, then, the epistle to the Hebrews does not begin as a letter would normally be expected to begin, it lacks both the name of its author and an indication of its intended recipients at the outset. One might then ask whether the absence of the formal epistolary opening is an indication that the text is not really a letter at all. While Christian tradition has long called the document a letter, the text itself does not claim letter status. As it begins it doesn't even look like a letter. Then, towards the end of the text, the author describes what he has written as a "word of exhortation" (*logos tēs paraklēseōs:* Heb 13:22). In Greek, "word" (*logos*) ordinarily means a word, but it was also used to describe a saying, a story, a speech or an address. As a matter of fact, one who reads the text of Hebrews without the presupposition that it is a letter readily gets the impression that it is a discourse or the text of a speech. While letters, especially long letters, normally treat of different topics, there seems to be a single sustained argument that is developed in Hebrews. Moreover, the author frequently emphasizes his point by making reference to what he has "said" or is about to "say" (Heb 2:5; 5:11; 6:9; 8:1; 9:5). This is particularly clear in 5:11 where we read "about this we have much to say which is hard to explain" (*peri ou polus hēmin ho logos kai dusermēneutos legein*), when a letter-writer more likely would have written "about this we have much to write" (cf.1 Thess 4:9). Even the use of the plural "we" (5:11, and in 2:5 and 6:9) gives the impression of an orator's style.

The reader's initial impression that the text was originally intended for oral delivery rather than written transmission is confirmed by scholarly study of the text's style, vocabulary and content. Its style closely resembles that of the homilies preached in the synagogues of first-century Judaism, particularly the Hellenistic synagogues of the Jewish diaspora. We can recognize some stylistic similarity between Hebrews and Stephen's speech in Acts 7 or Philo of Alexandria's allegorical commentaries on Genesis. Given the internal consistency of the text and the positive results of comparative analysis, most of today's scholars consider that Hebrews is essentially a carefully constructed sermon. Its literary genre is that of the homily rather than that of the letter.

As a matter of fact, the only part of Hebrews that clearly calls to mind the epistolary form consists of a few verses that come at the very end of the text (Heb 13:19, 22-25). Since Paul's letters frequently end with a blessing, somewhat reminiscent of the Aaronic blessing of Num 6:24-26, one might be tempted to include the final blessing of the "epistle" to the Hebrews as part of its epistolary conclusion. The fact of the matter seems to be, however, that final blessings were the natural conclusion to homilies preached in the synagogue. If Paul's letters conclude with a benediction (e.g. 1 Thess 5:23), it is because he intended that his letters be read aloud to a group of Christians who had assembled together (see 1 Thess 5:27) and so borrowed from an existing liturgical practice as he brought his letters to an end. Paul's epistolary benedictions were an adaptation of the homiletic practice. Moreover, the style of the benediction found in Heb 13: 20-21 is typical of Hellenistic liturgical style, though the content of the blessing has been adapted in such a way as to be in conformity with the major developments of thought within the text.

The fact that the so-called epistle to the Hebrews is not really a letter but a homily sheds light upon some of the salient features of the text. The interchange between the expository and the exhortatory sections (Heb 2:1-4; 3:7-4:3; 6:4-8; 10:26-39; 12:25-29) of the text has long been recognized as one of its most striking features. In the light of the identification of the text as a homily, the purpose of this interchange comes into a more distinct focus. The author-homilist has attempted to draw from his dogmatic exposition motivation for the community which he was addressing. The use of the first person plural in the paraenesis or moral exhortation (e.g. 2:1; 4:11) and the vocative form of address (e.g. "holy brethren," *adelphoi hagioi*: 3:1) reflect the style of the orator and preacher. These are essentially rhetorical devices. The manner in which the sacred scriptures are exploited recalls that of Judaism's homiletic midrash, its way of using and explaining the scriptures in a homiletic context. Even such passages as 6:4-8, 10:26-31, and 12:16-17 which proclaim that there is no possibility of repentance from apostasy take on new meaning in the light of the fact that we are reading a homily. Homilies tend to exaggerate and make use of the device of hyperbole. It is of the nature of a homily to appeal to the emotions; the homily shares something of the function of *pathos* in Hellenistic rhetoric. The preacher's need to encourage and his call for conversion preclude the nuance and fine sense of distinction that are characteristic of the legal document and the theological treatise.

Its Theme

Most homilies have one major theme. This would seem to be the case with the "epistle" to the Hebrews. Its theme is Jesus the High Priest. (Oscar Cullmann; David L. Mealand; Paul Andriessen). This theme is carefully developed in a pattern of concentric presentations until it reaches its climax in the exposition of 7:1-10:18, where it is set off amidst two paraenetic sections (5:11-6:20 and 10:19-39). Indeed, the author's christological focus is manifest from the very opening of his exposition, as his formal prologue concentrates on the Son:

> In many and various ways God spoke of old to our fathers by the prophets; but in these last days he has spoken to us by a Son, whom he appointed the heir of all things, through whom also he created the world.
> He reflects the glory of God and bears the very stamp of his nature,
> upholding the universe by his word of power.
> When he had made purification for sins,
> he sat down at the right hand of the Majesty on high,
> having become as much superior to the angels
> as the name he has obtained is more excellent than theirs.
> (Heb 1:1-4)

Some authors (e.g. Jack T. Sanders, J.D.G. Dunn, Reinhard Deichgräber, and George W. Buchanan) believe that these verses are part of an early Christian hymn, whose wisdom motifs, especially in the allusions to Wis 7:25 and Ps 110:1, relate it to such other early Christian hymn material as is to be found in Col 1:15-17 and John 1:1-3, but set it off from the rest of the epistle to the Hebrews where nothing else is to be found which can be readily called "Wisdom Christology." According to this train of thought, the author of Hebrews would have considered it particularly useful to appropriate this hymn fragment because of the reminiscence of Ps 110:1 ("sit at my right hand") in verse 3. Rabbinic tradition (see the *Yalkut ha Makiri* on Ps 110) had used Psalm 110 in reference to

Abraham and the Messiah, for whom a throne was to be prepared (Isa 16:5), while the same psalm had come to acquire capital importance in the scriptural apologetic of early Christianity.

Other authors, however, (for example, Otto Michel, Leopold Sabourin and John P. Meier) dispute the notion that the author of Hebrews has made use of borrowed hymnic material for his prologue. With regard to the prologue's formal style, they take note of the relationship between the prologue and other poetic passages in the text (e.g. Heb 4:12-13; 7:3). As far as its content is concerned, this second group of authors suggests that the author of Hebrews was quite capable of developing such thoughts. Ps 110:1 functions almost as a refrain throughout the sermon, recurring at 1:3; 5:5-6; 7:17; 8:1 and 10:13, while the author frequently capitalizes on the title of Son as he develops his Christological exposition (Heb 3:6; 4:14; 5:8; 6:6; 7:3, 28; 10:29.).

While acknowledging that there are substantial reasons for suggesting that the author of Hebrews might well have made use of a previous composition, the commentator must interpret the text of the prologue as it presently exists. Its four verses serve the author's purpose well since they offer a potentially powerful presentation of the subject of his homily. The development of thought proceeds in two major movements, whose essential unity is underscored insofar as both movements of thought are expressed in one sentence in the original Greek text of Heb 1:1-4.

The first movement of thought (vv.1-2), with God as its object, provides a broad theological perspective for the exposition which is to follow. God is the Revealer, the Creator, and the Consummator. The thought is developed antithetically, as the past and those who lived in it ("of old to our fathers") are contrasted with the present and those who live in it ("in these last days ... to us"), and the many ("in many and various ways ... the prophets") are contrasted with the one ("a Son ... the heir"). These contrasts serve to highlight the singularity and the superiority of the Son (*huios*), whose role in the consummation and creation of all things is already set forth.

The second movement of thought focuses on the Son

himself (vv.3-4). Whereas the verbs of verses 1-2 all had God as their subject, all the verbs of verses 3-4 relate to the Son, but each of these verbs occurs in dependent clauses. Initially three participial clauses (1."reflects" and "bears" [the Greek text uses one participle "*ōn,*" literally "being," to suggest the idea which is rendered in English by these two verbs in the RSV]; 2."upholding;" 3."had made") present the Son as sharing in the divine nature, as having a providential role in the sustenance of the universe, and as having atoned for sin. Thus qualified, the Son is presented as having sat at the right hand of God, in fulfillment of Ps 110:1 (see Ps 110:5). A participial clause affirms the superiority of the Son over the angels. Then the prologue reaches its climax on the note of the more excellent name received by the Son. The Greek text is, in fact, so arranged that the last word in the prologue, the one upon which the emphasis lies, is "name."

The more excellent name conferred upon the Son is precisely that—he is the Son. Among the ancient Semites, a name was far more than the somewhat arbitrary identification tag that it is in our contemporary Western culture. Even if he or she had been able to speak English, the ancient Jew could never say, as did Shakespeare, that "a rose by any other name would smell as sweet," nor would he or she understand how a name can be changed by means of a relatively simple judicial process. For the ancients a name indicated status, dignity, and function. Since it suggested status and dignity, it was possible to speak of a higher name and a lower name. A name also suggests relationships with others. Thus, as he begins the exposition in which the significance of the name of the Son will gradually unfold, the author of the epistle to the Hebrews focuses on two significant relationships enjoyed by the Son, his relationship with the angels and his relationship with humans.

The Son and the Angels

The Son's relationship with the angels is set out in a catena of scriptural passages (Heb 1:5-14), which pick up on the opening thought of the prologue, God who speaks (cf. 1:1, 5, 6,

7). The seven passages which have been cited, all but one taken from the psalms, are Ps 2:7; 2 Sam 7:14; Ps 97:7; 104:4; 45:7-8; 102:26-28; and 110:1. The first two citations are taken from Ps 2:7 ("You are my son, today I have begotten you") and 2 Sam 7:14 ("I will be his father, and he shall be my son"). These two quotations are linked together by means of the catchword "Son." These two verses of the Bible were classic in early Christian scriptural apologetic, precisely because they focused on the expectation of a son. In Hebrews, the two scriptures are linked together by means of a catchword, "Son." The use of catchwords, (the *gezerah shavah* principle) was one of the typical ways which Jewish rabbis used to bring scriptural passages together and thus develop a theme. By citing Ps 2:7, the author of Hebrews has made use of an enthronement formula, which he "explains" in rabbinic fashion by adducing the prophecy of Nathan (2 Sam 7:14). The idea of enthronement relates back to verse 2 with its idea that the Son has been "appointed" (*ethēken*), and suggests that the basic christological schema of Hebrews will be that of exaltation. One might also note that, by means of its reflection on the inheritance of the Son, verse 2 has made allusion to Ps 2:8.

With verse 6, the author introduces the notion of the presentation of the Son to the world. He is called the firstborn (*prōtotokos*), a title which was particularly significant in the Jewish world, especially because of the importance of the inheritance rights of the firstborn son. The enthronement idea is continued in verses 8-9, where the citation of Ps 45:7 implicitly affirms the divinity of Jesus—one of the rare times in the New Testament where Jesus is called "God" (*theos*; comp. 1:3; 3:4; see John 1:1; 20:28). The image of the enthroned Son allows the author to affirm that the angels worship him. The biblical tradition may well have designated the angels as "sons of God" (e.g. Ps 29:1; Job 1:6; 2:1; 38:7; and 1 Enoch 6:2; 13:8; 14:3; 101:1; perhaps Gen 6:2-4), but the Son is not merely one son among others, he is the firstborn and merits the worship due to the one who is enthroned forever. This reflection may have come about as a reaction to the community's tendency towards angel worship, a phenomenon not unknown in early Christian circles (see esp.Col 1:15-16; 2:18, but also Gal 3:19).

In the author's vision of things, the angels have been created as ministering servants; they do not sit upon the throne as does the Son. The author proclaims the superiority of Jesus, up to now identified only as the Son, over the angels. Then, after an interlude devoted to the unchangeability of God, the author returns to Ps 110:1 (v.13), the text to which the poem had made reference in verse 3. His manner of returning to the text with which he began is quite in keeping with rabbinic expository techniques, but it also demonstrates the author's literary artistry. He has formed the different scriptural passages into a single unit by means of a ring construction (or *inclusio*).

Psalm 110 is one of the Bible's greatest exaltation psalms; it is cited more than thirty times in the New Testament alone. The fuller citation of its first verse in Heb 1:13 (as compared with the brief allusion in v.3) intimates some idea of Christian hope since it professes the view that the enemies of the Son are to be conquered. Hope will prove to be a major theme of the epistle to the Hebrews, as will be the notion that the Son is priest forever according to the order of Melchizedek, a rather curious idea that occurs in the fourth verse of Ps 110.

The Son and His Brothers

After his magnificent proclamation, woven of scriptural citations, of the superiority of the Son over the angels, the author tips his preacher's hand by inserting an admonition (2:1-4) before continuing his exposition. He returns to his exposition in 2:5-18, where four scriptural passages (Ps 8:4-6; 22:22; Isa 8:17, 18) form the heart of his presentation. The three-verse citation of Psalm 8 in Heb 2:6-8 is one of the longest scriptural citations in the entire epistle to the Hebrews. It is linked to the earlier catena by means of two verbal links, "angels" and "under his feet." In the Psalter, Psalm 8 reflects on the creation of the human being, but the author of Hebrews comments on Psalm 8 in such a way as to make reference to Jesus, identified for the first time by his proper name in verse 9. His manner of commenting on the psalm is quite traditional. He has chosen to explicate some specific phrases in the psalm—a rabbinic procedure sometimes known as distributive exegesis—and has given an actualizing interpretation to the biblical text. His midrashic exposition interprets the text not in reference to its original utterance in the historical past, but in reference to its significance for the present—and the author's present is dominated by the Jesus event. Thus, he interprets a "little lower than the angels" with reference to Jesus' suffering, and his being "crowned with glory and honor" with reference to his enthronement (see v.5). While he continues with the theme of the Son's relationship with the angels (vv.7, 9, 16), his main point is to affirm Jesus' solidarity with human beings. Three times the author underscores Jesus' solidarity with other human beings: "...he who sanctifies and those who are sanctified all have one origin (v.11) ... he himself likewise partook of the same nature (v.14) ... made like his brethren in every respect" (v.17) It is this concern which permits him to refer to Jesus, for the first time, by means of his ordinary human name—Jesus (v.9), the name of the man who walked the lanes of Galilee and the streets of Jerusalem.

Jesus' solidarity with human beings allows him to be called by a new name, "brother" (v.12; cf.v.17). Recourse to a catena of scriptural citations (Ps 22:22; Isa 8:17, 18), beginning with a passage which not only contains "brother" as a key term, but also introduces cultural imagery into the author's exposition, enables the author to spell out the consequences of Jesus' solidarity. The brothers and sisters of Jesus are children of God (vv.10, 13). Jesus is the pioneer of salvation (*archēgos tēs sōtērias,* v.10).

In a final thought the author of Hebrews brings together the notion of Jesus' solidarity with humankind and his cultic imagery as he portrays Jesus as "a merciful and faithful high priest in the service of God (appointed) to make expiation for the sins of the people" (v.17). In fact, the author's thought has begun to focus on the Day of the Atonement (Yom Kippur), whose ritual (see Lev 16:29-34; 23:26; Num 29:7-11) will dominate much of what he is about to say (5:3; 7:27; 9:7). The first part of the rites appointed for the Day of Atonement consisted of the sacrifice of a bull and the sprinkling of its blood on the mercy seat for the expiation of the priest's own sins. This was followed by the sacrifice of a goat and the sprinkling of its blood for the sins of the people. Part two of the ritual was the scapegoat ceremony when the sins of the people were ritually placed on the head of a goat who was then banished to the wilderness. Taking a cue from Amos Wilder's notion that theopoetics is a function of the religious imagination, Paul Minear judges that Heb 2:5-3:6 is an exercise in theopoetics. It relies upon creative imagination (perhaps even a vision) in order to make a theological statement.

The author's use of cultic imagery will continue to dominate his christological exposition. Before continuing with his imaginative presentation of Jesus as priest (4:14), however, and even before entering upon the lengthy paraenesis (3:7-4:11) which Ernst Käsemann thought to have provided the key to the interpretation of the entire text, the author pauses to reflect on the superiority of Jesus, the Son, over Moses. This reflection functions as one of the three major comparisons in Hebrews, comparable to the comparisons between the Son and the angels which has preceded and that between the Son and the Aaronic priesthood which is to follow. The author has chosen to highlight the superiority of Christ over Moses by means of reflection on Num 12:7, a passage which rabbinic tradition had exploited to affirm the superiority of Moses over the angels. Having already demonstrated to his own satisfaction, if not to that of modern exegetes, that the Son is superior to angels, the homilist now demonstrates that the Son is even superior to Moses himself (comp.Gal 3:19; 2 Cor 3:7-18). He affirms that Moses was a faithful servant over God's household (his people), but that Jesus is faithful as a Son. The Jesus whom Christian faith confesses to be an apostle (that is, one who has been sent) and high priest is the faithful servant over God's household, which is the community of believers.

In Heb 1:5-3:6, the author of the epistle to the Hebrews has made use of different scriptural passages in such a fashion as to create two major tableaux. The result of his work is that he has presented to his listeners (and those of us who have read his text) an expository diptych at the beginning of his work. The first panel (1:5-14) focuses on the title Son, the major expository theme of the homily. It clearly presents Jesus as God, to such an extent that Heb 1:3, 8 are among the clearest expressions of Jesus' divine status in the entire New Testament. As Son, this panel presents Jesus as far superior to the angels, who are only servants. As Son, Jesus is enthroned and sits at the right hand of God (Ps 110:1). The christology of this panel can be described as an exaltation christology. The method adopted by the author in developing his first tableau essentially consists of the compilation of a catena of scriptural verses.

The second panel (Heb 2:5-18), linked to the first by means of a paraenetic passage (Heb 2:1-4) which serves as a hinge between the two descriptive panels, focuses on the title brother and calls Jesus by his human name. It clearly presents Jesus as a human being, to such an extent that it is frequently observed that no text in the New Testament, except the gospels, is more concerned with the humanity of Jesus than the epistle to the Hebrews (Rudolf Bultmann, Robert H. Strachan, E.F. Scott, James Moffatt, James Dukes, Edwyn C. Hoskyns, and C.N. Davey). This panel presents Jesus as the son who is brother, as a little lower than the angels for a while, and adds, almost as an appendage, that Jesus is even superior to Moses whom contemporary thought judged to be superior to the angels. As brother, Jesus is in solidarity with other human beings and shares their sufferings (2:18). This type of christology might be described as an Adam christology (James D.G. Dunn). The method adopted by the homilist to construct his second christological panel is that of the homiletic midrash on scriptural texts.

Jesus, the High Priest

The second panel of the magnificent christological diptych with which the author of Hebrews begins his homily finished with the theopoetic vision of Jesus as a merciful and faithful high priest in the service of God (2:17). In his subsequent development, the homilist seems to have divided the question. The theme of Jesus' fidelity is picked up in the comparison between Jesus and Moses (3:5-6) and functions as a key element in the great paraenetic interlude of 3:7-4:11. The theme of Jesus the merciful high priest is the object of the expository reflections in 4:14-5:10.

The homilist begins his exposition by recalling the confessional statement that Jesus is a great high priest (4:14), just as he had done in 3:1 ("consider Jesus, the apostle and high priest of our confession"). Jesus' mercy is highlighted in the brief exhortation of 4:14-16. Then the homilist begins to develop his thoughts on priesthood by setting forth the qualifications of those called to the Aaronic priesthood. Every high priest (*pas archiereus*, 5:1), he proclaims, is called to be a mediator before God on behalf of his fellow human beings. Every high priest is bound to be compassionate and to offer sacrifice on behalf of others (at this point the homilist makes reference to the Day of Atonement) because he is one of them in weakness and sin. Every high priest must be appointed to that office by God himself.

Having thus prepared the profile of the high priest, the homilist is ready to show that Jesus fulfilled each of the three conditions for the high priestly office. Jesus was an effective mediator; his human pleas to God had been heard (3:7). Jesus is compassionate because he has suffered (5:8; cf. 4:15). Nonetheless, the homilist's chief concern is to show that Jesus has been appointed high priest by God. He does so by citing two scriptural passages: Ps 2:7, "You are my son, today I have begotten you," and Ps 110:4, "You are a priest forever after the order of Melchizedek," two passages which had been introduced in the scriptural catena of chapter 1. The homilist brings this series of reflections on Jesus' priesthood to a close with the thought that Jesus "became the source of eternal salvation to all who obey him, being designated by God a high priest after the order of Melchizedek" (5:9-10). By returning to the confessional theme of 4:14, the homilist has clearly set off this homiletic development as a distinct unit.

Melchizedek was the ancient Canaanite priest-king of Jerusalem, about whom a brief tale is told in Gen 14:17-24, but who is otherwise not mentioned in the Old Testament except for verse 4 of Ps 110. Early exegetical traditions about him were rather varied. In some circles, he was considered to have been the chief priest. Some rabbis interpreted the pertinent biblical material in such a way that Christians could not use it against them. A small papyrus found in a cave on the northwestern shore of the Dead Sea in 1948 (11 Q Melch) tells about a Melchizedek described as a heavenly redemptive figure associated with the divine judgment at the end of time. Speculation about the role and figure of the relatively obscure Melchizedek seems therefore to have been somewhat common in first-century Judaism. The homilist seems, therefore, to have been generally aware of these traditions, even if it be hardly likely that he actually read the text of 11 Q Melch.

In his first expository reflection on Jesus as the high priest, the homilist calls Jesus "Christ" (5:5) a loan word taken over into English from the Greek (*Christos*, derived from the verb *chriō*, to rub with oil or anoint). The Greek Bible (the LXX or Septuagint) had used this term to translate the Hebrew *Messiah*, literally, the anointed one. According to the Old Testament the high priest was anointed as priest (Lev 4:16). Prior to 5:5 the homilist had used the title "Christ" for Jesus only once before, namely in 3:14, where it suggests Jesus as a heavenly figure ruling over his house. In 5:5 the title continues to suggest Jesus' heavenly status because, as we have seen (1:5), the homilist uses Ps 2:7 to suggest Jesus' exaltation and heavenly enthronement. In short, it seems that the idea suggested by the homilist's use of the Christ title is that of a heavenly priest-king.

As the author begins his expository reflection, however, he indicates that it was "Jesus, the Son of God" who was the great high priest (4:14). Like other first-century Christians the homilist used Jesus' personal name to refer to him as a human being with a personal human history. Consciously the homilist has called Jesus by his human name as he recalls the passion in verse 7 (cf. Matt 26:38-46; 27:46; Mark 15:34). Even more strikingly, however, the homilist seems to bring together his idea of Jesus' sonship and his vision of Jesus' priesthood. When he began this expository reflection on priesthood (4:14), it was the title of Son that he attributed to Jesus. At the end of his exposition (5:8-10), he sets Jesus forth as Son (v.8) and then proclaims that he has been designated by God as high priest according to the order of Melchizedek. It is almost as if the homilist wanted to emphasize the Son-high priest connection by bracketing his entire exposition on Jesus' high priesthood within the Son-high priest framework. Indeed, the scriptural passages which he cites together as the topic for this part of his homiletic reflection focus on sonship (Ps 2:7; verse 5) and priesthood (Ps 110:4; verse 6). Oscar Cullmann has suggested that in the epistle to the Hebrews the ideas of Jesus' sonship and his high priesthood are closely connected. His views in this regard seem to be quite correct. When the homilist was unfolding his panel on Jesus' sonship in chapter one he had used Ps 110:1 to present Jesus as the Son sitting at the right hand of God with his enemies at his feet (1:13; cf.v.3). In 8:1-2 he will develop his earlier idea to show that it is as high priest that Jesus sits at God's right hand, while in 10:12-14 he will indicate that it is because of Jesus' cultic activity that his enemies are to serve as his footstool.

The connection between Jesus the Son and Jesus the high priest deserves further reflection. In the world in which the homilist lived, a name suggested not only dignity and relationships but also one's function. It is well known that among the Jews the title "Son of God" was applied to those who belonged to God and did his will. As a nation Israel was frequently called the son of God (e.g. Deut 1:31; Isa 63:16; Hos 11:1), but even individuals were sometimes called the son of God, as, for example, the king in Ps 89:27 (*T. Levi* 17:2; *T. Jud.* 24:3, as well as the two classic passages appropriated by Christian apologetic, Ps 2:7 and 2 Sam 7:14) or the devout person in Wis 2:13, 18 (Sir 4:10; cf. *Pss. Sol.* 13:9; *Jub.* 19:29). In such passages as these the son of God title was used in a functional and relational sense, rather than in an ontological sense. Among the Jews this type of usage would not have been considered mere metaphor since names implied functions. A son was expected to act like a son, and one who acted like a son could be called a son. Our homilist seems to be spelling out the functional implications of Jesus' sonship as he develops the theme of Jesus, son and high priest.

High Priest According to the Order of Melchizedek

After his initial exposition on the high priesthood (4:14-5:10), the homilist interrupts his expository development to offer another long exhortation (5:11-6:20). In the last section of the exhortation (6:13-20), he focuses his thought on Abraham, the great patriarch of the Jewish people. Abraham is cited as one who had received the promise, confirmed by a divine oath. The homilist sets Abraham forth as a model for the community whom he was addressing (cf. 11:8-12; 17-19). In fact, the homilist is developing his argument rather subtly at this point. He will soon ask his hearers, and us too, to consider just how great Abraham is (7:4). In the meantime, he brings his exhortation to a conclusion with cultic imagery (6:19-20; see Lev 16:2, 12 for references to the tabernacle) and ends with a portrayal of Jesus as high priest forever according to the order of Melchizedek. That is the theme of chapter seven, which serves as the climax and fullest revelation of the homilist's vision of Jesus as the high priest. Interestingly enough, the title of Son which is of such importance in the first seven chapters of Hebrews, where it occurs thirteen times (cf. Heb 1:2, 5 [2x], 8; 2:6; 3:6; 4:14; 5:5, 8; 6:6) including three times in chapter seven (vv. 3, 5, 28), is used by the homilist only one more time after chapter seven (cf. 10:29). It is almost as if, once having explained the functional significance of the Son title, so that his hearers understand that the title of Son implies Jesus' priesthood, the homilist has no need to return explicitly to his keynote theme.

In chapter seven of his homily, however, he brings his exposition of the Son title to a magnificent climax as he waxes eloquently on Jesus as the high priest. The leitmotif of his reflection is obviously Ps 110:4, "The Lord has sworn and he will not change his mind, 'You are a priest forever after the order of Melchizedek,'" which is cited explicitly in verses 3, 11 and 15, and presented, allusively, as the theme verse (technically, the *lemma*) in 6:20. The chief explanatory passage is Gen 14:17-24:

> After his return from the defeat of Ched-or-laomer and the kings who were with him, the king of Sodom went out to meet him at the Valley of Shaveh (that is, the King's Valley). And Melchizedek king of Salem brought out bread and wine; he was priest of God Most High. And he blessed him and said, "Blessed be Abram by God Most High, maker of heaven and earth; and blessed be God Most High, who has delivered your enemies into your hand!" And Abram gave him a tenth of everything. And the king of Sodom said to Abram, "Give me the persons, but take the goods for yourself." But Abram said to the king of Sodom, "I have sworn to the Lord God most high, maker of heaven and earth, that I would not take a thread or a sandal-thong or anything that is yours, lest you should say 'I have made Abram rich.' I will take nothing but what the young men have eaten, and the share of the men who went with me; let Aner, Eshcol and Mamre take their share."

The homilist has introduced the Genesis passage into his reflection by means of the name Melchizedek, which serves as a catchword to link up this scripture with Ps 110:4. André Feuillet, a French exegete, has explained that these two Old Testament passages (Ps 110:4 and Gen 14:17-24)—along with the fourth servant canticle of Deutero-Isaiah (Isa 52:13-53:12, cf.Zech 12:10), a text which Feuillet thinks provided the homilist with the most immediate biblical antecedent for his thoughts on the sacrificial and priestly role of Jesus, even though the only clear allusion to the canticle in the entire homily is to be found in Heb 9:28 (cf.Isa 53:12)—are most significant for the homilist's exposition of the doctrine of the priesthood of Christ. The homilist has cited excerpts from the Genesis narrative in verses 1-2 and 4 of chapter seven, and makes allusion to the explanatory text in verses 7 and 10.

This exposition of Jesus' high priesthood not only brings the homilist's reflections on Jesus' priesthood to a climax; it also sets the stage for him to introduce a third movement of thought on the superiority of Jesus. In chapter one he had presented Jesus as superior to the angels; in chapter five, as superior to Moses; now he will present Jesus as superior to the

Aaronic priesthood. To do so, he will show the superiority of the priesthood of Melchizedek over that of Aaron, all the while showing that the real meaning of the priesthood of Melchizedek is revealed in the priesthood of Jesus. This perspective comes clearly to the fore in verse 3, when the homilist reminds us that Melchizedek resembles the Son of God. His thought proceeds by reflecting on the type and antitype rather than on a present reality and its historical precedent, as would the thought of a modern-day homilist. In Hebrews 7, the homilist proceeds according to usual rabbinic practice as he cites the Genesis story and then comments on it.

The significance of the name continues to occupy the homilist's attention as he focuses on the name Melchizedek (v.2)—popular etymology was a favorite resource in late Judaism's interpretation of the scriptures—but he also reflects on the fact that the scriptures do not relate essential biographical facts about Melchizedek. The Bible does not tell us when Melchizedek was born or when he died, who his mother was or who his father was. With a deft application of the inclusion and exclusion principle (*ribbui u-mu'it*), the homilist is able to exploit the biblical silence as an indication of the permanency of Melchizedek's priesthood (v.3). Then he turns to the heart of his argument (vv.4-9). Since it is obvious that a superior blesses an inferior, Melchizedek who blessed Abraham is obviously superior to him as well as to the hierarchical priesthood descendant from Abraham through Levi. In support of the notion that Melchizedek's priesthood is superior to that of Levi, he adds: "One might even say that Levi himself, who receives tithes, paid tithes through Abraham, for he was still in the loins of his ancestor when Melchizedek met him" (vv.9-10).

Although tradition occasionally regarded Melchizedek as the first priest, it was the permanence of the priesthood ("for ever," *eis ton aiōna*, 6:20 or "continually," *eis to diēnekes*, 7:3) which provides the essential point of the homilist's comparison between the priesthood of Jesus and that of Melchizedek, as well as the essential point of comparison between the Jesus-Melchizedek priesthood and the levitical priesthood. It may well have been timelessness which led the homilist to describe

Jesus as "*high priest* according to the order of Melchizedek" (5:10; 6:20). The scriptures call Melchizedek a priest (*hiereus*); they do not characterize him as a high priest (*archiereus*). The homilist obviously has Jesus in mind when he speaks of the high priest, but the prefix of the Greek term for high priest (*archiereus*, with the prefix, *arch* from *archē*, meaning beginning or timeless first principles) intimates timelessness, according to a suggestion made by Mark Kiley.

To be sure, there was a difficulty to be faced in the consideration of Jesus as a priest. Within Israel, priesthood was hereditary; priests belonged to the tribe of Levi. Jesus, however, belonged to the tribe of Judah (7:14). The homilist faced that difficulty squarely by stating that Melchizedek, the prototypical priest, did not receive the priesthood in hereditary fashion (of his father nothing is known, he is *apatōr*, fatherless, v.3) nor did he receive priesthood according to the norms of the law (v.16). The non-hereditary extra-legal priesthood of Melchizedek serves as a type of the priesthood of Jesus.

Many different points of view can be exploited in the comparison between the priesthood of Jesus and the priesthood of the levitical order. Previously the homilist had reminded his hearers of the importance of a divine oath (6:13-18); now he tells them that the priesthood of Jesus was established on the basis of an oath whereas that of the levites was not so established (7:20-21). Another reason for the superiority of the priesthood of Jesus over that of the levites was that Jesus was perfect. He was holy, blameless, unstained, separated from sinners, and exalted above the heavens (7:26). The homilist's dialectic manner of thinking comes to the fore as he presents a series of antitheses which point to the uniqueness and superiority of Jesus' priesthood: the one and the many, the weak and the perfect, the good and the better, the old and the new, the earthly and the heavenly. Ultimately, however, it is Jesus' dignity as Son which constitutes the new dimension of his priesthood over and against that of the levitical order (7:28).

These antitheses are exploited in the following chapter (Heb 8) when the homilist first compares the places where the priesthood is exercised and its sacrifices offered and then presents Jesus as the mediator of the new and better covenant. Whereas the tabernacle was constructed according to a plan conveyed to Moses, it is but a copy and shadow of the heavenly sanctuary where Jesus exercises his ministry. The tabernacle was, of course, sacred because it contained the stone tablets (cf.9:4) with the covenantal prescriptions. Thus, the homilist can turn his thoughts to the covenant and the superiority of the covenant, founded on better and more secure promises, mediated by Jesus. Once again, a catena of scriptural passages (Jer 31:31-34 [cited again in 10:16-17, where it is the longest single citation in Heb] Exod 19:5-6; 10:16-17; and 2 Kings 6:16) is employed to establish that the old covenant has become obsolete (Heb 8:13).

An Overview

According to Graham Hughes, it is his preoccupation with the history of the covenants which produces the homilist's double understanding of Jesus, with the categories which Hughes labels pioneer and priest, for as pioneer "Jesus stood firmly within the history of this people who must look to the future believingly, while as priest he is now the means of their participating, already, in the eschatological realities." Indeed, this double perspective on Jesus runs throughout the author's homily (comp. Heb 13:8). Initially, he had presented Jesus, as son and brother, as sharing the nature of God and sharing a human nature. As he develops his thoughts on Jesus' priesthood, the homilist affirms Jesus' solidarity with humans whose sufferings he had shared, with the result that Jesus is able to be a compassionate priest. He also affirms that, as the timeless one, Jesus is a priest forever.

The author's double perspective on Jesus undergirds his entire christological exposition, whose essential theme is that Jesus, son, is high priest. These christological titles, "Son" (*Huios*) (Heb 1:2,5,8; 3:6; 4:14; 5:5,8; 6:6; 7:3,28; 10:29; cf.2:6), and "High priest" (*Archiereus* Heb 2:17; 3:1; 4:14,15; 5:1,5,10; 6:20; 7:26,27,28; 8:1,3; 9:7,11,25; 10:11; 13:11) are key to the homilist's christological exposition, yet each of them is not without significant reference to us human beings since other "sons" (*huioi*, 2:10; cf 2:11-12; 12:5-8) are brought to glory, and one of the qualifications of Jesus as priest has been fulfilled in his having suffered and been tempted (2:18) as we humans have suffered and been tempted.

If his use of the "Son" and "High priest" titles epitomize the homilist's christology, it must also be recognized that the author has a predilection for the simple name Jesus (2:9; 3:1; 4:14; 6:20; 7:22; 10:19; 12:2, 24; 13:12). This preference for the absolute use of Jesus' personal name, that is, without further qualification, corresponds to the homilist's great interest in the humanity of Jesus. Only three times does the homilist speak of "Jesus Christ" (10:10; 13:3, 21), but he often rather simply speaks about "the Christ," thereby expressing his interest in Jesus as the Messiah or anointed one. Nonetheless, he makes it quite clear that he has understood this "anointing" in a rather singular fashion. For the homilist, Jesus is presented as the anointed one insofar as he is priest and king, indeed, according to the order of Melchizedek.

Frequently (16 times in all) the homilist speaks of "the Lord" (*ho Kurios*), but most of his references to the Lord are in the scriptural passages which he has cited. In his use of these biblical passages—with the exception of Ps 101:26 (cf. Heb 1:10)—he normally preserves the sense of the traditional text where *Kurios*-Lord is a manner of speaking about Yahweh, the God of the patriarchs (Heb 7:21 [Ps 110:4]; 8:8-11 [4 times: Jer 31:31-34]; 10:16 [Jer 31:33]; 10:30 [Ps 135:14]; 12:5-6 [twice: Prov 3:11-12]; 13:6 [Ps 118:6]). Twice in the latter part of the homily, the homilist even refers to Yahweh as "the Lord" on his own account (Heb 8:2; 12:14). In contrast only once does the homilist call Jesus "the Lord" (*ho Kurios*; 2:3); once he calls him "our Lord" (*ho Kurios hēmon*; 7:14); once he refers to him as "our Lord Jesus" (*ho Kurios hēmon Iēsous*; 13:20); and once he applies a passage of scripture which employs the title "Lord" to Jesus in such a way that Jesus is implicitly called Lord (Ps 101:26 in Heb 1:10). Thus, it is hardly likely that "Lord" is the superior name given to Jesus (Heb 1:4). Those who think that "Lord" is the superior name (e.g. J.H. Ulrichsen) seem to have been unduly swayed by Phil

2:9-11, where the "name above every other name" is clearly that of "the Lord."

In sum, the homilist spoke about Jesus by means of the traditional titles ascribed to him in early Christianity—Jesus, Christ, the Lord, Son, even God—but he has used these titles in his own particular fashion so as to confirm the uniqueness of Jesus and present him in a light that is proper to the homilist himself among New Testament authors. His particular vision of Jesus makes use of the "high priest" (*archiereus*; Heb 2:17; 3:1; 4:14,15; 5:5,10; 6:20; 7:26; 8:1; 9:11) and priest (*hiereus*; Heb 5:6; 7:11,15,17,21; 8:4; 10:11,21) titles, but he combines his use of these titles with royal imagery and a portrayal of Melchizedek, the priest-king, as a type of the priesthood of the Son.

The homilist fills out his vision of this unique Son who is priest by means of many other titles, most of which are relatively rare in the New Testament. The result is that one striking way in which the epistle to the Hebrews differs from other New Testament books is the fact that it contains a plethora of christological titles. In this litany we find that Jesus is the heir (*klēronomos*; 1:2); the firstborn (*prōtotokos*; 1:6); the apostle (*apostolos*; 3:1); the great shepherd of the sheep (*poimēn*; 13:20); the pioneer (*archēgos*; of salvation, 2:10; of faith, 12:2); the cause of salvation (*aitios*; 5:9); the perfector of faith (*teleiōtēs*; 12:2); the forerunner (*prodromos*; 6:20); the sanctifier (*ho hagiazōn*; 2:11); the guarantor (*egguos*; 7:22); the builder of the house (*ho kataskeuasas*; 3:3); the minister in the sanctuary (*leiturgos*; 8:2); the mediator (*mesitēs*; 8:6; 9:15; 12:24); and perhaps even the "Word" (*logos*, as Swetnam suggests in reference to the hymn fragment in 4:12-13). Many of these titles are used only once in the entire homily. Some of them are not used at all in the New Testament outside the epistle to the Hebrews. Their cumulative effect is to provide the reader of this homily with exceptionally rich christological imagery.

Almost as striking as the richness of the imagery is the soteriology (the understanding of salvation) which it implies. The mediator of the new covenant (8:6; 9:15; 12:24) is the source of salvation (5:9). Some of the christological titles used by the homilist portray Jesus as a human being who has participated in the journey to salvation, only to arrive there before all others (heir, firstborn, perfector, forerunner, and pioneer); while others portray the heavenly Son who mediates salvation to his earthly brothers and sisters (shepherd, builder, cause of salvation, sanctifier, perfector, guarantor, mediator, minister, and even apostle—insofar as the rabbis occasionally called the priest the *shaliach* or apostle of God and especially used this terminology when they were describing the role of the high priest on the Day of Atonement).

Paraenesis

Jesus as the apostle and high priest is the object of the Christian confession of faith (cf.3:1; 4:14; 13:15), to which the homilist urges his listeners and readers to hold fast (4:14; 10:23). This type of exhortation would seem to imply that at least some members of the homilist's community were in danger of losing their faith. At least one scholar (George E. Rice) even thinks that the danger of apostasy is the central concern in each of the homily's five sections (which Rice identifies as 1:5-2:4; 2:5-4:13; 4:14-6:8; 6:9-10:39; 11:1-12:29). While Rice's interpretation of the homily may be an overstatement of the situation, it is clear that the homilist's community is beset with difficulties and that these difficulties constitute a danger for the community. Indeed, one dimension of the homilist's portrayal of the human Jesus is to present him as a model of obedience and faithful endurance. Truly human, as we are human, Jesus was tempted. He remained faithful. As he was like us, so we should be like him, imitating his faithful endurance in the midst of trial and temptation.

Today there is general agreement among scholars that the homilist's magnificent portrayal of Christ ultimately served his paraenetic interest. He has identified his own work as a "word of exhortation" (*ho logos tēs paraklēseōs*; 13:22). Diplomatically he mentions that he has written only briefly, but that understatement is mere literary convention (cf.Paul Andriessen who draws our attention to similar usage in the Epistle of

Barnabas). In fact, apart from Rom and 1 Cor, the "epistle" to the Hebrews is the longest epistle in the New Testament. One of the factors that contributes to its length is the number of very explicit exhortations that are scattered here and there throughout the text (2:1-4; 3:7-4:11; 4:14-16; 5:11-6:12; 10:19-39; 12:1-13:17). Besides these obvious passages, where exhortation is the homilist's chief purpose, a paraenetic interest seems to have influenced much of the rest of his exposition.

In Greek, "exhortation" (*paraklēsis*) suggests warning and/or encouragement. Both of these aspects seem to run through the homilist's exhortative remarks. Sometimes his tone is that of the good pastor whose concern is to encourage a beleaguered flock, as has been suggested by K.M. Woschitz who thinks that the central issue of the entire epistle is the homilist's desire to show that it is indeed worthwhile to be a Christian. At other times the tone of the homilist is that of the uncompromising prophet who warns his listeners that they have only one chance—and no more (6:4-8; 10:26-31; 12:16-17). Of course, the homilist does not think that he alone has responsibility for exhorting the community; others have responsibility for that task as well (3:13; 10:25). Well aware that what he has to say is difficult (5:11), the homilist has chosen to exercise his responsibility because he knows the community and its needs. Thus, "the exhortation to heed, to hear and obey, is," as Juliana Casey wrote, "a significant and constant leitmotif in Hebrews."

One who reads the homily today would be able to appreciate better the nature of its exhortations if one could establish beyond all reasonable doubt an understanding of the circumstances, in which the homily was composed. Unfortunately we have only the text itself as a basis for reconstituting these circumstances, and scholarly opinion differs widely in its evaluation of what precisely those circumstances were. Some think of an active persecution (e.g. H.M. Parker who suggests the persecution of Diocletian), while others think that the real danger is fascination with Gnostic speculation (e.g. Robert Jewett who thinks that the homily is a response to the Lycus Valley heresy). Still others think that the danger to faith was not really so acute, holding that the intensity of the exhortation was principally due to the homilist's conviction that the final times have already begun and that the presence of these times generates a sense of urgency (e.g. Paul Andriessen).

It is clear that the homilist has appealed to his community in much the same way that he made his christological exposition, that is, he uses the scriptures in such a way as to apply them to the present situation. The fundamental role of the homilist's use of scriptures is a paraenetic one. Some German authors (e.g. Berthold Klappart and Erich Grässer) have observed that every major biblical citation or group of citations in Hebrews has as its express objective a word of exhortation. This is certainly true in the first extended paraenetic unit in the homily (3:7-4:11) where Ps 95 is cited at length (vv.7-11 in Heb 3:7-11) and commented upon in midrashic fashion, with the text of the psalm being explicitly cited again in 3:15 (vv.7-8); 4:3 (v.11), 5 (v.11), and 7 (vv.7-8). Israel's wanderings in the wilderness at the time of the Exodus serve as a model and as a warning for the homilist's own generation. He warns his contemporaries that they are not to falter in the midst of their own crisis.

The series of warnings scattered throughout the homily (2:1-4; 3:7-4:11; 6:4-8; 10:26-31) leads up to the triple warning of 12:15-17. There, immediately after a short exhortation (v.14), the homilist warns his congregation to see to it that no one fall from grace, that no root of bitterness spring up, and that no one become immoral and irreligious as Esau was. These last two warnings are phrased in such a way that the listener familiar with the Jewish scriptures would catch the references to Deut 29:17 and the Genesis story about Jacob's son (Gen 25:33-34; 26:34; 27:30-40).

It is, however, the pastor who recapitulates the history of God's people (Heb 11) ... Abel ... Enoch ... Noah ... Abraham ... Sarah ... Moses ... Rahab ... Gideon ... David ... Samuel ... reminding his congregation that these heroes (and heroines!) of faith "did not receive what was promised since God had foreseen something better for us" (11:39-40). These witnesses, whose example culminates in the example of Jesus himself (12:2), should encourage the congregation to endure. Because the Kingdom is unshakeable, they should lift their drooping heads and raise their sagging spirits.

They have been invited into God's rest but they must hold fast. Fidelity, patient endurance, obedience should characterize the way of life for this wandering generation. Wandering they may be, but all is not lost since they have the sworn promise of a sabbath rest for the faithful people of God (4:9) and the reality of a great and compassionate high priest who takes pity on them. The today (*sēmeron*) of Ps 95 represents the eternal call of God to his people, ever inviting them to remain faithful and not fall away from the living God (4:7-10; 3:12).

The homilist's community had suffered (10:32-35; 12:3-13) and could expect more suffering still (13:13-14). Those to whom the homily was addressed had obviously not yet suffered death—but that seems to have been not an unlikely possibility (12:4). Some members of the community had been imprisoned (10:34; 13:3; cf.11:36). The conditions in which the community lived were serious indeed; but no less a difficulty seems to have been the danger of slipping away from God and the true confession of faith (13:9). In such circumstances, it was imperative that the members of the community push on to maturity (5:14-6:1). Milk is suitable for children, but not for them.

Ceslas Spicq has drawn attention to the homilist's synthesis of christology, soteriology, and eschatology within his paraenetic contexts. While Christ is the model, and salvation ("rest") the goal, it is eschatology which provides the horizon for the homilist's exhortation and imparts a sense of urgency to his message. Christ will appear a second time (9:28). The Day is drawing near (10:25). The earth will be shaken once again (12:26, with reference to Ps 68:9). After death comes judgment (9:27). The Lord will judge his people (10:30, with reference to Deut 32:36). It is a fearful thing to fall into the hands of the living God (10:31). With reminders like these the homilist conveyed a sense of urgency to people living in the final times.

Exhortations to practice Christian charity are liberally sprinkled throughout the New Testament. These are sometimes given rather specific form. The author of the Acts of the Apostles has provided an ideal vision of the early Christians in Jerusalem sharing their goods with one another (Acts 2:42-47). Paul exhorted the Roman Christians to practice hospitality

(Rom 12:13; cf.1 Tim 3:2; 5:10; Tit 1:8; 1 Pet 4:9). Church leaders are to turn away from avarice (1 Tim 3:3; 2 Tim 3:2). In similar fashion, the homilist exhorts the community to show hospitality (13:2), to share possessions (13:16), and to avoid money-grubbing (13:5). These apparently common exhortations take on new meaning in the light of the fact that some members of the community have already experienced the expropriation of their property (10:34).

While a paraenetic intent can be discerned throughout the entire homily, the final chapter of the epistle to the Hebrews is a litany of concrete exhortations. It opens with an exhortation to foster sibling love (cf.1 Thess 4:9; Rom 12:10). Hospitality is encouraged. The homilist urges his community to hold marriage in high esteem. Honor is to be paid to leaders, whose way of life serves as an example for the community (13:7, 17). Disruptive teaching is to be shunned. Good is to be done (13:16) and, presumably, evil avoided. These various exhortations reflect, albeit with greater specificity, the homilist's earlier exhortation that the community strive for peace with all (12:14). This type of serial exhortation, with the various injunctions given in staccato fashion, is typical of the final section of many letters in the New Testament.

There are, nonetheless, features of the homilist's serial articulation of moral exhortation which are somewhat atypical. Rather unusual in New Testament paraenesis, but rather consistent with the author's way of developing his thought, is the homilist's way of using the ancient Jewish scriptures in his exhortations. Passages such as Deut 31:6,8; Gen 28:15, and Ps 117:6 serve as biblical warrants for the implied exhortation to rely on divine providence rather than on the accumulation of monetary wealth. The memory of the divine beings who visited Abraham (Gen 18:2-3; cf. Gen 19:1-3) is evoked in the exhortation to practise hospitality.

Decidedly atypical is the homilist's description of the moral life in cultic terms (e.g. 13:16). Even Heb 13:13, which some authors think provides the key to the author's entire paraenesis, is redolent with cultic imagery. Indeed, in the words of William Manson, "in Hebrews the whole pattern of Christian life is conceived in terms of Christian worship." Such a conception is unique among the texts of the New Testament. So, too, however, is the author's portrayal of Christ as the heavenly priest-king who has passed through the heavens (4:14). His use of cultic imagery provides for his unique understanding of Christ and gives a distinct configuration to the Christian life. Could it be otherwise when Christ is Son among sons (and daughters), a brother to the children of God, and the pioneer and perfector of the faith?

Who Wrote Hebrews?

Since the homilist did not sign his work, the epistle to the Hebrews must be considered an anonymous work. Reading the work gives one the impression that its author was a well-educated individual, well versed in the Greek language and familiar with Jewish exegetical traditions. As such, the author of Hebrews can be identified as a Hellenistic Jew. Beyond that affirmation, little can be said about the author of the homily on the basis of the text which he has left us.

In the first part of the third century, Origen (ca.185-ca.254), the great theologian and biblical interpreter from Alexandria, shared his reflections on the author of the text. He wrote: "...the thoughts are those of the Apostle (Paul), but the phraseology and the composition are those of someone who recalled to mind the teachings of the Apostle and who, as it were, had made notes on what was said by the teacher. If any church, then, holds this Epistle to be Paul's let it be commended for this, for not without reason have the men of old handed it down as Paul's. Who the author of the Epistle is God truly knows, but the account that has reached us from some is that Clement, who was bishop of the Romans, wrote the Epistle; from others, that Luke, who wrote the Gospel and the Acts, is the author."

It was Origen's teacher, Clement of Alexandria, who had suggested that Luke had translated a Pauline epistle written in Hebrew (Eusebius, *Ecclesiastical History* VI. 14,2; PG 20, 549). Remarks made by a man who may have been the founder of the Alexandrian school, Pantaenus (d. ca. 190), seem to indicate that Paul was the author of the epistle. Origen himself had his doubts because "the epistle ... does not possess the Apostle's rudeness of speech, that is, in style, but the Epistle is better Greek in the composition of its diction, as anyone who knows how to distinguish difference of phraseology would admit" (Eusebius, *Ecclesiastical History* VI, 25,11; PG 20, 584). Hence, he wrote "God only knows" (*to men alēthēs theos oiden*) who the author is.

If Origen has passed along the conjecture that the homily had been written by Clement of Rome (d. ca. 96 A.D.), it is because several expressions in Clement's letter to the Corinthians are quite akin to some expressions found in Hebrews. Both portray Jesus as the high priest (see the studies of Michael Mees and Gerd Theissen in this regard), and both offer remarkably similar catenae of scriptural citations. These similarities may well suggest that Clement was familiar with Hebrews—which, in any case, he does not ascribe to Paul— but they are hardly so numerous nor so striking as to establish a case for Clement of Rome having been the author of the homily. That the early Roman tradition did not attribute Hebrews to Paul is further suggested by the fact that Marcion did not include the epistle in his *Apostolikon*, though it must be admitted that his own biased view of what was authentically Pauline would have led him to drop the epistle from his collection even if he had known of a tradition ascribing it to Paul. At the turn of the third century, Gaius, the Roman anti-Montanist, did not consider Hebrews to be one of Paul's works. By the time that Eusebius wrote his *Ecclesiastical History* in the fourth century, however, the Roman tradition was that Hebrews had been written by Paul. By this time the Roman church was in substantial agreement with the Greek and Syrian churches as to Paul's composition of the "epistle."

The oldest extant manuscript of Hebrews, the Chester Beatty papyrus (P^{46}, ca.200 A.D.) situates Hebrews at a place in the New Testament between Rom and 1 Cor, thereby suggesting that it was written by the Apostle, but this manuscript evidence is unique among the ancient manuscripts which contain the homily. In most of the manuscript tradition, Hebrews is to be found after the letters to the churches (2

Thess), while in the manuscripts of the western tradition it is often placed after Philemon. The placement of Hebrews in the western manuscript tradition is evidence of the general western hesitancy to accept Hebrews as a composition of the Apostle. As a matter of fact, Tertullian, writing in North Africa at the end of the second century, cites Hebrews (*De pudicitia*, 20; PL 2, 1021) according to a tradition which ascribed it to Barnabas. Barnabas had levitical origins (Acts 4:36) and the connection between Hebrews and Timothy (Heb 13:23) made one think of Barnabas as a likely author of the composition.

It has only been since the latter part of the fourth century that the western tradition has generally recognized Paul as the author of Hebrews. In large measure, that was due to the influence of eastern writers and such western figures as Hilary and Jerome who nonetheless echoed the doubts of the African church (cf. *Ep*. LIII, 8; PL 22, 548). Both of these Fathers of the Church had studied in the East. Nevertheless, some manuscripts transcribed in the ninth century (the Codex Augiensis [F] and the Codex Bornerianus [G]) have omitted Hebrews from their collection of New Testament texts, and the placement of Hebrews after the "private letters" of Paul in the western tradition is subtle evidence of the lingering doubts about Pauline authorship that continued in the Western church throughout the first millennium of Christian history.

The Internal Evidence

Hebrews' anonymity and the ambiguous evidence of the Church's early traditions, as articulated by some of the Fathers and attested by the manuscript tradition, is such as to raise serious questions about the author of the homily. The early Alexandrian tradition focused on Paul as the most likely author. This tradition was soon attested in the other eastern churches and would become dominant throughout the entire Church from about 400 A.D. In the ninth century, Bassin the Syrian was able to give four pages of argumentation in favor of Pauline authorship. That type of conviction was representative of the traditions of the eastern Christian churches. However, doubts remained, principally within the western churches, and these would come to the surface at the time of the Renaissance and the Protestant Reformation.

In fact, the issue of the author of the epistle to the Hebrews is more an issue for the study of the tradition of the church than it is a study relevant to the interpretation of the text itself. The exegetical study of Hebrews leads quickly to the conclusion that Hebrews could not have been written by Paul. Even Origen had noted that the language and style were not those of Paul. In fact, of the 912 different words in Hebrews (whose Greek text contains 4955 words) 292 are not used in Paul's letters, and of these 152 do not occur elsewhere in the New Testament. Some of Paul's favorite words are hardly used in Hebrews (e.g. *ekklēsia*, "church," which is found only in a citation of Ps 21:23 in Heb 2:12); some are used with a different meaning (e.g. *apostolos*, "apostle," used of Christ in Heb 3:1); and some are not used at all (e.g. *euaggelion*, "gospel," which Paul uses 69 times.) The classical and rhetorical style of Hebrews is quite different from the passion and crisp expression found in Paul's letters. While Paul's own language is rather simple, the Greek text of the epistle to the Hebrews is about the most elegant in the entire New Testament.

Christology is the main theme of Hebrews; it is likewise the central object of Paul's proclamation of the gospel. Yet there are vast differences between the homilist's appreciation of Christ and Paul's proclamation of him. While the difference between Paul's passionate attachment to Christ (cf. Rom 8:35-39; Gal 2:19-20) and the homilist's dispassionate disquisition (e.g. Heb 3:1-2; 4:14,16; 12:2-3; 13:8) may be partially attributable to the difference between the literary form of a letter and that of a homily, the discriminating reader must recognize that there are discernible differences between the respective authors' points of view on Jesus. These differences are evidenced in their choice of christological titles. The author of Hebrews focuses on the high priesthood of Jesus and uses the titles of Son, priest, and high priest in his christological exposition. The high priesthood theme is completely lacking in Paul, whose principal christological titles are Lord and Christ.

As an example of their different ways of speaking about

Jesus, we might note that Paul refers to "Jesus Christ the Lord" (the personal name of Jesus with both titles) some fifteen times in the letter to the Romans alone, but that this full designation of Jesus does not occur even once in the entire epistle to the Hebrews. There is, however, considerable difference in the authors' respective choice of christological schemas. Paul's favorite models are those of the crucifixion (e.g. 1 Cor 2:2) and resurrection (1 Thess 1:10) of Jesus. These schemas are virtually absent from Hebrews (see, however, 12:2), whose principal christological schema is that of exaltation. While Paul has little to say about Jesus' humanity, this is a major focus in the homilist's portrayal of Jesus. Finally, Paul's christology is clearly rooted in the earlier tradition of the church (e.g. 1 Cor 15:3-6), while the homilist's derives from his own theopoetic vision.

These christological differences, so obvious because of the centrality of Christ in the writings of Paul as well as in the text of the homilist, are a sign of broad differences in general theological outlook between Hebrews and the letters of Paul. In this regard, Albert Vanhoye has written about a difference in spirituality and of theological orientation. Surely, there is some difference in the understanding of the notion of faith itself. For the homilist, faith is really a matter of hope (11:1); the faith that is confessed is one which has a strong doctrinal and intellectual content. For Paul, faith is a response to the gospel which has been preached; it is essentially a matter of personal relationship. While Paul writes frequently about the Spirit, the homilist says very little about the Holy Spirit. In his letters to the Galatians and to the Romans Paul had to deal with the reality of the Torah and the demands that it makes; when the homilist refers to the Law it is principally to its cultic prescriptions that he makes reference.

In his christological and paraenetic expositions, the homilist uses the Jewish scriptures to great advantage. Much has been written about the scriptures which he used, particularly with regard to his principles of interpretation. Among twentieth-century exegetes, it has been commonly held that the homilist's way of interpreting the scriptures had much in common with Philo of Alexandria's allegorical interpretation of the scriptures. Today, however, scholarly interpretation has moved away from that point of view (e.g. Ronald Williamson, Stanley G. Sowers) to one which suggests that the homilist employed traditional Jewish principles of interpretation (e.g. Graham Hughes, Rinaldo Fabris) to whatever biblical text was locally available to him (e.g. J. C. McCullough). Extended citations and midrashic reflections on the scriptural texts are characteristic features of the way in which the homilist develops his thoughts. Paul was likewise aware of the traditional Jewish exegetical principles, but his letters rarely cite more than a single verse of the scriptures at one time, and nowhere does he offer an example of that sustained reflection on biblical texts which is such a striking feature of Hebrews.

The Anonymity of Hebrews

In sum, reflection upon the contents of Hebrews hardly suggests that it was composed by Paul whose thought and style of writing is well known to us because of the many letters which he has left us. This almost brings us back to square one in asking about the author of Hebrews. "Only God knows," Origen's rejoinder, seems as valid today as it did at the beginning of the third century. Origen was aware of speculation as to the possible role of Clement of Rome or the evangelist Luke in the production of the Greek text of Hebrews. Tertullian knew of a tradition that ascribed the work to Barnabas. In recent years, commentators have suggested a variety of names as possibly being the individual behind the homily which has come down to us. Clement, Barnabas and Luke, Philip, Silvanus, Peter, Aristion, Priscilla, Jude, and Apollos are among the names that have been cited. Most frequently (e.g. Martin Luther, Theodore Zahn, Ceslas Spicq, Jean Héring) it is the name of Apollos which comes to the fore. This preference is due to the fact that Apollos and his particular skills (cf. Acts 18:24-28; 1 Cor 1:12; 3:6; 4:6) are comparatively well-known.

We do not know the identity of the author of Hebrews. We know something of his skill and his vision. We know something of his Hellenistic Jewish Christian background and of his closeness to the community for which he wrote. We know that he was a Christian of the second generation (Heb 2:3). Yet he remains anonymous.

Frequently the determination of the place and date of an author's composition provide useful information in the search for an author's identity. Unfortunately this type of information is not easy to come by in the case of the epistle to the Hebrews. Some scholars (e.g. John A.T. Robinson and George W. Buchanan) have argued that a text so obviously concerned with Jewish cult as is the epistle to the Hebrews would certainly have mentioned the destruction of the Jerusalem temple, had the text been written after 70 A.D. Hebrews does not refer to the razing of the temple, but the argument from silence is always a difficult one to manage. As for the fact that Hebrews speaks of sacrificial offerings as if they were currently taking place (8:3-4; 9:6-7; 10:1-2), important Jewish authorities, such as the historian Flavius Josephus (*Against Apion,* 2, 77) and commentators on the Mishnah, wrote in similar fashion even though they were writing long after the destruction of the temple.

Since Hebrews was apparently cited by Clement of Rome in about 96 A.D., the text must have been written before that date. On the other hand, its author was a second-generation Christian (2:3) who writes about leaders who have gone before (13:7). Heb 10:32 speaks of the past times as if they belonged to a somewhat distant past. Heb 13:5 implies that the community was relatively well-off. All of these considerations suggest that the epistle was written during the last third of the first century A.D. That suggestion is confirmed by the studies of the most recent German language commentator on Hebrews, Herbert Braun, who opines that Hebrews was written between 80 and 90 A.D.

If Hebrews offers few clues as to the time of its composition, it offers still fewer clues as to the place of its composition. The only self-evident clue is 13:24, "Those who come from Italy send you greetings," but that clue is really ambiguous. "Those who come from Italy" (*hoi apo tēs Italias*) are really "the Italians." The verse says that the author of the homily is sending greetings from a group of Italians who were associated with him. This makes it quite likely that the homily was being sent to a community of Christians in Italy. More likely than not, that community was located in Rome.

The verse which has just been cited (13:24) is an integral part of that relatively small number of verses at the end of Hebrews which suggest that the text had been sent at some time or other. These verses give the epistle something of the form of a letter. This epistolary conclusion (Heb 13:19,22-25) has attracted a fair amount of scholarly attention. It is generally thought that these verses are an addition to the original text. Thereafter scholarly opinion is divided. Some scholars (e.g. William Wrede, C.C. Torrey) have suggested that the verses are a later addition, designed to give a Pauline appearance to a non-Pauline text. Some authors think that it was Paul himself who added the epistolary codicil to another's writing (e.g. the seventeenth-century Guilielmus Estius, as well as such recent commentators as Paul Gächter and Jean Héring). Some think that it was at least partially composed so as to give the homily the appearance of a letter and thus ensure its entrance into the canon (e.g. G.W.Buchanan). Perhaps the epistolary conclusion was added simply when the text of the homily was being sent to another church (e.g. Albert Vanhoye). In any case, although these few verses add a Pauline flair to the end of the text they cannot serve as evidence that the text was written by Paul.

Thus, Hebrews really is an anonymous composition. We should respect the anonymity which the author has chosen for his work. Those responsible for the reform of the lectionary designed for use in Roman Catholic churches after the Second Vatican Council have chosen to do so. Each of the lections from Hebrews is introduced with the simple formula, "A reading from the letter to the Hebrews" (apart, that is, from the reading of Heb 4:14-16; 5:7-9 on Good Friday and of Heb 1:1-6 during the dawn Mass of Christmas day. These readings are introduced by "A reading from the letter of Paul to the Hebrews.").

What happens when this homily is read as an anonymous composition, independent of Paul? What happens when, as it were, this epistle is freed from the shackles of the Pauline tradition and read in its own right, as its author apparently intended it to be read? Then the author's magnificent christological vision, the product of his unique theopoetic imagination, is appreciated in its own light. A striking vision of Jesus is to be had. This vision is not considered to be less significant because it is compared to other visions. Rather, it shines forth in its own particular splendor. Indeed the anonymous author has shared with the readers of his homily a vision which provides another insight into the multivalent reality of the Jesus event. His work was written to encourage believers; and so it should.

A Brief Bibliography

Brown, Raymond E. "The Epistle to the Hebrews," in Raymond E. Brown and John P. Meier, *Antioch and Rome: New Testament Cradles of Catholic Christianity.* New York: Paulist, 1983, 139-158.

Bruce, F.F. "Recent Contributions to the Understanding of Hebrews," *ExpTim* 80 (1969) 260-264.

Casey, Juliana M. *Hebrews.* NTM 18. Wilmington: Glazier, 1980.

Childs, Brevard S. *The New Testament as Canon: An Introduction.* Philadelphia: Fortress, 1984, 400-418.

Fitzmyer, Joseph A. "'Now this Melchizedek...' (Heb 7:1)," *CBQ* 25 (1963) 305-321.

Havener, Ivan. "A Concerned Pastor," *TBT* 24 (1986) 223-227.

Horton, Fred L. *The Melchizedek Tradition: A Critical Examination of the Sources to the Fifth Century A.D. and in the Epistle to the Hebrews* SNTS MS, 30. Cambridge: University Press, 1976.

Hutaff, Margaret D. "The Epistle to the Hebrews," *TBT* 99 (1978) 1816-1824.

McCullough, J.C. "The Old Testament Quotations in Hebrews," *NTS* 26 (1979-1980) 363-379.

McCullough, J. C. "Some Recent Developments in Research on the Epistle to the Hebrews," *IBS* 2 (1980) 141-165; 3 (1981) 28-45.

McGehee, Michael. "Hebrews: The Letter Which is Not a Letter," *TBT* 24 (1986) 213-216.

2
Ancient Writers

Upon reflection it should not prove to be much of a surprise that Hebrews is an anonymous composition, especially when one takes with the seriousness which it deserves the fact that Hebrews is not really a letter. In terms of its content, almost seventy-five percent of the New Testament is to be found in six of its longest books, all of which are anonymous compositions—Matthew, Mark, Luke, John, Acts, and Hebrews. Since the first letter of John also appears in the New Testament as an anonymous composition, it can also be added to this list of major works.

The Anonymity of Jewish and Christian Religious Literature

The anonymity of the major writings in the New Testament is not without parallel in the Old Testament, where many of the principal books are in fact anonymous. The five books of the Pentateuch (Gen, Exod, Lev, Num, Deut) are frequently called the five books of Moses but it is only the book of Deuteronomy that lays any specific claim to Mosaic authorship (Deut 1:1), and that claim is more than a bit suspect since Deuteronomy describes the death of Moses (Deut 34). In fact, taken as a group, the historical books of the Old Testament (Jos, Jud, 1-2 Sam, 1-2 Kings, 1-2 Chron, 1-2 Macc) are generally anonymous. This is in keeping with the practices of the cultural situation within which they were written.

Most of the written works of the ancient Near East are anonymous compositions. The practice by which an author lays claim to his compositions by appending a colophon or by citing his name at the beginning of his work seems to have begun in Greece around the sixth century B.C. Although many later Jewish authors adopted the Greek practice, the custom of "signing" one's own work was not universally followed in the Jewish world, not even during Hellenistic times when such noteworthy Hellenistic Jewish authors as the philosopher, Philo of Alexandria, and the historian, Flavius Josephus, left their works unsigned.

Although the four gospels were written outside of Palestine, they have their origins in a Jewish environment. Mark, who created the gospel genre, was probably a Palestinian Jewish Christian who composed his gospel in Rome. It is not unlikely that the authors of at least two of the other gospels (Matt, John) were Jewish Christians. Luke, to whom Christian tradition has attributed the third gospel, made use of Mark in the composition of his gospel and like his predecessors, left his work unsigned—a practice that he maintained in the composition of the Acts of the Apostles, the second part of his two-part work. That Luke should have followed Mark in composing an anonymous gospel is a bit surprising insofar as he has furnished his version of the gospel with a short preface (Luke 1:1-4) which bears remarkable similarity with the prefaces of different Greek historical and scientific works. Despite the obvious Hellenism of his prologue, Luke has nonetheless composed both his gospel and the Acts of the Apostles as anonymous works.

While the rootedness of the canonical gospels in the Jewish world of first-century Palestine may be a singularly important factor in their having been written in anonymous fashion, two additional factors have undoubtably made their contribution to the anonymity of the gospels. The first of these is that the gospels are witnesses to the faith of a community of believers. This is most apparent in the latest of the canonical gospels, the Gospel according to John, in which the evangelist employs the first person plural in order to express his community's point of view. This use of the "Johannine we" is to be found in John 1:14, 16, 45; 3:11; 4:22, 42; 6:5, 68, 69; 9:4; 11:16; 14:22; 16:30; 20:25; and 21:24, some twenty-nine times altogether. Although the Synoptists, Matthew, Mark and Luke, do not use an editorial we in this fashion, form-critical analysis of their respective gospels has long highlighted the importance of the community's transmission of the traditions on which the synoptic gospels are based. Each of them represents an edited form of the community's tradition.

In the early days of form-criticism some of its more radical proponents presented the synoptic evangelists as virtually nothing more than anonymous compilers of community traditions. Fortunately the development of redaction criticism during the 1960's redressed the situation somewhat and restored each of the synoptic writers to the status of an author and theologian in his own right. Nonetheless, the insight that each of the evangelists served as a spokesperson for a faith community remains one of the lasting contributions of the form-critical study of the gospels.

From the perspective of their literary analyses of his work, the early form-critics (for example, Karl Ludwig Schmidt and Rudolf Bultmann) highlighted the notion that Mark, the author of the first written gospel was a spokesperson and a tradent of tradition. From quite another perspective, ancient Christian tradition had also claimed that Mark's gospel was the work of a spokesman. Eusebius of Caesarea, the fourth-century historian, had written about Papias, bishop of Hieropolis (Asia Minor) in the early second century. Papias is quoted as saying that the presbyter used to say that Mark was Peter's interpreter and wrote down accurately what he remembered (*Ecclesiastical History*, III, 39, 15; PG 20,300.) In modern terms we could almost say that Eusebius, Papias, and the presbyter considered Mark to have been Peter's ghost-writer. Throughout the patristic era the gospel of Mark was considered to be Peter's gospel. Its apostolic authority was derived not from Mark who wrote it but from Peter whose testimony it was considered to contain.

Although Matthew and Luke have modified considerably the gospel of Mark upon which they based their own versions of the gospel, they followed the pathfinder in likewise producing works that were anonymous. It was only towards the end of the second century that the anonymity of the gospels was somewhat dispelled. Then the Christian churches began to experience a need to distinguish one gospel from another. Titles began to be added to the manuscript copies of the respective gospels. Subsequently, Christian tradition came to identify the four canonical gospels as "the gospel according to Matthew ... Mark ... Luke, and ... John."

In addition to the gospels' Jewish context and their relationships with their respective Christian communities, there was another important factor which contributed to the anonymity of the gospels. That is the conviction that the Spirit himself is the author of these works. Unlike Josephus, who appended to his *Jewish Antiquities* an epilogue in the first person in which he reflected on the work that he had just completed and discussed his future literary intentions (*Jewish Antiquities,* XX, 12, 1), none of the Synoptists offers an autobiographical reflection on his work. Alone among the gospels, the fourth is relatively explicit about the sources of its traditions (John 19:35) and the purpose of its composition (John 20:30-31). Yet it is also the Fourth Gospel which explicitly affirms the role of the Spirit in the remembrance of the traditions about Jesus (John 14:26; cf.16:13; comp. Matt 10:19-20; Mark 13:11; Luke 12:11-12).

The role of Spirit-inspired prophets was so esteemed in the early Church that Papias could state: "I did not suppose that information from books helped me so much as that from a living and abiding voice" (Eusebius, *Ecclesiastical History*, III, 39, 4; PG 20, 297). For his part, Paul was very conscious that he possessed the Spirit (1 Cor 7:40) and that it was in the power of the Spirit that he proclaimed the gospel (1 Thess 1:5). Commenting upon the situation of the Christian communities of those earliest times, Kurt Aland has written: "The one, who, in those days, instructed the Christian society did so according to the Spirit. He was but the pen moved by the Spirit." Indeed some commentators have suggested—without, in my judgment, sufficient proof—that the classic comment on the inspiration of the Scriptures (2 Tim 3:16-17) is a reflection on Christian writings. To the extent that this interpretation of the passage can be established, it serves as an indication that the earliest writings of Christian authors were presumed to have the Spirit as their origin and the Spirit as the source of their authority.

Jewish Religious Traditions

By most indications the Old Testament's book of Deuteronomy is a work dating from the seventh century B.C. It comes from a time long after the death of Moses, so long afterwards that his place of burial was no longer known (Deut 34:16). Its language and its concerns reflect the times in which it was written. Essentially Deuteronomy is structured along a pattern outlined in the Decalogue. Its obvious intention was to make relevant and update the Jewish tradition (see, for example, Deut 5:2-3). There are good reasons to think that the book of Deuteronomy was composed as a reformulation of the Jewish law during the intensive religious reform of Josiah (621 B.C). It is quite likely that Deuteronomy was "the book of the covenant which had been found in the house of the Lord" (2 Kgs 23:2) during Josiah's reform.

Nevertheless, the book of Deuteronomy purports to relate the words of Moses (Deut 1:1; cf. Deut 5:1, 29:1). This fact tells us something rather important about the Jewish religious tradition, namely, its tendency to attribute to the heroes of its tradition a body of material that did not actually come from the hero himself. Since Moses was the great lawgiver of Israel, laws and reformulated laws were easily attributed to him as they were in the book of Deuteronomy. Nearly half the psalms, including Psalm 110 (see Mark 12:36 and par.), are attributed to David, "the sweet psalmist of Israel" (2 Sam 23:1). Entire genres of literature were attributed to these important names in Israel's history.

A similar phenomenon is to be noted within the Old Testament's prophetic literature, particularly with regard to the book of Isaiah. Scholars are presently accustomed to distinguish a second and a third part, respectively chapters 40-55 (Deutero-Isaiah) and chapters 56-66 (Trito-Isaiah) from the older part of the book, chapters 1-39. Only this older part of the book dates from Isaiah's era in the eighth century B.C. Deutero-Isaiah seems to come from the mid-sixth century B.C., while Trito-Isaiah comes from the last quarter of the sixth century.

In fact, the history of the book of Isaiah is rather complex. One should not naively assume that even the first part of the book was the work of the prophet himself. Although Isaiah is commonly known as one of the writing prophets, a circle or "school" of his disciples seems to have been actually responsible for the written composition of the oracles found in the book of Isaiah. Moreover, in addition to the Deutero- and Trito-Isaiah which were added onto the original text at a much later date, there also appears to have been an occasional interpolation into the Isaiah text. These interpolations have also resulted in the attribution to Isaiah of material that did not actually come from him.

David G. Meade has recently published a study (*Pseudonymity and Canon*, Tübingen, Mohr, 1986) which places this development of the Isaian tradition within a context which sheds considerable light upon its development. That context is the general Jewish and biblical understanding of prophetism. Meade highlights four of its salient features. The first is the divine nature of the prophetic word. Ultimately the prophetic word is not the word of the prophet, but the word of Yahweh. The fact that the source of prophetic revelation was one (cf. Jewish henotheism-monotheism) provides a second characteristic feature of the prophetic word, namely, its unity or consistency. The prophetic word partakes of the unified or coherent message of Yahweh. This does not imply the uniformity of all prophetic utterance; rather it suggests that each prophetic utterance fits into a larger whole.

A third feature of the prophetic word is its autonomous character. Once spoken the prophetic word enters into its own independent history; it is almost separable from the prophet himself. Modern linguistic analysts will undoubtedly recognize in this feature an element that has to do with the performative function of religious language. Finally there is the interpretive nature of the prophetic word. Since there was no normative mode of revelation, for example, a vision, an auditory experience, or an inspired reflection on previous tradition, the real emphasis was on the interpretation of revelation. The prophet was one who made sense of a revelatory experience. Prophets were part of a living tradition. Retelling earlier stories was not foreign to their task, as James Sanders and other proponents of canonical criticism have recently pointed out.

Within the broad context of Jewish prophetism, later oracles ascribed to Isaiah can be regarded as a "creative reinterpretation of the oracles of Isaiah." They constitute an actualization of the tradition (*Vergegenwärtigung*).They attempt to make the one revelation and the one tradition pertinent and relevant to a new situation. The one who actualizes the tradition remains personally anonymous because Isaiah is recognized as the head of the tradition. Thus, "the anonymous/pseudonymous expansion of the Isaianic corpus is a recognition that Isaiah had become *part* of the tradition, and *the resultant literary attribution of that corpus must be regarded more as a claim to authoritative tradition by the participants in the process, and less a claim to actual authorship by Isaiah of Jerusalem"* (D.G. Meade, his emphasis).

Meade maintains that something quite similar has happened within Israel's wisdom tradition, generally ascribed to Solomon. Wisdom literature typically had its origin in the royal court, but the source of wisdom is located in God the Creator. An important feature of the wisdom tradition is the authority that it attributes to its representatives, especially the king. In the Jewish tradition Solomon is esteemed as the wise king *par excellence* (see 1 Kgs 11:41). The widely attested link between Solomon and Israel's wisdom tradition may well suggest that wisdom as a national tradition originated during the reign of Solomon. Solomon is consequently esteemed as the patron and father of Israel's wisdom tradition. Indeed, an old Christian text, the Muratorian Fragment, states that the book of Wisdom was written by the friends of Solomon in his honor (*Sapientia ab amicis Solomonis in honorem ipsius scripta*).

In the literary attribution of Israel's wisdom tradition, its perceived historical origins play an important role. The book of Proverbs, for example, begins with this superscription: "The proverbs of Solomon, son of David, King of Israel" (Prov 1:1). According to Meade, this superscription represents far more than a mere literary form; it is a theological claim to an authoritative tradition, that specifically Israelite form of the wisdom tradition which began to take shape in the reign of Solomon.

Like prophetic utterance, wise *dicta* have a source that is divine, a message that is coherent because it is based on the divine order of creation, and a somewhat autonomous nature as is shown by its proverbial quality. Yet wisdom is also interpretive insofar as it depends not only on the passing along of a tradition but also upon a creative application of that tradition to contemporary life.

The foundational role attributed to Solomon in Israel's wisdom tradition and the understanding of wisdom that prevailed at the time made it possible to attribute to Solomon not only anthologies such as the book of Proverbs, but also fully developed works, such as Qoheleth and Wisdom. Qoheleth gives the words of the preacher (= Qoheleth), the son of David, king in Jerusalem (Qoh 1:1), but nonetheless suggests that the reign of Solomon is in the past (Qoh 1:12, 16; 2:9). The book of Wisdom implies that it is from Solomon (compare Wis 7, esp. the autobiographical note of vv. 7-14, with the prayer of Solomon in 1 Kgs 3:5-15). According to Meade, the Solomonic attribution, whether of collective works such as Proverbs or fully developed works such as Qoheleth, is "primarily an assertion of authoritative tradition, not a statement of literary origins."

Another type of Jewish literature in which the phenomenon of pseudonymity functions in a remarkable visible fashion is apocalyptic literature. Most Jewish apocalyptic literature has not entered into the biblical canon of the Christian church, but belongs to what is usually called intertestamental literature. Most of Jewish apocalyptic literature was composed during a period just less than three centuries long (ca. 170 B.C.-100 A.D.). The book of Daniel is the primary biblical example of Jewish apocalyptic. Scholars believe that the book was written during the reign of Antiochus Epiphanes (ca. 175-164 B.C.) but it appears under the name of Daniel, an ancient but relatively obscure figure who lived at the time of the Babylonian exile (Ezek 14:14; 28:3).

Scholars have long noted that the choice of the pseudonyms, as patrons of apocalyptic revelation, is not entirely gratuitous. The Apocalypse of Abraham capitalizes on the traditions contained in Gen 15, while 1 Enoch makes use of Gen 5:21-24. Baruch and Ezra figure prominently in the apocalyptic literature of the first century A.D. Their roles in Jewish history at the time of the fall of Jerusalem in 587 B.C. have made them appropriate choices to address the problems confronting Jerusalem after the events of 68-70 A.D.

Apocalyptic literature makes use of earlier, older prophetic literature by making frequent allusions to it. Indeed, it is sometimes suggested that one of the factors which gave rise to the production of Jewish apocalyptic literature is the belief that prophecy had ceased in the land of Israel. Jewish apocalyptic literature is then, at least to a large extent, a reworking of the prophetic tradition(s) in order to make them applicable to a new situation. In other words, writes Meade, "authorship or attribution is inseparably tied to authoritative tradition." This is not only because the apocalyptic writers made use of earlier prophecy but also, as Meade suggests, because the apocalyptists identify with their heroes in terms of wisdom. The heroes of apocalyptic literature are wise men and scribes (see Dan 1:4; *1 Enoch* 12:4; 4 Ezra 14:40, 50; *2 Bár* 38:4). Thus wisdom is the real point of contact between the apocalyptists and their heroes.

A striking feature of apocalyptic literature is its panoramic vision of history. Its deterministic view of all history provides an element of hope in uneasy times. Meade sees this feature of apocalyptic literature as a development of the uniform and coherent quality of revelation. This feature of apocalyptic literature, together with its expressed conviction of having been inspired, the autonomy implied by its use long after the demise of the pseudonymous hero, and its interpretive character, combine in apocalyptic literature, as in the development of the prophetic and wisdom traditions, to promote literature in which the real author is lost in anonymity. In this respect,—among others, in fact—there is a similarity among apocalyptic literature, prophetic literature, and wisdom literature. The author of Jewish apocalyptic literature has invested his authority in a pseudonym as he sought to reinterpret the tradition and apply it to his own times.

According to Meade's analysis, in all three of these instances within Jewish religious literature—prophetism, the wisdom tradition, and apocalyptic literature—pseudonymity serves as a means for the actualization of tradition. At bottom pseudonymity is the literary expression of a theological claim that a given work is a faithful interpretation of an authoritative tradition.

Actualization may take place in a variety of ways. There is textual actualization when oracles are reinterpreted; contextual actualization when the tradition provides the context for actualization as, for example, in Deutero-Isaiah, and configurational actualization when originally independent traditions are drawn to and assembled harmoniously around an earlier tradition. Notwithstanding this variety, the actualization of tradition is always an attempt to reinterpret a core tradition for a new and often different life situation. Should it be considered erroneous, the basis for judgment is not the use of a pseudonymous patronym, the basis for judgment is infidelity to tradition.

The Composition of Early Christian Literature

If, like Hebrews, the lengthiest of the early Christian writings were anonymous compositions, can anything be said about the way in which they were written? Much of the recent New Testament research has been devoted to just this issue. This book is not the place to attempt a summary of this vast amount of literature, but its aim might be furthered if some reflection is brought to bear on some features of the composition of the gospels and the Acts of the Apostles. The application of the various methods developed by form-criticism, the history of traditions, and redaction-criticism shows that none of the gospel accounts are verbatim reports of what Jesus said and did. Vatican Council II's Dogmatic Constitution on Divine Revelation summarized the real situation when it stated: "The sacred authors wrote the four Gospels, selecting some things from the many which had been handed on by word of mouth or in writing, reducing some of them to a synthesis, explicating some things in view of the situation of their churches, and preserving the form of proclamation but always in such fashion that they tell us the honest truth about Jesus " (*Dei Verbum*, 19).

That a complex process of tradition, synthesizing, editing and explicating lies behind each of the gospels is readily apparent when the various forms of the sayings of Jesus are compared among themselves. For example, Matthew has dropped from Mark's version of Jesus' saying on divorce the clause "and if she divorces her husband and marries another, she commits adultery" and added a problematic phrase "except for unchastity" to Mark's "whoever divorces his wife and marries another commits adultery" (Matt 19:9; Mark 10:11-12). Luke preserves a form of the tradition in which it is said that Jesus cast out demons "by the finger of God" (Luke 11:20), while Matthew's version of the saying holds that it is "by the Spirit of God" (Matt 12:28) that Jesus performed exorcisms. Different words are even attributed to the voice from heaven which was heard on the occasion of Jesus' baptism. Whereas Mark and Luke have a statement in the form of direct address (Mark 1:11; Luke 3:22), Matthew has a presentation statement in the third person singular (Matt 3:17).

The evangelists have also composed speeches which they have placed on Jesus' lips. Noteworthy in this regard is Matthew who composed five major discourses (The Sermon on the Mount, 5-7; The Missionary Discourse, 10; The Parables, 13; The Exhortation to Church Leaders, 18; and The Eschatological Discourse, 24-25) around which he has articulated his entire gospel. None of these sermons exist in quite this form in the other synoptic gospels. Matthew has compiled the material for these sermons on the basis of sayings attributed to Jesus in his written sources (Mark and the hypothetical Q-source) and the oral traditions handed down to him. Moreover, some of the sayings within the Matthean discourses of Jesus seem to have been formulated within the evangelist's own community and it is not unlikely that some of them are Matthew's own creation.

That an evangelist should have compiled a speech and placed it on the lips of Jesus is not something that would be acceptable according to modern canons of reporting. At most, we are familiar with anonymous speechwriters who have composed a text to be delivered by someone else who then lays claim to it by delivering it in public, but the practice of attributing speeches to important figures was fully in keeping with ancient literary customs. Ancient historians freely composed speeches for their own purposes and then attributed these speeches to the heroes and heroines of their sagas.

The Hellenistic Jewish historian, Flavius Josephus (ca. 37-ca. 100), introduced his *Jewish Antiquities* with a description of the procedure that he intended to follow: "The precise details of our Scripture records will . . . be set forth, each in its place, as my narrative proceeds, that being the procedure that I have promised to follow throughout this work, neither adding nor omitting anything" (*Jewish Antiquities*, Proem, 3). Subsequently, in the context of a description of Isaac's deliverance from child sacrifice (*Jewish Antiquities*, I, 13, 3), Josephus attributes a long speech to Abraham even though Genesis 22:8 attributes only a single sentence to Abraham. Later on, Josephus places a speech on the lips of Herod, encouraging his soldiers on to victory (*Jewish Antiquities*, XV, 5. 3), but Josephus himself gives a quite different version of this speech in the *Jewish Wars* (I, 19, 4).

A Roman contemporary of Josephus, Publius Cornelius Tacitus (ca. 55-120) is well known for his *Annals*, an early second century work in which he described the persecution of Christians by Nero. In Book Eleven of the *Annals* Tacitus described a speech purportedly delivered by the Emperor Claudius on the occasion of the conferral of the *ius honorum* on the Gauls (*Annals*, XI, 24). This speech is totally different from the one in the historical records discovered at Lyons in 1524.

If authors like Tacitus and Josephus, respected historians in the Hellenistic world, freely composed speeches which, essentially, provide an interpretation of the events which were being described, it is not implausible that Luke, a Hellenist and something of a historian, would have followed a similar procedure in composing the Acts of the Apostles. In fact, he has clearly done so. Almost one quarter of the Acts consists of twenty-four speeches, variously attributed to Peter and Paul, Stephen and James. All of these "speakers" speak the language of Luke. They speak on their topics in a way that is consistent with Luke's overall purpose in composing Acts. Contemporary scholars, therefore, consider that these various speeches of the Acts of the Apostles are Lukan compositions, written by the author of Acts according to the accepted literary customs of his time.

Letters

Even older than this early Christian "literature" (the Gospels and Acts) are the letters of Paul. Biblical scholars commonly acknowledged that Paul's letters are the oldest extant Christian texts. The first of Paul's letters was written about twenty years before the first of the gospels. Many different factors came together to produce this situation. A variety of social and theological realities had generally inhibited the production of religious literature among the first generations of Christians. The early Palestinian Christians were largely illiterate. They were, at any rate, not a "bookish" community, as the British scholar C.H. Dodd once explained. These Christians were, moreover, Christian Jews. To a large extent, they continued to worship in the temple and attend the synagogue, probably until as late as the eighties, approximately half a century after the death and resurrection of Jesus. In the religious life of Judaism, the Torah and other ancient writings, inspired by God, enjoyed a pride of place. For "the people of the book" there was simply no place for a competitive set of religious writings.

Even if their religious understanding had allowed for the composition of their own religious texts, and their social condition had made it possible, it is quite unlikely that the first generations of Christians would have produced a religious literature. Their expectation of an imminent Parousia (the glorious presence of the Lord Jesus Christ at the end of time) would have prompted them to consider such literary endeavors to be somewhat futile. Moreover, the esteem paid to the living testimony of inspired Christian prophets, to which Papias testified almost a full century after the death and resurrection of Jesus, also served to inhibit the development of their own religious literature among early Christians. It was only after they had begun to come to grips with the reality of the delay of the Parousia, with their own religious identity as distinct from Judaism, and with the death of the first generations of authentic Christian prophets, that Christian communities experienced a need to produce their own literature. Our canonical gospels are the result of this new situation.

Letters were, however, another matter. Of itself, the epistolary genre is not religious literature. Letters might occasionally touch upon religious topics. During the Hellenistic period the epistolary salutation customarily included a health wish—in fact, an implicit prayer. The body of the Hellenistic letter (its *homilia*) typically began with a prayer of thanksgiving. In addition, there might have been an occasional mention of a religious subject in a letter. By and large, however, letters did not generally deal with religious topics and were not considered to be religious literature.

Letters, moreover, are occasional compositions. The letters of antiquity, like those of our times, were written in rather specific sets of circumstances. Letters were not written for posterity's sake. They were not "literature" in the ordinary sense of the term. Hence, the conditions which impeded the development of a properly religious literature among the early Christians did not prevent itinerant preachers from writing to those whom they had met and evangelized.

Missionaries did not need to have texts with them when they preached the gospel. They might have had available small collections of pertinent scriptural citations or perhaps of Jesus' sayings, but that is another matter. Missionaries, however, did have a need to maintain contact with the communities which they had evangelized. Sustained contact was particularly desirable when problems arose within neophyte churches or when recent converts had need of an encouraging word. The itinerary of early Christian evangelists made it difficult for them to sustain or renew contacts with those to whom they had preached. Letters could help to satisfy the need for some contact between a missionary and newly evangelized Christians.

Paul clearly considered his personal presence to be the ideal response to the needs of the community (1 Thess 2:17-18). Frequently it was impossible for Paul himself to return to one of his beloved communities when it had need of his apostolic presence. In such instances Paul would try to send an emissary, such as Timothy to Thessalonica (1 Thess 3:1-2) or Titus to Corinth (2 Cor 12:17-18; cf. 2 Tim 4:10). A less desirable, though still effective way of responding authoritatively to the needs of his churches was through letters. "The Pauline letters," William G. Doty writes, "were at best a makeshift substitute for Paul's presence with the addressees." So far as we know, Paul was the first Christian missionary to have written a letter or at least the first to have written a Christian letter. His initiative in this regard is such that Helmut Koester has described Paul's first letter (1 Thess, written in about 50 or 51 A.D.) as an "experiment in Christian writing."

Within Hellenistic epistolary literature Paul's letters represent a unique development. By and large, they are much longer than the letters found among the ancient papyri, discovered towards the end of the nineteenth century. They are even longer than the extant letters of figures such as Plutarch and Cicero. It is not their length, however, which constitutes the most distinctive feature of the Pauline letter. That distinction falls to their apostolic character.

Paul's letters are clearly a development of the Hellenistic personal letter. Paul's letters and the Hellenistic personal letters have the same general purpose. They express friendship, impart information, and serve as an attenuated form of personal presence. With the exception of the letter to the Romans, written to a community which Paul had not yet visited, Paul's letters reflect the deeply seated bonds that link him to the communities which he has evangelized. Yet it is in his capacity as an apostle that Paul expresses a desire to visit and be with the community. His message is authoritative because it comes from an apostle of Christ. Indeed, Paul's letters are always written from an apostolic perspective. In this respect, they are never merely personal letters; they are always apostolic letters.

Nonetheless, the model on the basis of which Paul developed the apostolic letter is the Hellenistic personal letter. Hellenistic personal letters typically began in stereotyped fashion. The name of the one writing the letter is mentioned as the first word in the correspondence. The name of the author was immediately followed by the name of the addressee. Paul continued this custom as he wrote his apostolic letters. It was all the more important for Paul to cite his own name, and occasionally provide himself with an appropriate title—apostle, servant, or prisoner—insofar as he usually developed his argument on the basis of his previous experience with that community and his present solidarity with them. Since Paul's letters were real letters and bear his name, the oldest literature in the New Testament is literature which has been signed.

The Composition of Letters

When writing his letters, Paul occasionally made use of a secretary, that is, an *amanuensis* or scribe. One of his scribes was Tertius, who appended his own greetings to Paul's letter to the Romans (Rom 16:22). We do not know the names of any other secretaries employed by Paul, but scholars have occasionally suggested that the names which appear in the salutation of Paul's letters may very well be those of the scribes who have physically written the letters (e.g. Timothy in the case of 1 Thess). Nonetheless, there are positive indications that Paul did employ secretaries in the composition of at least some of his other letters. For example, towards the end of his first letter to the Corinthians Paul notes that he is writing a greeting in his own hand (1 Cor 16:21). In Gal 6:11, Paul writes: "See with what large letters I am writing to you with my own hand," thereby suggesting that it was possible to distinguish between the calligraphy of the main text and the handwriting of the subscription. The extant Greek papyri show that, during the period more or less contemporary with Paul's letter-writing activity, it was quite common for the writers of letters to use secretaries. Two different forms of handwriting are clearly discernible in many of these ancient texts. In most of these cases the author of the letter has apparently appended a subscription in which he takes leave of his addressee, sends greetings, and adds the date. Some of the papyri tell why the author employed a secretary. Occasionally the reason simply was that the author himself wrote too slowly. Sometimes the author's own analphabetism caused him to make use of a secretary's services. Richard N. Longenecker has suggested that the facility of having writing materials at hand might have been yet another reason for employing an *amanuensis*.

In the Roman world it was common practice for statesmen and men of letters to use secretaries in the composition of their letters. The Roman Emperor Julius Caesar (100-44 B.C.) is reported to have employed different secretaries as he simultaneously dictated four letters (see Pliny, *Natural History*, VII, 25, 91). His contemporary, Cicero (106-43 B.C.) the orator and Roman consul, was known to have used Tiro and Spintharus as secretaries (see *Ad Atticum*, XIII, 25, 3), even in the composition of personal letters to his friends and members of his family. A century later, Quintillian, the Roman rhetorician (ca. 35-100 A.D.), gave evidence of a negative attitude towards the use of secretaries. The practice of using secretaries was, however, fairly common. Cicero alleges that his own busyness was a major factor in his use of secretaries (*Ad Quintum fratrum*, II, 16, 1; *Ad Atticum*, II, 23, 1). One's poor handwriting, failing eyesight or illness, and the demands of travel seem to be other reasons prompting the use of secretaries for the writing of letters during Roman times.

Not all secretaries had the same capabilities; some were more qualified than others. Although the evidence for the practice in the Hellenistic world is difficult to evaluate, it is clear that at least some Roman secretaries had developed a system of shorthand for taking dictation. Cicero dictated to Spintharus on a syllable-by-syllable basis (*syllabatim*), but he was accustomed to dictate major sections (*totas periochas*) to Tiro, his favorite secretary (*Ad Atticum*, XIII, 25, 3). Many scholars (Otto Roller, William J. Albright, Gordon Bahr, and Richard Longenecker, pace F.R.M. Hitchcock et al.) think that ancient *amanuenses* enjoyed a great deal of freedom in the physical composition of the letters that had been dictated. According to these scholars the word-for-word dictation of letters was a relatively rare phenomenon.

Paul, then, was acting as a man of his own times and culture when he employed secretaries in the composition of his letters and added a subscription in his own hand. Although it is difficult to establish the case with full surety, it is even quite likely that Paul used a secretary in the composition of most of his letters. Otto Roller, the German scholar who produced the classic study on the use of secretaries in the Hellenistic world more than a half-century ago, thought that Paul had fully written out in his own hand only the short letter to Philemon and the longer letter to the Galatians (compare Phlm 19 with Gal 6:11).

Given the diversity of talents of ancient secretaries and the various ways in which they were used, it is quite probable that Paul made use of a variety of *amanuenses* and employed different techniques of dictation in the composition of his various letters. This variety is partially responsible for the differences of vocabulary and style that can be discerned when the various letters of Paul are compared with one another. Small differences exist in the midst of that remarkable similarity of vocabulary, style, and thought which has led scholars to write about Paul's language, his style of writing, and his theology.

When secretaries are employed for letter writing, we consider the author to be the one who is ultimately responsible for the letter. The author is the person in whose name and under whose direction the letter is sent no matter who actually composed the text. This person can be held responsible for everything within the letter. When the signature is added, this signature attests to this person's authorship of the text.

Similarly, although Paul employed scribes for the physical composition of his letters, he must be considered to be their real author.

Pseudonymity and Pseudepigraphy

A written work is properly considered to be pseudonymous when its author is deliberately identified by a name other than the author's real name. In our culture, pseudonyms are generally invented. In such cases, we speak of pen names, or noms de plumes, such as those of Mark Twain and George Sand. In antiquity, the pseudonyms used were generally names borrowed from figures from the past. In these cases pseudonymity was tantamount to pseudepigraphy, that is, the ascription of a written composition to someone other than the real author.

When the name of a real author is confused with that of a more famous namesake or when later tradition erroneously attributes an anonymous work to a known historical figure, the phenomenon is, strictly speaking, misappropriation, rather than pseudepigraphy. Nonetheless several authors (e.g. Martin Rist, Horst Balz) who have studied the phenomenon of biblical and extrabiblical pseudepigraphy use the terms pseudonymous and pseudepigraphal rather loosely and apply them to works that are really anonymous. Other authors are, however, more judicious in their choice of terms, and use the terminology of "secondary pseudonymity" to designate those anonymous works, traditionally, but falsely, attributed to an ancient writer.

In the ancient world, pseudonymity was not an exclusively Jewish phenomenon. Indeed, the pseudonymous works in the Bible are but a small part of antiquity's pseudonymous legacy. Some of it was religious and some of it was not. Following the earlier work of Josef Sint (1960), Wolfgang Speyer (1971) distinguished three different forms of religious pseudepigraphy in ancient times: genuine religious pseudepigraphy, forged religious pseudepigraphy, and fictional religious pseudepigraphy. Allowing for Speyer's use of oxymoron, genuine religious pseudepigraphy is to be found in the oracle or other religious work which has God as its author. Forged religious pseudepigraphy is present when there was a deliberate imitation of a religious oracle. Fictional religious pseudepigraphy is a poetic and literary device by which authors offer their compositions as if they were oracular.

Since the phenomenon of pseudepigraphy was in ancient times not restricted to religious literature, Horst Balz in a 1969 study distinguished four general categories of pseudepigraphy: 1) literary fictions; 2) works that have become pseudonymous in the tradition; 3) the traditions of the ancient schools; and 4) self-conscious falsifications. The category of literary fictions includes the speeches composed by such ancient historians as Herodotus, Thucydides, and Josephus as well as those oracles (Sint and Speyer's "genuine religious pseudepigraphy"), revelations, and hymns whose *Sitz-im-Leben* or life situation is a setting of community worship. Among the works that became pseudonymous in the tradition are the epic poetry attributed to Homer, Aesop's fables, and medical texts attributed to Hippocrates, discourses to Demosthenes, and philosophical speculations to Pythagoras. The traditions of the ancient schools include works produced by disciples in imitation of their masters, such as the pseudo-socratic, the pseudo-hippocratic, and pseudo-platonic texts, as well as a whole series of works by the academic, peripatetic, and stoic philosophers. The miscellaneous category of self-conscious falsifications includes a wide range of works composed for a variety of different reasons.

Bruce Metzger chose the term "literary forgery" to identify the works belonging to this last category. A literary forgery is essentially a piece of work created or modified with the express intention of deceiving its readers. The practice seems to have originated in the third or fourth century B.C. According to Galen, the Greek physician and writer (129- ca. 199 A.D.), literary forgeries began to abound as the kings of Egypt and Pergamum vied with one another in attempts to increase the holdings of their respective libraries. Indeed, the foundation of the great public libraries of antiquity, that of Alexandria founded by Ptolemy Philadelphus (283-246 B.C.) and that of

Pergamum established by Eumenes II (197-159 B.C.), created a demand for copies of the works of revered authors. Because payment was offered to those who produced books for the libraries, financial gain was frequently the motivating factor behind the composition of many of antiquity's literary forgeries. Yet, monetary greed was not the only motivation for the production of spurious works. Motives ran from the most noble to the most base and most trivial. Thanks, love, respect, or friendship sometimes prompted the production of pseudonymous works, as, for example, when a student wanted to honor a revered master. Sometimes it was modesty, real or alleged, that prompted an author to write pseudonymously. In many historical works, dramatic and literary interests prompted the attribution of pseudonymous speeches to various heroes. The Pythagoreans and Platonists held that falsehood, the "noble falsehood," was acceptable in support of religion. Some ancient works were composed pseudonymously because an exaggerated respect for the past tended to undermine the authority of later compositions. Occasionally pseudonymity was a way in which an author tried to obtain a readership for his work. Some authors chose a pseudonym in order to make use of the authority and prestige of an ancient figure when they themselves did not enjoy much authority and prestige. Sometimes it was pure malice which prompted the composition of a literary forgery, as happened, for example, in the case of some works which were written in order to attack or vilify one's enemies.

No matter the reasons why they were written, pseudonymous works used all possible means to give an impression of authority, importance, and trustworthiness. Indeed, pseudonymous works are similar to orthonymous works in this respect. Both the author who signs his work and the writer who attributes his work to another, for whatever reason, want their works to be read and appreciated.

Certain techniques were, however, particularly important for pseudonymous authors. In the Greek schools, works written in honor of a master or in dependence upon him were expected to be modelled after those of the master. *Mimēsis* (imitation) was a valued rhetorical and literary device.

Pseudonymous works intended to deceive become even more convincing to the extent that they imitated the vocabulary and phraseology, the syntax and style, the ideas and ideology of the pseudonym. The use of archaic language or a reference to past events as if they were contemporary occurrences contributed to the verisimilitude of a pseudonymous work. The pseudonymity of a work could be intensified and contextualized by means of occasional references to the time, place, and circumstances of the pseudonym as well as by references to his presumed situation or alleged personal data. Under the rubric of the techniques of pseudonymous writing, one could cite many interpolations into or additions to earlier, authentic works as well as the stories of "finding ancient books" in temples, archives, libraries, and graves.

Norbert Brox has suggested that pseudonymity supposes a lack of critical sense and a certain amount of gullibility and naiveté on the part of its readers. To some degree, that represents an accurate assessment of the situation, but the phenomenon is not always to be judged so negatively. Some of the ancients were critical readers. Taking advantage of a reader's gullibility was not always a factor at issue in literary deception.

Cicero thought that it was permissible for rhetoricians to lie in the course of their historical descriptions so that their speech might be more forceful (*Concessum est rhetoribus ementiri in historiis ut aliquid dicere possint agrutius*; *Brutus*, 11, 42). As has been mentioned, various Pythagorean and Platonist philosophers espoused the doctrine of the noble falsehood. Indeed, Plato himself stated that deception is a "useful means" (*pharmakon chrēsimon; Ab Polit.* II, 282c) or a "human means" (*Ab Polit. II, 382d-III, 383a*).

Porphyry, a second-century (A.D.) Neoplatonic philosopher, distinguished the authentic works of Pythagoras from those which had been forged. He counts 280 books among the "authentic" works, but only eighty of these are judged to have come from Pythagoras himself. The rest come from noble men who belong to Pythagoras' circle or his party, or who were heirs to his wisdom. Tertullian, the second-century Christian, is often cited as having remarked that "it is allowable that that which disciples publish should be regarded as their master's work" (*Adversus Marcionem,* IV, 5; PL 2, 567).

On the other hand, Suetonius, the first-century Roman biographer (ca.69-122 A.D.) states that Augustus condemned those who wrote *sub alieno nomine* ("under another name"), but the reason for the condemnation appears to be not so much the pseudonymity itself as the fact that it maligned the one to whom the work was attributed (*Aug* 55; cfr. 51, 1). Galen often lamented the fact that spurious interpolations had been made not only into the works of Hippocrates, but also into his very own works by devious and uncritical authors. Galen tells the story about his having overheard the comment of an educated man who had begun to peruse a work falsely attributed to him. He had read only two lines when he tossed it aside as a forgery because "the style isn't Galen's." Indeed, this learned man of letters and of medicine was so incensed by forgeries circulated in his name that he wrote a little book, entitled *On His Own Works* (*Peri tōn idiōn bibliōn*), in which he lists the works that he himself had written.

Galen developed a fairly critical method for the identification of interpolations. A couple of centuries later, Jerome (ca. 342-420), exposed a forgery that had been attributed to him. He, too, developed a series of criteria for distinguishing between authentic works and forgeries. Among his considerations were the following: Is the work inferior in subject matter when compared to other works by the alleged author? When was the work written, and how does this date agree with other historical evidence? Does the work conflict with or contradict the known works of the author? Does the style of the work correspond to that of the author, his language, and the period in which he wrote?

Pseudepigraphal Letters

What about letters? Were letters, ostensibly signed documents, sometimes attributed to someone other than their real authors? Bruce Metzger has responded: "Among the several kinds of literary forgeries in antiquity, arising from diverse motives, that of producing spurious epistles seems to have been most assiduously practiced. There is scarcely an illustrious personality in Greek literature or history from Themistocles down to Alexander, who was not credited with a more or less extensive correspondence." The German scholars Horst Balz and Norbert Brox concur with this assessment, but Brox also notes that the practice of epistolary forgery was more common among the Greeks than it was among the Romans. Indeed, the striking individuality of epistolary style makes it relatively easy to imitate and forge letters. As a result, forged correspondence was a fairly common phenomenon in both pagan and Christian antiquity.

How is such correspondence to be judged? In the case of letters there is virtually no possibility of "secondary pseudonymity" or misappropriation. By nature, letters are signed texts. Thus, the pseudonymity of letters is very explicit. Moreover, since letters are signed by their authors, pseudonymous letters are pseudepigraphical, that is, they purport to have been written by the person whose name appears, in Hellenistic style, at the head of the letter.

A modern person might judge the ancient practice of epistolary pseudepigraphy in the same way that he would judge the forgery of a letter at the present time. A general and spontaneous judgment would be a judgment made too hastily and applied too universally. In antiquity, the production of pseudonymous letters was prompted by almost as many different kinds of factors as provoked the composition of other kinds of pseudonymous writing.

Historians occasionally composed and used letters in much the same way as they composed and used speeches, that is, to provide either a dramatic quality for their narrative or an interpretation for the events which they were describing. In the judgment of some biblical scholars, the letter to the churches of Antioch, Syria and Cilicia in Acts 15:23-29 is a letter of this sort. The letters to the seven churches of Asia are merely literary creations (Rev 1:4-5; 2:1-3:22). The letter of Demetrius to Jonathan (1 Macc 11:30-37) might have been similarly composed by the author of Maccabees.

On the other hand, fifty letters attributed to the philosopher

Epicurus were far from innocent. According to Diogenes Laertius, the biographer of the Greek philosophers, these obscene letters were composed by a Stoic named Diotimus who wrote in order to defame the philosopher, for whom he had no use (*The Lives and Opinions of Eminent Philosophers,* X, 3).

The practice of composing forged letters for rather base motives could easily be subject matter for a chapter in early Church history. Heretics frequently found a means of gaining credibility for their doctrines by publishing them under a false name. According to one forged letter, Jerome is alleged to have attributed the translation of the Bible into Latin (the Latin Vulgate edition) to the folly of his youth. A faulty exposition on the Trinity was included in a collection of Cyprian's letters. These and other examples of blatant falsification come from a period in the history of the early church when it had already become customary for Christian writers to acknowledge their own writings.

Might it not have been possible for an earlier generation of Christian writers to have composed letters in Paul's name, thereby honoring him and invoking his authority? While the idea may initially seem a bit farfetched, it would not have been without precedent in Hellenistic Judaism. The letter of Jeremiah claims to be a copy of a letter sent by the prophet in 597 B.C. to those Jews who were about to be deported to Babylon. Its contents appear to be a disquisition upon Jer 10:11. Roman Catholic tradition considers it to be an integral part of the canonical Bible. In the history of the biblical manuscripts, the letter (Ep. Jer.) sometimes appears as an independent work while at other times it appears as the sixth chapter of the book of Baruch. The letter of Jeremiah has nothing, however, to do with Baruch, Jeremiah's disciple. Most scholars consider that it was written during the Hellenistic period, most probably in the second century B.C.

A famous Jewish letter of uncertain origin is the letter of Aristeas. The letter is best known for its legend about the origin of the Septuagint, the standard Greek translation of the Bible. According to the story, Ptolemy Philadelphus desired to have a copy, in Greek, of the Hebrew law for his library in

Alexandria. He engaged seventy-two translators for his work. Working simultaneously, though independently, these seventy-two men produced a translation of the Pentateuch. Later the legend was expanded so that the entire Greek Bible came to be known as the Septuagint (LXX), from the Greek "seventy," in honor of its reputed translators. The letter of Aristeas, in which this tradition is contained, claims to have been written by a certain Aristeas, an official in the Egyptian court, during the reign of Ptolemy Philadelphus. This datum would place the composition of the letter in the first half of the third century B.C. Scholarly opinion has been unable to date the letter with certainty. Opinions range from about 200 B.C. to 33 A.D., but all agree that the letter of Aristeas was written much later than the reign of Ptolemy Philadelphus.

New Testament Pseudepigrapha?

Since the development of the historical-critical method of biblical interpretation during the eighteenth and nineteenth centuries, many questions have been raised as to the authorship of the biblical books. Some of the inquiries focused on the books that were actually anonymous compositions, later attributed to various ancient "authors." Critical scholarship has also asked questions about the authorship of some biblical books which seemingly claim, explicitly or implicitly, to have been written by some noted figure from the Jewish or Christian tradition. Some scholars believed that pseudonymity represented the Hellenization of the ancient Jewish tradition of anonymous religious literature. Indeed, critical scholarship rapidly came to the consensus judgment that Jewish apocalyptic literature was basically pseudonymous. Apocalyptic writings are generically attributed to names from the real author's "normative past."

In the troubled times in which Jewish apocalyptic literature was written, mere anonymity would have sufficed to hide the authors' real identities. Jewish apocalyptic literature is, nonetheless, generally pseudonymous rather than simply anonymous. There even seems to be some connection between the various apocalyptic works and their pseudonyms. How is this phenomenon to be explained?

R.H. Charles, D.S. Russell and other scholars have attempted to elucidate apocalyptic literature's pseudonymous character. Charles, for example, cited the widespread belief that prophecy had ceased at the time of Ezra. He also drew attention to the growing supremacy of the Law within Judaism. Along with such later authors as Eva Osswald, Horst Balz, and Donald Guthrie, he hypothesized that since the time of canonical revelation was believed to have come to its end, later religious works had to borrow canonical names. For his part, Russell made use of H. Wheeler Robinson's notion of corporate personality to suggest that there was a mixing of individual and group identity. Differences between Semitic and Western conceptions of time were cited so as to suggest that the Semitic mind would provide a sort of contemporaneity between an author and his patron. Reflections on the Hebrew understanding of the name gave rise to a notion of extended personality whereby it was suggested that by appropriating the name of a patronym an apocalyptic author became as it were an extension of the personality of his hero.

The suggestion that a variety of factors might have contributed to the formation of the apocalyptic pseudepigrapha prompts one to ask if there might not have existed various factors which contributed to the formation of Christian pseudepigrapha. The question is all the more intriguing in that literary pseudonymity and pseudepigraphy were quite common in the Hellenistic world in which the earliest Christian literature was composed. Moreover, it is well known that the earliest expressions of Christianity were culturally conditioned. An important aspect of the cultural incarnation of Christianity was the transposition of the gospel message from a Jewish *weltanschauung* and its attendant institutions into a Hellenistic framework and its pertinent institutions.

Only a relatively small percentage of the New Testament's contents actually claim to have been written by a given individual in early Christianity. For the various reasons briefly reviewed earlier on in this chapter, literary ascription is characteristic only of the New Testament's epistolary literature.

Thirteen "letters" are attributed to Paul, that is, according to the canonical order, Romans, 1-2 Corinthians, Galatians, Ephesians, Philippians, Colossians, 1-2 Thessalonians, 1-2 Timothy, Titus, and Philemon. Four general letters are attributed to other authors, namely, James, 1-2 Peter, and Jude. As for the Johannine letters, 1 John is in fact anonymous, while 2-3 John are attributed to "the elder."

Upon analysis, it appears that some of these "letters" are not really letters; they are documents made to appear like letters. With regard to these texts, which only seem to be like letters, one might ask the question that scholarship has raised with regard to the so-called Epistle of Barnabas. If its epistolary form is artificial, might not the name of its apparent author likewise be a literary device? Most contemporary students of early Christian history answer yes to this question. They hold that the Epistle of Barnabas was the work of an Alexandrian Christian who wrote towards the end of the first century A.D., rather than a letter written by Barnabas, the sometime companion of Paul.

In evaluating the situation of the New Testament letters which are really not letters, many critical scholars have implied that pseudonymity was a relatively innocent literary device used by ancient authors and that it was easily recognized by their contemporaries. These scholars were disinclined to use pejorative terms like fraud or forgery when speaking about the possibility of New Testament pseudonymity and pseudepigraphy. Shortly after the turn of the century, Adolf Jülicher, for example, explained that "it is only to the advantage of an exceedingly narrow view of history that we should attach ideas of fraud and deceit to writing published by men of a later generation under cover of some honored name in the past." For many of the scholars who shared similar views, epistolary pseudepigraphy was simply a stylistic device.

Recent studies on the phenomenon of pseudonymity in the ancient Greek, Roman, and Jewish cultures indicate that it is simplistic to speak about pseudonymity/pseudepigraphy as a mere literary device. Pseudonymity and pseudepigraphy were widespread in the ancient world, but they arose from different motivations, served different purposes, and were judged differently even by their contemporaries. Nonetheless, pseudonymity and pseudepigraphy were, in any case, sufficiently common in both Hellenism and Judaism during the first century of Christianity as to make it quite plausible for Christians to have written pseudonymously. For these Christians the possibility of Christian pseudonymous writings was further enhanced by the way in which religious traditions had been passed down and attributed to figures from the past, within both the Jewish and the Christian traditions.

If early Christian pseudepigraphical literature really existed, was its pseudonymity merely a variant on and a development of the anonymity of early Christian literature (so, eventually, thought Kurt Aland)? Or might not early Christian pseudepigraphical literature be the result of a coming together of a Jewish-Christian religious tradition which ascribed materials and specific genres to heroes of the past (Moses, Solomon, Jesus, for example) and a cultural situation (Hellenism) which allowed for the ambivalent phenomenon of pseudepigraphical epistolary writing?

Possibility is not reality. Each case must be judged on its own merits, but the contemporary biblical scholar must at least deal with the possibility that some of the canonical New Testament texts are in fact pseudonymous. There are relatively few contemporary biblical scholars who would claim that the epistles of Peter, James, and Jude were written by men who belonged to the group of Jesus' twelve disciples.

What about the epistles of Paul? Unlike Peter, James, and Jude, Paul is known to have written letters. He developed a form of the apostolic letter which prompted imitation by later writers whose works have been incorporated into the New Testament (for example, 1 Pet and the letters of Rev 2:1-3:22). Paul's influence on the history of early Christianity was so significant that Luke portrayed Paul as the means by which the Holy Spirit carried the proclamation of the gospel to the ends of the earth (Acts 1:8). A critical reading of Acts, however, shows that Luke's portrayal of Paul is highly stylized. From the tradition about Paul, Luke has created a portrait of the apostle which was pertinent to his own historical situation.

Some contemporary authors use the term "Paulinism" to

indicate, in a rather loose fashion, that body of thought and group of writers who have been influenced by Paul. This does not mean that these various writers had direct interaction among themselves; it simply implies that they were dependent upon a tradition in which Paul was singularly revered. Some scholars are a bit more specific. Hans Conzelmann and Jean Giblet, for example, speak of a Pauline school, in the fashion in which other scholars speak of a Matthean (Krister Stendahl) or a Johannine school (R. Alan Culpepper). Had there really existed a Pauline school, it would have been a relatively easy matter for the members of the school to write in the name of Paul. The practice would have had a precedent in the various Hellenistic schools and, among Jews, in the "schools" of the prophets. Within the Pauline school, the practice of the art of *mimēsis* could well have occasioned the production of Pauline epistolary pseudepigrapha.

Even apart from the existence of a Pauline school—for which evidence is highly circumstantial—might not the figure of Paul have been sufficiently important for the writing of apostolic letters under his name? Might not some local churches have had need of an actualized Pauline tradition? Questions such as these can not be answered in the abstract. Only an examination of the Pauline letters themselves can provide the elements for a response.

Fortunately, there are thirteen letters attributed to Paul in the canonical Pauline corpus. Long ago men like Galen and Jerome recognized that stylistic comparison is a major consideration in determining whether a work is authentic or not. To this criterion of stylistic homogeneity one can add that of thematic homogeneity. Issues of stylistic and thematic homogeneity are the major considerations to be weighed when one asks about the existence of deutero-Pauline works. If they did exist, which books in the New Testament are deutero-Pauline (i.e. not written by him, but attributed to him)? Pseudonymity is a cloak for anonymity, but is there more to it than that? How are the deutero-Pauline letters to be interpreted? What does the phenomenon of canonical Pauline pseudepigraphy really mean? These are the questions to be considered in the following chapters.

A Brief Bibliography

Aland, Kurt. "The Problem of Anonymity and Pseudonymity in Christian Literature of the First Two Centuries," *JTS* 12 (1961) 39-49.

Beckwith, Roger. "The Ancient Attitude to Pseudonymity," in *The Old Testament Canon of the New Testament Church: and its Background in Early Judaism.* Grand Rapids: Eerdmans, 1985, 346-358.

Dalton, W.J. "Pseudepigraphy in the New Testament," *Catholic Theological Review* 5 (1983) 29-35.

Dunn, James D.G. "The Problem of Pseudonymity," in *The Living Word.* London: SCM, 1987, 65-85.

Fenton, J. C. "Pseudonymity in the New Testament," *Theology* 58 (1955) 51-56.

Koch, Klaus. "Pseudonymous Writing," in Keith Crim, ed., *IDBSup,* 712-714.

Longenecker, Richard N. "Ancient Amanuenses and the Pauline Epistles," in R.N. Longenecker and M.C. Tenney, eds., *New Dimensions in New Testament Study.* Grand Rapids: Zondervan, 1974, 281-297.

Meade, David G. *Pseudonymity and Canon.* WUNT, 39. Tübingen: Mohr, 1986.

Metzger, Bruce M. "Literary Forgeries and Canonical Pseudepigrapha," *JBL* 91 (1972) 3-24.

Rist, Martin. "Pseudepigraphy and the Early Christians," in D. E. Aune, ed., *Studies in New Testament and Early Christian Literature.* NovTSup, 33. Leiden: Brill, 1972, 75-91.

Stowers, Stanley K. *Letter-Writing in Greco-Roman Antiquity.* Philadelphia: Westminster, 1986.

White, John L. "Paul and the Apostolic Letter Tradition," *CBQ* 45 (1983) 433-444.

White, John L. *Light from Ancient Letters.* Philadelphia: Fortress, 1986.

3

The Pastoral Epistles

Since the middle of the eighteenth century, the two epistles to Timothy and the letter to Titus have commonly been known as the pastoral epistles. D.N. Bardot called the epistle to Titus a pastoral epistle in 1703, but it was not until 1753 that this terminology was first used as a descriptive title for all three letters. Paul Anton employed this title in his book, *Essays on the Pastoral Epistles* (*Abhandlungen der Pastoralbriefe*). Anton's choice of this descriptive title was motivated by his idea that the three epistles contain "divine instruction for all church servants and the true original of a church constitution according to God's will."

Even a cursory reading of the epistles shows that the use of this title is quite appropriate for the texts. The first epistle to Timothy indicates that Paul left Timothy behind in the Asia Minor city of Ephesus to provide pastoral care there while he himself continued on to Macedonia (1 Tim 1:3-6; cf. 2 Tim 1:18; 4:12), while the epistle to Titus indicates that Titus had been similarly left behind in Crete while Paul continued on with his missionary journey (Titus 1:5). Subsequent tradition, as Eusebius of Caesarea already mentioned in his fourth century *Ecclesiastical History* revered Timothy as the first bishop of Ephesus and Titus as the first bishop of Crete. From this point of view, the addressees of the pastoral epistles are indeed pastors. Moreover, the content of the three epistles is mainly concerned with the pastoral responsibilities of those to whom the texts are addressed.

The pastoral epistles were not included in the *Apostolikon* of Marcion, a second-century Roman heretic who had an inordinate preference for the writings of Paul. Tertullian suggested that Marcion deliberately excluded the three texts from his collection of Pauline writings, but it cannot be proved that Marcion ever knew about their existence. Later in the century (ca.172) Tatian, the founder of a heretical sect in Syria, accepted the epistle to Titus but seems to have rejected the two epistles to Timothy. By the end of the second century, however, Christians universally accepted the three pastoral epistles as letters of Paul the apostle to his chief co-workers. In its review of the various epistles of Paul, the Muratorian fragment expressed a common judgment when it stated: "...to Titus one (epistle), and to Timothy two (epistles) were put in writing from personal inclination and attachment, to be in honor however with the Catholic Church for the ordering of ecclesiastical discipline."

This widely accepted opinion held the day until the beginning of the nineteenth century, when various scholars—particularly German scholars inspired by the Enlightenment—began to express doubts about Paul's authorship of one or another of these epistles. In 1804, J.E.C. Schmidt expressed reservations about the authenticity of 1 Timothy. In the following year, Edward Evanson, while apparently holding to the Pauline authorship of 1 (and 2) Timothy, expressed doubts as to the authenticity of Titus. In 1807, Friedrich Schleiermacher launched the first systematic attack against the Pauline authorship of 1 Timothy. He argued that the linguistic differences between that epistle and 2 Timothy and Titus were so great as to make it virtually impossible for the author of 2 Timothy and Titus to have written 1 Timothy as well. He also noted that the biographical information on Paul given by 1 Timothy was not consistent with what is otherwise known about the apostle. Schleiermacher readily admitted that there were substantial similarities among the three texts, but suggested that these resulted from the author of 1 Timothy having borrowed from the other two epistles.

In 1812, Johann Gottfried Eichhorn, a professor at the University of Göttingen, published the second volume of his influential *Introduction to the New Testament* (*Einleitung in das Neue Testament*). In this work he drew attention to the distinctive religious language of all three pastoral epistles and suggested that this vocabulary was so distinctive as to make it unlikely that Paul was the author of these texts. One generation later (1835), the Tübingen scholar, Ferdinand Christian Baur, vigorously denied the Pauline authorship of 1 Timothy and noted that there were sufficient links between the polemical argumentation of the pastoral epistles and second-century gnosticism as to warrant the conclusion that the three epistles were written sometime during the second century— several decades, therefore, after Paul's death.

During the course of the nineteenth century, German critical scholarship gradually came to a consensus that the epistles to Timothy and Titus had not been written by Paul. This point of view was expressed in various Introductions to the New Testament that appeared in the second half of the century, as, for example, those of de Wette (1858), Baur (1879, 2nd ed.), and Holtzmann (1885). In his Introduction, Holtzmann collated the various arguments against the Pauline authorship of the pastorals. Since then, an ever increasing number of scholars has been proposing the view that neither of the epistles to Timothy nor the letter to Titus was the work of Paul the apostle. Writing in 1986, David G. Meade could state that the pseudonymity of the pastoral epistles is "a foregone conclusion."

One scholar's judgment that the pseudonymity of 1-2 Timothy and Titus is a foregone conclusion and a consensus among German language scholars that the pastorals were not written by Paul do not mean that all scholars are in agreement on the matter. There are still some scholars, particularly in more conservative circles, who maintain the Pauline authorship of these epistles. Pierre Dornier, for example, in an important French language commentary written in 1969 argued for the Pauline authorship of the pastorals. In 1981, Jakob Van Bruggen proposed that 1 Timothy and Titus were written during Paul's third missionary journey and that 2 Timothy was written during Paul's first imprisonment in Rome. A year later M.K. Loane likewise attempted to situate all three epistles within the context of Paul's own life and teaching. In his 1984 commentary on the pastorals, Gordon D. Fee argued that all three epistles were written by Paul, a point of view that he urged once again with specific reference to 1 Timothy in a 1986 article. In that same year Anthony Kenny proposed that a stylometric examination of the Pauline corpus allowed for the Pauline authorship of the epistle to Titus alone to be called into question. In the meantime, Michael Prior had defended a doctoral thesis at the University of London with the title, *Second Timothy: A Personal Letter of Paul* (1985).

Despite the demurrers coming from more conservative scholarship, most twentieth-century scholars remain nonetheless convinced that the apostle Paul did not write any of the pastoral epistles. They differ among themselves, however, in their judgments as to the relationship between the pastorals and the apostle. Some authors (e.g. Otto Roller) maintain that the epistles were written by an *amanuensis* or scribe. In their estimation, Paul's secretary was ultimately responsible for the linguistic and theological differences between the pastorals and the other Pauline epistles. Other scholars think that the pastorals were written by an author who used excerpts from Paul's own letters as he composed his three pseudonymous works. This view was proposed by P.N. Harrison (*The Problem of the Pastoral Epistles*, Oxford, 1921), and it was maintained by Anthony T. Hanson in his first commentary on the epistles (1966). It is also reflected in the writings of some continental European scholars, such as Gottfried Holtz (1965) and Pierre Dornier (1969). Yet another group of scholars holds that the author of the pastorals was a first-century Christian author who held Paul in high esteem. The evangelist Luke, tentatively proposed as the author of the pastorals by Heinrich August Schott in 1830, is cited as their most likely author by such recent scholars as C.F.D. Moule, August Strobel, Stephen G. Wilson, and Jerome D. Quinn.

The view that is easily preponderant, however, is that there is a fairly loose relationship between Paul and the pastoral epistles which bear his name. In the late 1950s, Lucien Cerfaux, professor of New Testament at the Catholic University of Louvain in Belgium and a member of the Pontifical Biblical

Commission, prudently suggested that "there is good reason not to use the pastoral letters in truly erudite studies without due prudence, whether there is question of defining the theology of the Apostle, or an attempt to reconstruct the history of primitive Christianity." By the end of the sixties, Norbert Brox had published *The Pastoral Letters (Die Pastoralbriefe*, Regensburg, Pustet, 1969), the first thoroughgoing commentary on these epistles written by a Catholic author from the point of view that Paul was not their author.

If Paul was not the author of the pastorals, who was? Hans von Campenhausen has suggested that Polycarp of Smyrna (ca.69-ca.155 A.D.) wrote the pastoral epistles, but most contemporary scholars, who are determined to identify the author of the epistles by name, light upon Luke as the most likely candidate to have written the documents. A far greater number of scholars, however, prefer not to specify a particular individual as the likely author of these epistles. They are comfortable with the notion that these texts are, under the cover of pseudonymity, really anonymous compositions.

When pressed, most contemporary scholars think that the pastorals were written either towards the very end of the first century or in the first decades of the second century. One scholar who considers that the pastorals reflect the state of the church in the years between 80 and 100 A.D. and therefore situates their composition within that time frame is Elliott C. Maloney. On the other hand, scholars such as Martin Rist, David G. Meade, Paul D. Hanson, and Dennis R. MacDonald believe that the pastorals reflect a development of the Pauline tradition which is most likely to be situated in Asia Minor during the early years of the second century, indeed rather close to the very turn of the century according to Anthony T. Hanson and Norbert Brox.

If indeed the pastoral epistles were written towards the turn of the second century, then it is quite possible that they were written not only after the death of Paul (sometime between 58 and 67 A.D., a likely possibility being 62 A.D. according to Robert Jewett's recent study of the chronology of Paul's life) but also after the deaths of Timothy (97 A.D.) and Titus (?). Accordingly, authors such as Werner Stenger and Josef

Zmijezski write about the "double pseudepigraphy" of the pastoral epistles. By that, they mean that both the apparent addressor and the apparent addressees of these texts fail to represent a simple historical referent. Since it has by now become common to call these texts "pastoral epistles," some commentators think it useful to designate their unknown author as "the pastor." Other commentators who nonetheless maintain the non-Pauline authorship of these texts continue to call their pseudonymous author "Paul," which they see as a useful code to designate the anonymous author. It is a convenient choice because it is faithful to the option of the author himself as well as being hallowed by centuries of Christian tradition.

The suggestion that the three epistles are doubly pseudepigraphical seems warranted when one begins to read the documents themselves. They share the form of the genuine Pauline letter, beginning with a mention of Paul, his addressee, and a greeting. This type of salutation was typical of Hellenistic personal letters and was used by Paul in his apostolic letters. As the apostolic letter form was developed by Paul, it was not unusual for him to add a title or qualification to his name as he greeted his addressees. No title is used in the first of his letters (1 Thess), but he calls himself an apostle in Romans, 1-2 Corinthians, and Galatians (cf. Eph 1:1 and Col 1:1), a servant of Christ Jesus in Philippians, and a prisoner for Jesus Christ in Philemon. Normally, the choice of a title indicates the capacity with respect to which Paul wishes to address the recipients of his correspondence. As John L. White says, Paul "explicitly refers to his status as apostle, when that is a factor in the situation at hand."

One could presume that the historical Paul would have no need of a self-introductory title in writing letters to Timothy and to Titus. Timothy was, in the words of C. H. Dodd, Paul's "chief lieutenant." Their close association is clearly attested in Paul's letters, as well as in the Acts of the Apostles. Although Luke does not mention the relationship between Paul and Titus, the name of Titus appears frequently in Paul's second letter to the Corinthians as well as in the letter to the Galatians.

The fact that Timothy and Titus were among Paul's

principal colleagues in the Hellenistic mission of the early Church makes the salutations of the epistles to Timothy and Titus so exceptional. Although the solemn salutations of the epistles to Timothy are relatively modest, the salutation of the epistle to Titus includes a rather long reflection on the nature of the apostolate: "Paul, a servant of God and an apostle of Jesus Christ, to further the faith of God's elect and their knowledge of the truth which accords with godliness, in hope of eternal life which God, who never lies, promised ages ago and at the proper time manifested in his word through the preaching with which I have been entrusted by command of God our Savior; to Titus my true child in a common faith" (Titus 1:1-4a).

Within the Pauline corpus, it is only the letter to the Romans which has a salutation as long and as solemn as that of the epistle to Titus, but the letter to the Romans was written to a Christian community which Paul had not evangelized and which he had not yet visited. In that situation, it would have been appropriate for Paul to introduce himself to the Roman Christians and share with them a common confession of faith (Rom 1:1-7a). A solemn introduction seems, however, to be somewhat out of place in a letter presumably written to a close companion and long-standing co-worker. Given the bonds of friendship and cooperation that linked Paul and Timothy with one another, it is also somewhat surprising that the two epistles to Timothy contain as formal a presentation of Paul as is found in 1 Corinthians ("Paul, called by the will of God to be an apostle of Christ Jesus...;" 1 Cor 1:1a), a letter written to a community divided within itself as to its reliance upon Paul and his apostolic authority.

The Language and Style of the Pastorals

What, in fact, are the reasons which have prompted so many scholars to doubt the Pauline authorship of the pastoral epistles? Since the time of Schleiermacher, scholars have regularly noted that the language and style of the pastorals is quite different from the language and style of the genuine

Pauline letters. In this regard, statistics are not entirely probative, but they can be helpful.

There are 3,482 words in the Greek text of the three pastoral epistles. The total vocabulary of the texts includes 901 different words. Apart from proper nouns, there are approximately 850 different words. 175 of these words are not found in any other book of the New Testament. Thus almost 20% of the general vocabulary of the pastorals is not used by Paul or by any other New Testament author. Words which occur only once in a given body of literature are called *hapax legomena* (or, in the singular, *hapax legomenon*). The Greek expression means "said once." Of the 175 *hapax legomena* of the pastorals, about sixty are not found in other first-century literature but do occur in the writings of the second-century Fathers of the Church.

While many of the *hapax legomena* found in the genuine Pauline letters come from the Greek Bible, this is not so frequently the case for the pastorals. Robert Morgenthaler, the undisputed authority in the field of New Testament vocabulary statistics, has pointed out that there are 335 words in the special vocabulary of the pastorals and that, proportionately, this special vocabulary appears two-and-a-half times as frequently as does Paul's special vocabulary in the genuine epistles. Moreover, of the 540 words common to the pastorals and to the authentic letters, only fifty represent typical Pauline vocabulary.

Statistics always need to be evaluated. The evaluation must be particularly nuanced in the case of texts as short as the pastoral epistles. In the case of the pastorals, the statistical data can be complemented by other evidence. For instance, the pastorals, lack many of the particles and shorter words that Paul commonly used—for example, "again" (*palin*), "as" (*hōste*), "then" (*ara*), and "wherefore" (*dio*). These omissions are significant because writers tend to use such short words almost unconsciously in their writings. In addition, some words from Paul's vocabulary can be found in the pastorals, but with a different meaning—for example, *archai* used by Paul to denote the principalities (Rom 8:38) but by the pastorals for human rulers (Titus 3:1) and the "in Christ" (*en*

Christō) formula, Paul's favored term to describe Christian existence, which is used in the pastorals as an almost bland equivalent for the adjective "Christian."

There are, moreover, some very characteristic Pauline concepts which are absent from the pastoral epistles. Among these are "righteousness" (*dikaiosunē*) and "body" [of Christ] (*sōma tou Christou*). "Body" is so characteristic of Paul that John A. T. Robinson has written that "the omission of the word altogether from the pastorals seems as decisive an argument against their Pauline authorship, at any rate in their present form, as any that can be advanced."

The choice of words, *lexis* according to the categories of Hellenistic rhetoric, is one element in an author's style; the other is what ancient authors called *synthesis*, or composition, that is, the way in which words were formed into phrases, phrases into clauses, and clauses into sentences. Paul's letters have a lively style, but the pastoral epistles seem to be singularly static and colorless. Their syntax is flatter and smoother than the syntax of Romans and Galatians. They lack the variety of stylistic refinements found in Paul. Their use of particles is less varied than Paul's, the sentences longer and more regular. According to Klaus Beyer the presence of "Greekisms" is far more preponderant in the pastorals than it is in the genuine Pauline letters, as a matter of fact, some ten to twenty times so according to his 1962 study.

Personal Data

One of the remarkable features of the pastoral epistles is the amount of biographical information which they contain. Some of this data is found in the so-called biographical fragments (2 Tim 1:16-18; 3:10-11; 4:1-2a, 6-22; Titus 3:12-15) which serve as the linchpin of the "Fragment Hypothesis" for the composition of the pastorals. Another element would be the number of persons mentioned in these epistles. Many of them do not appear in the New Testament outside of the pastorals. This would be the case for Eunice and Lois, the mother and grandmother of Timothy (2 Tim 1:5), the heretics

Hymenaeus, Alexander, and Philetus (1 Tim 1:20; 2 Tim 2:17; see 2 Tim 4:14), the supportive Onesiphorus (2 Tim 1:16; 4:19), the Asian deserters Phygelus and Hermogenes (2 Tim 1:15), Paul's companions Artemas (Titus 3:12), Crescens (2 Tim 4:10), Eubulus, Pudens, Linus, and Claudia (2 Tim 4:21), and Zenas the lawyer (Titus 3:13).

There are also many references to the historical situation within which the epistles were presumably composed. Chief among the historical circumstances would have been the time that Paul and Timothy worked together in Ephesus just before Paul's journey to Macedonia and the composition of 1 Timothy (see 1 Tim 1:3). There is also the Pauline mission to Crete which terminated with Titus' having been left behind to continue the work (see Titus 1:5). At the time of writing 2 Timothy, Paul is presumed to be imprisoned in Rome (2 Tim 1:8, 16-17; 2:9). In 1807, Schleiermacher had noted that it was almost impossible to reconcile the biographical information about Paul contained in the pastorals with what is otherwise known about him. In fact, the historical situation presumed by the pastorals does not tally with information contained in the Acts of the Apostles and the genuine letters of Paul.

Since the genuine letters provide only incidental bits of biographical data about Paul—far less, in fact, than the amount provided in the pastorals—the lack of correspondence between the information of Paul's letters and that of the pastorals is not excessively problematic. Much more serious is the matter of the relationship between the information of the pastorals and that of the Acts. To be sure, the Acts of the Apostles is not a history in the modern sense of the term, still less does it purport to provide the reader with a full biography of Paul. Nonetheless, the Acts of the Apostles does enjoy a significant historical foundation.

Acts tells us of Paul's three-year stay in Ephesus and his departure from there to Macedonia (Acts 20:1-2). However, it also tells us that Timothy, rather than having been left behind in Ephesus on that occasion, was actually sent ahead to Macedonia as Paul's front man (Acts 19:22). Acts tells us about Paul's two-year stay in Rome under house arrest (Acts 28:16-31), but does not mention any missionary activity of

Paul in Crete. While Paul was on his way to Rome, his ship sailed off the coast of Crete and dropped anchor for a while in the port of Fair Havens (Acts 27:7-13; see v. 21), but he himself does not seem to have set foot on the island.

If the circumstances to which the pastorals refer are historical, they must have taken place some time after Paul's two-year imprisonment in Rome. In his encomium of the Roman martyrs, Clement of Rome, writing in 96 A.D., stated that Paul "taught righteousness to the whole world, and after reaching the confines of the West (*epi terma tēs duseos elthōn*), and having given testimony before rulers, passed from the world and was taken up to the Holy Place, having become the outstanding model of endurance" (*1 Clem.* 5:7). With these words, Clement suggested that Paul had realized his dream of preaching the gospel in Spain (see Rom 15:24,28). That tradition is echoed in the late second-century *Acts of Peter* and the *Muratorian Canon*. The existence of these ancient traditions shows that Paul might have carried on some missionary activity after his Roman imprisonment, but they do not include any mention of a new visit to Ephesus or a missionary trip to Crete. As for a second Roman imprisonment, to which allusion is apparently made in 2 Tim 1:8, 16-17, and 2:9, the earliest witness is the fourth-century church historian, Eusebius of Caesarea (*Ecclesiastical History,* II, 22, 2; PG 20, 195).

Those who hold that the pastorals are genuine writings of Paul the Apostle must postulate not only this second Roman imprisonment, but also trips to Ephesus and Crete after the period in Paul's life described by Luke in the Acts of the Apostles. Most contemporary scholars believe that the historical evidence is too meager to warrant such postulation. They believe that the best way of dealing with the discrepancy between the information of Acts and that of the pastorals is the suggestion that the epistles are pseudonymous and that the biographical information which they contain is at best anachronous.

The History of the Church

A third factor in the evaluation of the question of the authorship of the pastorals has been the relationship between the epistles and the broader history of the early church. Not a few of the early critical scholars believed that the pastorals were written in an attempt to combat various heretical movements of the early second century. Some took a cue from the warning against "contradictions of what is falsely called knowledge" (*antitheseis tēs pseudōnumou gnōseōs*, 1 Tim 6:20) to suggest that the pastorals were directed against the second-century Roman heretic, Marcion, who wrote a major work called *The Antitheses* (*Antitheseis*), in which he set in opposition to one another the Creator God of the Old Testament and the loving God of the New Testament. This point of view led Marcion to reject the Old Testament completely. Some scholars who held that the pastorals were directed against Marcion and Marcionism believe that 2 Tim 3:16 was designed as an apology for the Jewish scriptures.

Other early critical scholars held that the heresy against which the polemic of the pastorals was directed was second-century gnosticism. The name covers many different forms of teaching, all characterized by an undue emphasis on *gnōsis* ("knowledge"; see 1 Tim 6:20). Since gnostic systems of thought are essentially dualistic, much speculation is directed to the origins of the universe (see 1 Tim 1:4; 4:7; 2 Tim 4:3-4; Titus 1:14; 3:9). This dualism included a disdain for matter and the human body. As far as ethics are concerned, gnostic dualism typically led either to blatant licentiousness or to an undue asceticism with prohibitions on the use of food and sex (see 1 Tim 4:3-4; Titus 1:14-15; cf. 1 Tim 2:15; 3:2; 5:23; Titus 1:6). Gnosticism fosters an elitism and a radical division between the haves (i.e. those who have "knowledge") and the have-nots (see 1 Tim 1:2, 4-5). Christian gnosticism typically affirms that the resurrection of the dead has already taken place for those who possess *gnōsis* (see 2 Tim 2:18).

These and similar ideas are found in a number of second-century sects, for example, those associated with the names of Valentinus and Basilides. The second-century gnostic heresy is chiefly known to us through the writings of various Fathers of the Church who combatted the gnostic sectarian movement among Christians. The recent discovery of ancient manuscripts, for example those found at Nag Hammadi in Upper Egypt in 1946, has shown that gnosticism is not an exclusively Christian phenomenon nor was it restricted to the second century. The second-century Christian gnostic sects were but specific manifestations of a broader phenomenon.

Today, "gnosticism" is used virtually as an umbrella term to cover a wide range of popular dualistic philosophical thought which highly esteems "knowledge" and the prophets through which it is given. Pierre Dornier suggests that the erroneous teaching against which the argumentation of the pastorals is directed is pre-gnostic, while others think that the pastor was trying to deal with an early form of gnosticism. Some scholars note that occasionally gnosticizing and Jewish thoughts were intermingled. Indeed, there is a fair amount of similarity between the dualism of popular gnostic thought and the dualism of the Essene writings found among Qumran's Dead Sea Scrolls. This fact allows other elements of the pastoral epistles to be put into somewhat sharper focus. The pastor's worry is the men of the circumcision party (*hoi ek tēs peritomēs*; Titus 1:10). They want to be teachers of the Law (1 Tim 1:7) and start quarrels about the Law (Titus 3:9). They pay heed to Jewish myths and commandments, and seem to be concerned about matters of ritual impurity (Titus 1:14-15). Thus, Stephen Wilson describes the pastor's opponents as "Jewish gnostics," while Anthony Hanson, taking his lead from Martin Dibelius and Hans Conzelmann, suggests that "Jewish protognosticism" would seem to be the best description of the heresy.

Church Order

While the contemporary evaluation of the gnostic phenomenon precludes using the identification of the pastor's opponents as gnostic as an ultimate argument for claiming that the pastoral epistles were composed during the second century, reflection on the church order promoted in the pastorals has also been used in the argumentation for their non- and post-Pauline character. Specifically, it has been suggested that the relatively well developed form of ecclesiastical structure, with its offices and officers, attested in the pastorals, is akin to that of the church in the second century. More often than not, it is argued that the monarchical episcopate and a threefold hierarchy (bishops, priests, and deacons) are second-century institutions. While it is clear that Ignatius of Antioch (ca. 35-ca. 107) was a strong proponent of the monarchical episcopate (see the letters written to various churches toward the end of his life, for example, *Eph* 2:2; *Magn* 3:1; *Trall* 2:2; 3:1) and that a threefold hierarchy of church orders existed during the second century, it is not at all clear that the church order attested in the pastorals was one that featured a monarchical episcopate and a threefold hierarchy.

The mere fact that all three terms, *episkopoi* (overseers or bishops), *presbuteroi* (presbyters or priests), and *diakonoi* (deacons or servants), appear in a single text as they do in 1 Timothy is a bit unusual, since all three terms are not found together in any other book of the New Testament. However, there seems to be some interchangeability between "overseers" (*episkopoi*) and "presbyters" (*presbuteroi*) in the pastor's use of these terms. Thus, it is probably best not to speak about a monarchical episcopate and a threefold hierarchy in the pastorals. It is better to take each text as it is, using the terminology of overseers, elders, and servants, and in this way avoiding the somewhat naive equation between forms of ministry in the pastor's vision of things and the forms of ministry that developed in the second century.

Although it is no longer possible for a scholar to maintain simply that the church order of the pastorals is the same as the church order of the second century, it remains clear that the pastor's churches are much more structured than were the Christian communities evangelized by Paul. They clearly represent a stage which, from a sociological perspective, might be called the institutionalization of the church, whereas the churches of the Pauline mission still enjoyed the sociological status of a movement. The charismatic principle was operative in the ordering of the Pauline churches; members of the local church fulfilled the necessary pastoral responsibilities. In contrast, the pastorals show a church structured according to various orders. These included the overseers (1 Tim 3:1-7; Titus 1:5-9), elders (see the elders' bill of rights in 1 Tim 5:17-22), servants (1 Tim 3:8-13), and widows (1 Tim 5:9-16). Some authors—Norbert Brox and Joachim Rohde, for example—believe that there is even a tendency towards the monarchical episcopate in the pastorals, while others think the *presbuterion* of 1 Tim 4:14 represents an abstract term ("the presbyterate") rather than a collective term ("the group of elders"). To the extent that these opinions represent valid interpretations of the pastorals, the church structure that they portray is far more developed than was the church structure of the Pauline foundations.

Theology

The study of an author's language is not simply an examination of an author's choice of vocabulary, the number and type of words that are used. What is important is not so much how many different words are used but how an author's thought is reflected in the words that have been used. An author's choice of words reflects the patterns of his or her thought. Thus, a comparison of the vocabulary of the pastorals with that of the genuine Pauline letters is not merely a matter of statistics; it is a comparative study of different signs and symbols of thought. The real differences that exist between the vocabulary of the pastorals and that of the genuine letters is symptomatic of the very real differences of thought, that is, in this case, differences of theology, among these different texts.

This is readily apparent when one considers that the pastorals do not employ such rich expressions from the Pauline theological register as "justification" and "body (of Christ)." The reality is also clear when one considers that some of Paul's most evocative expressions (e.g. the "in Christ" formula) are used in the pastorals, but with a connotation far different from that associated with those expressions in Paul's own writings. When differences of language have to do with vocabulary that is not quite as theologically pregnant as that in the examples just mentioned, the differences of vocabulary indicate differences of thought more subtly, but just as really. Indeed, it can be justifiably maintained that the differences of church structure and of ministry that can be discerned from a comparative reading of the pastorals and the authentic epistles are, in fact, an important indication of significant differences in the respective ecclesiologies (that is, the understanding of the church) of these different texts. In sum, the considerations that have been briefly reviewed thus far indicate that there are major theological differences between the pastoral epistles and the other Pauline writings.

According to Luke T. Johnson, the most telling objection to the authenticity of the pastorals is the criterion of theology and ethics. The already cited opinion of John A. T. Robinson was that the mere omission of "the body" concept was a sufficient indication of the inauthenticity of the pastorals. In the strict sense of the term, "theology" is the understanding of God or doctrine about God. One of the striking features of the theology (in this strict sense) of the pastoral epistles is the use of Hellenistic terminology in the description of God.

This is particularly apparent in the doxologies (e.g. 1 Tim 1:17; 6:15-16; 2 Tim 4:18) where, in the words of Jerome Quinn, "the words are those of Hellenism and the tune that of Jewish Hellenism." In the doxology of 2 Tim 4:18, the expression "for ever and ever" (*eis tous aiōnas tōn aiōnōn*), a solemn form characteristic of public confession, contrasts with the more simple "for evermore" (*eis tous aiōnas*) of Rom 16:27. For our purposes, more important than the form of the doxologies is their way of speaking about God. In 1 Tim 1:17, God is given the title "King of the ages" (*ho Basileus tōn aiōnōn*) and the attributes "one" (*monos*), "immortal" (*aphthartos*), and "invisible" (*aoratos*). In Titus 1:2, God is described as one who never lies (in Greek the adjective *apseudēs*, literally the "non-lying," an expression which is *hapax* in the New Testament). In Titus 2:13 God is called "great" (*megas*). This use of abstract attributes for God contrasts sharply with Pauline usage. The apostle prefers expressions which are more biblical and more concrete—for example, the living and true God (1 Thess 1:9) who tests our hearts (1 Thess 2:4). Similarly, philosophical and non-biblical is the hymnic language of the doxology found in 1 Tim 6:15-16. There God is celebrated as "the blessed and only Sovereign" (*ho makarios kai monos dunastēs*) "who alone has immortality and dwells in unapproachable light" (*ho monos echōn athanasian, phōs oikōn aprositon*). Moreover, the God of the pastorals is formulaically designated as "Savior" (*Sōtēr*, 1 Tim 1:1; 2:3; 4:10; Titus 1:3; 2:10; 3:4). The ultimate thought may well be that of the Jewish tradition, but the descriptive language is quite different from the evocative language of Paul who so often harks back to the biblical tradition itself.

Although the pastor's theology is clearly binitarian, rather than trinitarian, it is nonetheless surprising that his pneumatology (i.e. doctrine about or understanding of the Spirit) is so underdeveloped. Only four passages in the pastorals explicitly refer to the spirit of God (1 Tim 3:16; 4:1; 2 Tim 1:14; Titus 3:5). Among these four, there is one rather pedantic reference to the spirit of revelation, the spirit of prophecy, namely, "the Spirit expressly says that in later times some will depart from the faith" (1 Tim 4:1). Two of the passages explicitly mention the Holy Spirit in expressions that are as formulaic as they are theologically pregnant, that is, "the Holy Spirit who dwells in you" (2 Tim 1:14) and "renewal in the Holy Spirit" (Titus 3:5). Thus, Anthony Hanson thinks that "the author did not have a very clear theology of the Holy Spirit, and certainly did not rise to the level of the Pauline doctrine of the Spirit."

The pastor seems also to have had an understanding of "faith" (*pistis*) which is different from that of Paul. In Paul's own writings, faith is a dynamic concept. It denotes one's total response to the gospel which has been proclaimed, suggesting the very personal relationships which ensue from that response, particularly between the believer and God, the believer and the Lord Jesus, and the believer and the other members of the faith community. In the pastorals, "faith" seems to designate more the content of the gospel; it is the truth which is to be believed and maintained. To be sure, there are occasionally passages where the pastor's use of the term "faith" suggests a more subjective reality (e.g. 1 Tim 1:5, 14), but, by and large, he speaks of "faith" as an objective content. His "faith" is the *fides quae*, rather than the *fides qua*, of later theology. Among the passages in which "faith" designates the objective content of the gospel are 1 Tim 1:2, 4, 19; 3:9, 13; 4:1, 6; 5:8; 6:10, 12, 21; 2 Tim 2:18; 3:8; 4:7; Titus 1:1, 4, 13; 2:2.

Typical in this regard is 1 Tim 4:6, in which the pastor exhorts "Timothy" to be "a very good minister of Jesus Christ, nourished on the words of faith (*entrephomenos tois logois tēs pisteōs*) and of the good doctrine." The pastor's words remind the reader of the qualifications which are set out for the overseer who must "hold firm to the sure word as taught" (*tēn didachēn pistou logou*) (Titus 1:9). In 1 Tim 4:6, the pastor emphasizes the objective content of truth by putting the words of faith in apposition to good doctrine (*tēs kalēs didaskalias*, v.6) and in opposition to the pretensions of liars (*hupokrisei pseudologōn*, v. 2) and godless and silly myths (*bebēlous kai graōdeis muthous*, v.7).

The pastor's emphasis on faith as content is also reflected in his use of the formulaic expression "the saying is sure" (*pistos ho logos*), which echoes as a refrain throughout the epistles (1 Tim 1:15; 3:1; 4:9; 2 Tim 2:11; Titus 3:8), where it serves as an endorsement of the traditional material cited by the pastor in the course of his writings. Indeed, "tradition" (*parathēkē*) designates a deposit of truth to be maintained (1 Tim 6:20; 2 Tim 1:12) rather than a process of transmission as it does in 1 Cor 11:2, 23; and 15:3. The pastor's concern for orthodoxy is also reflected in his emphasis upon "sound doctrine"or "healthy teaching" (1 Tim 1:10; 6:2; 2 Tim 1:13; 4:3; Titus 1:9; 2:1; cf. Titus 1:13; 2:2). The expression, somewhat similar to the language of the philosophers, indicates not only that the teaching is reasonable, but also that it is beneficial to those who accept it.

In any comparison of the thought of the pastor with that of Paul, the emphasis must certainly lie upon what they have to say about christology and ethics. It is in their respective considerations of these two vital areas of Christian thinking and theology that we find the most noticeable differences between the reflections of Paul and those of the pastor. In his classic *Introduction to the New Testament,* Werner Georg Kümmel states the fact of the matter quite succinctly when he says that "there is evident here a completely different christological stance than in Paul... Still more striking ... is the description of Christian existence which one finds in the pastorals."

An Interlude

Before turning to an examination of the christology and ethics of the pastoral epistles, it might be helpful to reflect that exegesis, that is, the science of textual interpretation, has its own methodology. That methodology is quite unlike the methodology used in the physical sciences; it is also quite different from the methodology used in the behavioral sciences. It is, nonetheless, a methodology which is helpful because a number of indications tend to converge in a single direction without any one of them being absolutely probative. Rarely does the exegete enjoy the luxury of the singularly strong argument that is demonstrative in and of itself. On the other hand, there are many occasions when the science of exegesis is difficult to practice because the indications are all too few.

Four types of arguments are generally cited by critical scholars as indications that the pastoral epistles were not written by Paul. They are, as has been noted, the argument of vocabulary and style, the argument of biographical information, the argument of historical setting, and the argument of theological differences. Each of these arguments must be carefully evaluated. Differences of vocabulary and style, for example, do not *necessarily* indicate that two texts ultimately come from two different authors. For these differences to be truly significant, the length of the texts being compared must be taken into account. One must also consider the proportion of different vocabulary. There is also the factor of different circumstances. Differences of time and situation also account for some variety. An author's vocabulary changes with the passage of time, and it is certainly adapted to the audience or readership that is being addressed. Finally, the critic must at least entertain the possibility that a scribe has been employed for the actual writing of the texts. In the case of the pastorals there is no indication that an *amanuensis* has been used by "Paul," their author, but that possibility cannot be excluded.

When all of the variables are taken into consideration, it seems to the majority of scholars today that the differences of vocabulary and style between the pastorals and Paul's genuine letters cannot really be explained by the suggestion that the apostle wrote these epistles in his old age or that he had entrusted a good part of their formulation to his secretary. On balance, it would seem that the linguistic and stylistic differences are such that the epistles must have been written by someone other than the apostle Paul.

In our presentation of the argument of biographical information, it was noted that the data on Paul found in the pastorals cannot be integrated into the course of Paul's life such as it can be known from the Acts of the Apostles and Paul's letters. It is, of course, possible to postulate a fourth or fifth missionary journey of Paul, but that suggestion appears to be almost gratuitous and is rejected by most contemporary scholars without their being able to say absolutely that such a voyage did not take place.

As for the argument of historical situation, it has already been noted that the first authors who questioned the authenticity of the pastorals did so without benefit of the substantial historical information that has been available to scholars in the last few decades. All too readily did these earlier scholars identify the heresy combatted by the pastor with second-century Christian gnosticism. Just as readily did they equate the pastorals' church order with the structures and institutions of the second-century church. The finding of the Dead Sea Scrolls in 1948 and of the Nag Hammadi texts in 1946 have added different perspectives to this argument. There are some similarities between the organization of the Essenes at Qumran and the church of the pastorals. The study of the Nag

Hammadi manuscripts indicates that gnosticism was not merely a second-century Christian heresy. Thus, neither the "heresy" of the pastorals nor its church institutions require a second-century situation. However, it remains true that the churches of the pastorals are differently structured from the churches of the earlier and genuine Pauline letters. Moreover, it is clear that the pastor's way of dealing with the heretics, that is, generally by polemics and condemnation rather than by argument and refutation, is quite different from the way that the apostle had dealt with his opponents in the letters which he had written.

When attention is brought to bear upon the theological and other conceptual differences that obviously exist between the pastorals and the genuine letters of Paul, it is clear that sometimes the difference is often mainly a matter of emphasis. 1 Tim 1:8 proclaims that the Law is good, whereas Paul considers that the Law actually incites to sin (Rom 7:8) and carries on an extensive antinomian discussion in Romans and Galatians. However, Paul also says, albeit without emphasizing the point unduly, that "the law is holy, and the commandment is holy and just and good" (Rom 7:12). Moreover, just as different times and circumstances call for different vocabulary, so different times and circumstances evoke different types of theological reflection. Finally, one must take into consideration the various possibilities of development of thought. Even when due attention is paid to these various possibilities, contemporary scholars are more inclined to the view that the ideological differences between the pastorals and the other Pauline letters are more likely due to their having been written by an author other than Paul than their having been written by him in his declining years.

Of course, it is possible to begin a study of the pastorals by accepting at face value the tradition that attributes the pastorals to the apostle Paul. There are, however, considerable difficulties of interpretation to be faced by those who hold to the tradition. One such difficulty is precisely the fact that the epistles do not easily fit into the known biographical framework of the apostle's life. Another is that the apostle has taken to boasting about himself in his old age (see 1 Tim 1:12-17 and most of 2 Tim). This virtually requires that the old apostle underwent a change of character as he approached his declining years. Still another difficulty is "the assumption that Paul changed his original manner of speaking in his old age and adopted more worldly expressions, to express precisely those thoughts which form the very center of his Christianity." Whoever is unwilling to accept this assumption, Dibelius and Conzelmann have suggested, will deny the Pauline authorship of these epistles.

In sum, what the scholar must do, in trying to evaluate the authenticity of the pastorals, is weigh all the evidence and evaluate the cumulative effect of all the factors. As Hans von Campenhausen has written, "It is not the individual arguments against the genuineness, important as they are, which are decisive, but *their complete and comprehensive convergence* [my emphasis] against which there are no significant counter-arguments. This convergence includes the late and tendentious external witness, the strangeness and improbability of the inner and outer depiction of the life of Paul, the non-Pauline concept of the community's structure, the completely different bland speech. Above all, there is the consistent alteration in the content which is indeed connected with Paul but in such a manner as both to continue and alter his thought according to the dogmatic needs of a later time..."

A Further Reflection

Thus far we have treated the pastoral epistles as a small collection of writings within the Pauline corpus of the New Testament. In so doing, we have adopted descriptive terminology which has become customary during the past two centuries. Grouping the three epistles together in this fashion has the advantage of drawing attention to the fact that all three texts presuppose the same sort of false teachers, similar organizational structures, and comparable conditions in Ephesus and Crete. Writing about these epistles under a single rubric also has the advantage of highlighting their remarkably similar vocabulary, style, and thought. Thus, we have chosen to speak of the pastor as if one single, albeit anonymous, author has produced all three texts.

This way of treating the pastorals has, however, the decided disadvantage of drawing attention away from the real differences among the three epistles. The vocabulary of 2 Timothy is, for example, much closer to that of the genuine Pauline letters than is the vocabulary of 1 Timothy and Titus. There is, moreover, not a perfect consistency of thought among the three texts. In 1 Tim 4:14, for instance, the pastor indicates that Timothy was "ordained" in a rite in which there was an imposition of hands by the council of elders, whereas 2 Tim 1:6 suggests that Timothy had been "ordained" by Paul.

Some portion of the inconsistency of thought among the pastorals is undoubtedly due to the fact that their author employed different source materials. We should also note that the three epistles do not really have the same literary form. They are, in fact, epistles only in appearance. They certainly do not seem to be letters in the ordinary sense of that term, that is, occasional correspondence between one individual and another individual or between an individual and a group. It has already been suggested that the pastor's use of the names of Timothy and Titus in the salutation of the epistles is pseudepigraphical (see also 1 Tim 1:18; 6:20; and 2 Tim 4:10 for other mentions of Timothy and Titus). The farewell greeting of all three epistles is in the plural (1 Tim 6:21b; 2 Tim 4:22b; Titus 3:15b). This peculiarity shows that these "epistles" were really intended for a church or churches, rather than for the single individual to whom they are ostensibly addressed.

For many years, it was common for New Testament scholars to classify the pastorals as documents of church order, a literary genre to which German scholarship has given the name *Kirchenordnungen* (congregational rules). The pastorals were considered to have been the oldest examples of this type of ecclesiastical literature, which would have continued well into the fifth century with the publication of texts such as the *Didache* (early 1st cent.), the *Didascalia Apostolorum* (3rd cent.), the *Apostolic Church Order* (ca. 300 A.D.), the *Apostolic Constitutions* (4th cent.), and the *Testamentum Domini* (5th cent.). To classify 2 Timothy as a document of this type is misleading since it really does not give directives for church order. Most scholars believe that 2 Timothy should be classified as an apostolic testament. The literary form would be somewhat akin to the farewell discourses of Jewish and Christian literature (e.g. Acts 20:18-35), a literary genre which is essentially pseudonymous by nature. Recently, Benjamin Fiore has demonstrated that, from the standpoint of their literary form, the one common feature of the pastorals is their hortatory purpose, enshrined in the use of a variety of hortatory techniques. In this respect, the literary form of the pastorals is similar to that of the Socratic and pseudo-Socratic letters. Fiore has demonstrated that there exists, nonetheless, an important difference among the letters so that one should think of the pastor as having employed two different literary types. All three epistles can be considered as examples of the paraenetic letter, but 2 Timothy is personally hortatory whereas 1 Timothy and Titus are officially regulatory. With respect to their content, a further distinction can be made between these last two letters. Titus apparently contains directives for more recently established churches, whereas 1 Timothy contains directives for older, established communities. From this perspective, Titus may well have been written before 1 Timothy.

Christology

Since Hans Windisch's seminal study on the christology of the pastorals in 1935, it has been common for commentators on these epistles to make note of the christological diversity of the texts. Windisch underscored what he thought to be the pastor's lack of a unified and systematic christology when he wrote that the pastor has "no theological christology, but only teaching about Christ in the form of statements, formulas, and hymns which spring from various circles of teaching and teaching material." Windisch's thought in this regard was echoed in the important commentary by Martin Dibelius and Hans Conzelmann. They wrote: "...there is a diversity of christological perspectives which must not be combined to reconstruct 'the' christology of the pastorals. The unity does not lie in a particular christological conception (several types stand side by side with no sign of theological reflection). Rather, unity results from the constant emphasis upon the meaning of salvation for the present."

There is no small measure of truth in this type of reflection; nonetheless, some recent studies in German (especially those of Elpidius Pax, Victor Hasler, and Lorenz Oberlinner) have shown that the pastor's use of an epiphany schema provides him with a framework within which Pauline traditions and early christological formulae could be assembled. His use of the schema is associated with the christological titles, Savior *(Sōtēr)* and Lord *(Kurios)*. The use of these titles together with the epiphany schema allows the pastor to develop a functional or soteriological christology whose leitmotif is the manifestation of God's salvation in the appearance of Christ Jesus.

Apart from 2 Thess 2:8, the noun *epiphaneia*, "epiphany," "manifestation," or "appearance," appears in the New Testament only in the pastorals and it appears in all three of these texts (1 Tim 6:14; 2 Tim 1:10; 4:1, 8; Titus 2:13). The dominant notion is that of the appearance of the Lord Jesus Christ at the end of time. The pastor charges his addressees to keep the commandments until the appearance of our Lord Jesus Christ (1 Tim 6:14). In Titus 2:13, the manifestation of the glory of our great God and Savior Jesus Christ appears as the object of Christian hope, just as it does in 2 Tim 4:8 where the author's "Paul" expresses the conviction that "there is laid up for me the crown of righteousness, which the Lord, the righteous judge, will award to me on that Day, and not only to me but also to all who have loved his appearing."

Thoughts of the final appearance are also present in an exhortation of 2 Timothy when the pastor writes: "I charge you in the presence of God and of Christ Jesus who is to judge the living and the dead, and by his appearing and his kingdom" (2 Tim 4:1). Within the context of 2 Timothy, this exhortation has an unusual allure insofar as it does not immediately attribute the title "Lord" *(Kurios)* to the one who is to appear as judge. That lacuna is almost immediately rectified, in v. 8, where the pastor mentions the Lord, the righteous judge. One of the striking features of the christology of 2 Timothy, in comparison with that of 1 Timothy and Titus, is that the pastor tends to use the Lord title absolutely, that is, without being placed in apposition to the name of Jesus or being otherwise qualified. In fact he does so some fifteen times in this letter (2 Tim 1:16, 18 [2x]; 2:7, 14, 19 [2x], 22, 24; 3:11; 4:8, 14, 17, 18, 22). Thirteen of these uses of the title Lord have to do, either directly or indirectly, with judgment (i.e. all but 2:14 and 3:11).

In two of the four epiphany passages which have reference to the final appearance of Jesus, Jesus is called Savior *(Sōtēr,* 2 Tim 1:10 and Titus 2:13, specifically "our Savior" *(Sōtēr hēmon Iēsous),* a title that is also attributed to Jesus in Titus 2:4 and 3:6. This designation shows that the pastor judged that the appearance of Jesus would be a salvific experience for Christians,—he is not only Savior, but *our* Savior,—an idea which the pastor reinforced by presenting the appearance of Jesus as the object of Christian hope. The pastor's Paul awaits the crown of righteousness (2 Tim 4:8), while Onesiphorus can expect mercy on that Day, according to the pastor's prayer in 2 Tim 1:16-18.

In his function as Savior, Jesus is subordinate to God. The pastor expresses this aspect of his christology-soteriology by juxtaposing God and Christ Jesus in 2 Tim 4:1. He does so even more effectively in 1 Tim 6:14 where he complements the image of the appearance of our Lord Jesus Christ with the idea that this will be made manifest at the proper time by the blessed and only Sovereign (v. 15). In fact, the Greek text is so worded that "the blessed and only Sovereign" is the subject of the verb, allowing the pastor to enter into a veritable paean of praise for the God who has made manifest the appearance of our Lord Jesus Christ (vv. 15-16).

Of the five epiphany passages in the pastorals, the only one which does not pertain to the final, salvific appearance of Jesus is 2 Tim 1:10. There the pastor speaks of "the grace which he gave us in Christ Jesus ages ago, and now has manifested through the appearing of our Savior Christ Jesus, who abolished death and brought life and immortality to light through the gospel" (2 Tim 1:9-10). Once again we read that it is God who has made manifest the appearance of Jesus. His epiphany was in the power of God (v. 8) and in virtue of his own purpose (v. 9). However, the appearance of which the pastor speaks is not the final appearance on that Day; it is, rather, the appearance of Jesus who abolished death and brought life. It is clear that the pastor is speaking of the earthly presence of Jesus, his Incarnation and death, as an epiphany of salvation.

Two passages in the epistle to Titus remind us that the pastor really did consider the earthly presence of Jesus to be an epiphany. Before expressing his hope for the final, salvific presence of Jesus, the pastor announced that "the grace of God has appeared *(epephanē)* for the salvation of all men, training us to renounce irreligion and worldly passions, and to live sober, upright, and godly lives in this world" (Titus 2:11-12). The pastor's words clearly make reference to the earthly presence of Jesus, construed as a manifestation of the grace of God. Nonetheless, the earthly function of Jesus is that of teacher and model.

In parallel fashion, the pastor announces: "When the goodness and loving kindness of God our Savior appeared *(epephanē)*, he saved us" (Titus 3:4-5). The aorist tense of the last verb ("saved," *esōsen*) indicates that the pastor has in mind a once-and-for-all act in the past. Although some authors believe that the pastor's thought focuses in rather narrowly on the birth of Christ (e.g. Ceslas Spicq) or consider that goodness and loving kindness indicate some of the principal qualities of the human Jesus (e.g. Gottfried Holtz), it is more likely that the verse simply refers to the human presence of Jesus as a manifestation of the goodness and loving kindness of God. The pastor goes on to say that baptism is a key element in the process of salvation as he writes "not because of deeds done by us in righteousness, but in virtue of his own mercy, by the washing of regeneration and renewal in the Holy Spirit" (vv. 5-6). Since the pastor considers both the earthly presence of Jesus and his final appearance to be epiphanies of salvation, he understands that Christians live in the time between these salvific epiphanies. For them, the present age is an age of salvation.

The pastor's use of epiphanic language is rather restricted in

1 Timothy, the longest of his extant compositions. In this epistle, the pastor does not use the verb "to appear" *(epiphainō)* at all and uses the noun "appearance" *(epiphaneia)* only in 1 Tim 6:14, where it calls forth the great doxology of 1 Tim 6:15-16. In some respects, that doxology is parallel to the Christ hymn of 1 Tim 3:16: "He was manifested in the flesh, vindicated in the Spirit, seen by angels, preached among the nations, believed on in the world, taken up in glory." This hymn, apparently Jewish Christian in origin, presents in virtual chronological order the principal steps in the life of Jesus, from the Incarnation to the Ascension. In the opinion of Frederic Manns, the stich "seen by angels" *(ōpthē aggelois)* has reference to the descent of Jesus into hell. Jerome Murphy-O'Connor, however, believes that there is a strong possibility that the stich was an interpolation into the original hymn, added to emphasize the idea of tradition, namely, that the link between the past appearance of Jesus and the present is effected by human messengers (*aggeloi*). In his view, the hymn was originally a five-line composition which celebrated the God-given and God-perfected humanity of Jesus present in the world for a short period of time.

Some authors believe that this christological hymn was originally a three-line composition, each having two parts, which proclaimed the exaltation, presentation, and enthronement of Jesus. This theory seems unduly complicated. In my judgment, the hymn, certainly such as it has been used by the pastor, relates to the humanity of Jesus. It touches upon the principal moments in the story of the human Jesus.

The hymn represents one of the major christological statements of the pastorals. It begins with the confession that "he was manifested in the flesh" *(hos ephanerōthē en sarki)*. In Greek, "manifested" *(ephanerōthē)* comes from the verb *phaneroō*, "to manifest," which belongs to the same family of words as the verb *epiphainō*, "to appear," and the noun *epiphaneia*, "appearance." In sum, in the great christological hymn of 1 Tim 3:16, the pastor has once again presented the human presence of Jesus as an epiphany.

The epiphany schema employed by the pastor is one which he has taken over from the Hellenistic world in which he lived.

As a vehicle for expressing his christology, it has little in common with the history of salvation schema used so successfully by Luke in his gospel and the Acts of the Apostles. Use of the schema implies, according to Lewis Donelson, that Jesus has no immediate or direct contact with the church, or at least that the affirmation of such a contact is not of primary concern for the pastor. This would, in fact, seem to be the case. The pastorals are notably deficient in the use of theological language that would describe immediate relationships between Christ, the church, and its members. One has only to think of the avoidance of the "in Christ" formula as a description of the Christian life, of the fact that the church is not described as the body of Christ, and of the relative infrequency of the Lord title (especially of the expression "our Lord," *Kurios hēmon*; see, nonetheless, 1 Tim 1:2, 12, 14; 6:3, 14), with the striking exception of 2 Timothy where "Lord" almost always designates the one awaited at the end of time.

On the other hand, use of the epiphany schema has allowed the pastor to integrate, even if somewhat superficially, disparate christological material. He has made use of a Jewish-Christian hymn in 1 Tim 3:16 and has employed some material from Paul's letter to the Philippians in 2 Tim 4:1-8. Use of the epiphany schema has also allowed the pastor to use some titles for Jesus rather effectively. Thus he is called Savior (2 Tim 1:10; Titus 1:4; 2:13; 3:6) in reference to his first appearance (2 Tim 1:10; Titus 3:6) as well as in reference to his final appearance (Titus 2:13). It is in regard to the final appearance that Jesus is called Lord in 2 Timothy.

The pastor's striking use of these christological titles has prompted Peter Trummer to label his christology a "title christology." By that Trummer meant that the pastor preferred to express his christology by a judicious use of titles rather than by a sustained christological exposition. The pastor's use of christological titles is, in fact, remarkable. Not once does he employ the title of Son, which served the homilist so effectively in the letter to the Hebrews. Rarely does the pastor employ the title Lord (*Kurios*), and never does he use it in conjunction with the resurrection schema, so central to the thought of Paul the apostle.

Every time that the pastor mentions the name of Jesus he does so with the Christ title in apposition. Among the thirty-one occurrences of the name of Jesus in the pastorals, there is not one that is not accompanied by the Christ title. Normally the pastor prefers to call Jesus "Christ Jesus." He uses this sequence, a title followed by the name, twenty-six of the thirty-one times that he mentions Jesus' name (1 Tim 1:1 [2x], 2, 12, 14, 15, 16; 2:5; 3:13; 4:6; 5:21; 6:13; 2 Tim 1:1 [2x], 2, 9, 10, 13; 2:1, 3, 10; 3:12, 15; 4:1; Titus 1:4; 2:13). It is almost as if Christ Jesus is the name by which the pastor knew of Jesus. On only five occasions did he invert the order, calling Jesus "Jesus Christ" (1 Tim 6:3, 14; 2 Tim 2:8; Titus 1:1; 3:6).

On the other hand, it is also striking that the pastor almost never (see 1 Tim 5:11 for the exception) employs the Christ title by itself. The Christ title does not merit his attention and "Christ" seems to have enjoyed virtually no formal significance in the pastor's writing. The Christ title is extremely rich from the standpoint of the history of salvation, but that is not the pastor's chosen christological schema.

A particularly remarkable feature of the pastor's title christology is that he uses Savior and Lord interchangeably for God and for Jesus. Lord, used of Jesus in the "our Lord" formula of 1 Timothy (1:2, 12, 14; 6:3, 14) and so frequently of Jesus in his capacity as epiphanic judge in 2 Timothy (e.g. 1:16, 18), is used of God in 1 Tim 6:15 and perhaps in 2 Tim 1:18, as well. Savior is used of Christ in 2 Tim 1:10; Titus 1:4; 2:13 and 3:6, but of God in 1 Tim 1:1; 2:3; 4:10; Titus 1:3; 2:10; and 3:4.

There is also a strong possibility that Jesus is called God in Titus 2:13, a passage that the editors of the *New Jerusalem Bible* describe as "a clear statement of the divinity of Christ." Commentators are divided among themselves as to whether the reference is to the appearance of the glory of the great God and the appearance of our Savior, thus a double appearance, or to the appearance of the glory of our great God and Savior, thus a single appearance. The Greek text is difficult to interpret with the result that some modern English language translations (e.g. the RSV, the NEB, the JB and the new JB) suggest a single appearance, while others (e.g. the NAB) suggest a double appearance. In his commentary, Norbert Brox has judiciously noted that the theological meaning of the text does not depend on a solution to this thorny problem. The author's point is that the appearance of Jesus is the manifestation of divine salvation. It is, in fact, this conviction which seems to provide the conceptual framework within which the pastor was so easily able to exchange his hieratic titles between God and Jesus.

The pastor's lack of interest in the history of salvation schema does not mean that he was uninterested in the earthly presence of Jesus. Far from being uninterested in that earthly presence, the pastor has valorized the earthly presence of Jesus by means of his epiphany schema. Some aspects of Jesus' earthly presence are more important than others. He highlights the role of Jesus as the teacher (Titus 2:11-14) and model (1 Tim 6:13) of the ethical life. In the words of Lewis Donelson, "his impact appears to focus upon the ethical life, making virtues possible, providing teaching standards for virtue, and regarding virtue on judgment day. Thus, Jesus saves, because virtues save."

The pastor does not seem to have attached any salvific value to the cross of Christ as such (note the absence of any specific reference to the death of Jesus in the christological hymn of 1 Tim 3:16; cf. Phil 2:8), but he nonetheless makes unexpected reference to the passion of Jesus when he writes about his testimony before Pontius Pilate (1 Tim 6:13). This reference may well be part of the pastor's theology of suffering (see 2 Tim 2:3), of which Paul is a primary example (2 Tim 1:8; 2:3-13). The pastor, moreover, affirms that Jesus came into the world to save sinners (1 Tim 1:15) and that he is the single mediator between God and man, a mediator who gave himself as a ransom for all (1 Tim 2:5-6). The pastor knows of Jesus' resurrection and his Davidic origins (2 Tim 2:8), but has apparently chosen not to emphasize these realities. Moreover, he does not seem to have affirmed the pre-existence of Christ Jesus. Nonetheless, the christology of the hymn reproduced in 1 Tim 3:16 has what Werner Stenger has called "cosmic dimensions."

Paraenesis

Three features of the pastor's ethical exhortation strike the reader immediately. They are Jesus' function as teacher and judge of the ethical life, the exemplarity of Paul, and what Dibelius and Conzelmann call the "ideal of good Christian citizenship," identified by other commentators as the bourgeois morality of the pastoral epistles.

The pastor's epiphanic christology provides him with a framework within which he can present Jesus as one who articulated the ethical content of the Christian life in the teaching given during his first epiphany and as one who, at the time of the second epiphany, will reward or punish according to one's life of virtue or of vice. This point of view is expressed quite clearly in Titus 2:11-14: "For the grace of God has appeared for the salvation of all men training us to renounce irreligion and worldly passions, and to live sober, upright, and godly lives in this world, awaiting our blessed hope, the appearing of the glory of our great God and Savior Jesus Christ, who gave himself for us to redeem us from all iniquity and to purify for himself a people of his own who are zealous for good deeds."

The projection of Paul as a model or paradigm of the ethical life (see esp. 1 Tim 1:3-20; 2 Tim 1:3-18; 3:1-4:8) was consistent with the times in which the pastorals were written. A fair amount of literature contemporary with the pastorals used a personal paradigm as a vehicle to give content and shape to ethical teaching. In the pseudonymus Cynic letters attributed to Crates, Crates is idealized and serves as paradigm of ethical conduct according to the standards of the Cynics. The appeal to a model found in so much of the Cynic literature was particularly developed in the Socratic epistles, a collection of letters written under the name of Socrates and characterized by a distinctively Cynic point of view. The recent studies of Fiore and Donelson highlight the great similarities that exist between the Socratics' use of the idealized philosopher as a paradigm for ethical behavior and the pastorals' use of the idealized apostle in a similar fashion.

Contrast, in the form of antithesis, is a characteristic feature of the paraenesis of the Socratic epistles. It serves to identify and to promote a particular way of life. This hortatory device is used by the pastor very effectively, in accordance with his interests which are both paraenetic and polemical. The widows to be respected are contrasted with idlers, gossips, and busybodies (1 Tim 5:9-13). As God's stewards, overseers are contrasted with those insubordinate men, empty talkers, and deceitful persons to whom a damning statement of local wisdom can be applied, namely, that "Cretans are always liars, evil beasts, deadly gluttons" (Titus 1:12).

Phygelus and Hermogenes, who abandoned Paul, are sharply contrasted with Onesiphorus and his household, who not only provided for Paul at Ephesus, but, came to his assistance during the presumed Roman imprisonment (2 Tim 1:15-18). Whereas Demas, who was in love with the world, abandoned Paul, Luke stood steadfastly by him (2 Tim 4:10-11a). Alexander the coppersmith brought great harm to Paul and opposed the teaching of the apostle, whereas Timothy is expected to render aid to Paul and to remain steadfast in the teaching of the apostle (2 Tim 4:14; cf. vv. 5, 9, 13).

The pastor highlights the exemplary stature of Paul by adducing various lists of sinners and sins, such as "the lawless and disobedient, the ungodly and sinners, the unholy and profane, murders of fathers and mothers, manslayers, immoral persons, sodomites, kidnapers, liars, perjurers, etc.," a list found in 1 Tim 1:9-10 (see also 1 Tim 6:4-5; 2 Tim 3:2-5; Titus 3:3). The use of a then-now schema in 1 Tim 1:13-16 represents another antithetical device by means of which the pastor emphasizes Paul as his ethical ideal. Paul had been the foremost of sinners; now he must be considered as the greatest of saints.

What qualities of Paul are particularly valued? A brief sketch is offered in 2 Tim 3:10 where the pastor writes of Paul's teaching, conduct, and aim in life, and then of his faith, patience, love, and steadfastness. Taken cumulatively, the list functions to characterize Paul as an integrated model of the ethical life. Its first three items are broad categories, while the final four spell out some particular features of Paul's exemplary behavior. Paul's faithful endurance in the midst of being persecuted and imprisoned serves as a main theme of the pastor's theology of suffering (e.g. 2 Tim 3:11). In contrast, Paul's former life of blasphemy, persecution of the church, and insulting of God (cf. Titus 3:3) illustrate patterns of conduct to be avoided by those who would follow the model of the new Paul, saint and ethical paradigm.

The ideal of good citizenship is depicted in a number of passages (e.g. 1 Tim 2:2; 3:8) which portray the quiet life as something of an ideal. The descriptions make use of common terminology and constitute a profile remarkably akin to what Philo has called "the quiet life of an ordinary citizen" *(De Vita Mos.* 2, 235). The emphasis lies on such civil virtues as fidelity, temperance, prudence, rationality, piety, and financial integrity. The language used to indicate these virtues is commonly found in pagan ethical literature contemporary with the pastor's own times. His own emphasis on the quiet virtues seems to have been prompted by his need to counter the ultra-moralizing tendencies of the "heretics." Their disdain for the ordinariness of life in this world contrasts sharply with the vision of that ethical life in the world which the pastor portrays as characteristic of Christian existence in the age between epiphanies.

In terms of the paraenetic techniques which he uses, the pastor's listing of sinners gave him the opportunity to rehearse a list of vices similar to those found among the Stoics. He seems to have been familiar with the Stoic ethical catalogues, that is, the so-called catalogues of virtues and vices. Many of his ethical terms, including some which are *hapax* in the New Testament, are to be found in the Stoic and Cynic lists. The pastor's listing of the duties of those belonging to various ecclesiastical orders, especially the overseers (1 Tim 3:2-7; Titus 1:6-9), the servants (1 Tim 3:8-13), and widows (1 Tim 5:9-10), allows him to use rather effectively not only the categories of the catalogues of virtues, but also the categories of the traditional domestic codes.

In fact, the pastor's understanding of the ethical life seems to consist of the appropriation of rational ethical categories as a description of the Christian life within the literary context of a series of paraenetic texts. There is little doubt that the pastor offers a rationalist ethical description of Christian existence. One need only think of his idea of the good and pure conscience (1 Tim 1:5, 19; 1 Tim 3:9; 2 Tim 1:3). He stresses the importance of good works (1 Tim 2:10; 2 Tim 3:17; Titus 2:14; cf. 1 Tim 6:18). He urges that we "lead a quiet and peaceable life, godly and respectful in every way." In the pastor's judgment, such a life is good *(kalos)*, but it is also acceptable in the sight of God *(apodektos enōpion tou theou;* see 1 Tim 2:2-3).

As a summary description of proper Christian behavior, the pastor writes about "piety" *(eusebeia;* 1 Tim 2:2; 4:7-8; 6:3, 5-6, 11; 2 Tim 3:5; Titus 1:1). In the Hellenistic world in which the pastor lived, piety suggested not only cultic duties, but also general behavior which was pleasing to the gods. It is in the latter sense, albeit within a monotheistic frame of reference, that the pastor extols the virtue of piety. One of his characteristic statements in this regard is to be found in the contrast between the irreligion *(asebeian)* and worldly passions to be avoided, and the sober, upright, and godly life *(eusebōs,* an adverbial form) to be lived in this world (Titus 2:12).

Many commentators have noted that these three qualities represent four of the cardinal virtues of classic antiquity. According to the classic list of Diogenes Laertius (*The Lives and Opinions of Eminent Philosophers,* III,80), the biographer of the ancient philosophers, the cardinal virtues were prudence, justice, temperance, and fortitude. Justice ("upright") and temperance ("sober") are cited by the pastor in Titus 2:12. The pastor's "piety" does not appear on Laertius' list of the cardinal virtues, but piety is cited among the four cardinal virtues—the number four is standard—by Aeschylus and in some of Plato's earlier works. Thus, it seems that the pastor was proclaiming the importance of the cardinal virtues as a pattern of life for Christian moral behavior. The three virtues of Titus 2:12, functioning as a canon of the cardinal virtues, are, in the judgment of S.G. Mott, "a code for virtue in the full sense."

Among the elements of the ethical life to which the pastor draws particular attention are temperance (1 Tim 3:3, 8; 5:23), the civic virtues (e.g. Titus 3:1), and various virtues pertaining to the domestic sphere and sexual responsibility. Overseers and servants must be faithful to their marriage, and manage their children and households well (1 Tim 3:2, 4, 12). Within the pastor's social world, slavery was a fact of life. Echoing the accepted canons of appropriate behavior, he exhorts slaves to be faithful, responsible, and obedient (1 Tim 6:1-2; Titus 2:9-10). Women are to love their husbands and children (Titus 2:4). A false asceticism should not tempt them to avoid childbearing (1 Tim 2:15). When the pastor urges women to be sensible, chaste, domestic, kind, and submissive to their husbands, he is once again reflecting the behavioral standards of his day.

In the area of financial responsiblity and the use of wealth, the pastor requires that overseers and servants be not greedy and avaricious (1 Tim 3:3, 8). As a negative example, Demas is cited as someone who has deserted Paul because of his undue love for the present world (2 Tim 4:10). The pastor's words seem to reflect the Jewish wisdom tradition (see Job 1:21; Qoh 5:14) as he urges Christians to be content with their state of material well-being and warns them of the allure of money (1 Tim 6:6-10). Some of the pastor's "flock" were financially well-off. He urged those so-endowed not to be haughty, but to keep their focus on "God who richly furnishes us with everything to enjoy." But that is not all. Those who are rich are exhorted to be generous with the goods which they possess (1 Tim 6:17-19).

More remains to be said about the content of the pastor's paraenesis. However, the limited scope of the present work precludes an in-depth treatment of the moral exhortation of the pastoral epistles, just as it makes it impossible to offer anything more than a mere summary of some of the highlights of the pastor's christological appreciation. Nonetheless, one other feature of the pastor's paraenesis deserves to be mentioned before this brief overview is brought to a close. This is the close relationship between sound doctrine and correct ethical behavior that the pastor has emphasized in a variety of ways.

The link between teaching and conduct is intimated in the brief sketch of the Pauline model drawn in 2 Tim 3:10. It is present in the pastor's exploitation of the epiphanic schema as he portrays Jesus who has appeared in order to teach us how to live (Titus 2:11-12). It is to be found in the pastor's understanding of the scriptures, which are "profitable for teaching, for reproof *(pros elegmon)*, for correction *(pros epanorthōsin)*, and for training in righteousness *(pros paideian tēn en dikaiosunē)*, that the man of God may be complete, equipped for every good work" (2 Tim 3:16-17). It is reflected in his thoughts on the role of "Timothy" who is to "teach and urge these duties," that is, to offer that "teaching which accords with godliness" *(tē kat'eusebeian didaskalia)* (1 Tim 6:2b-4).

While there are many different ways in which the pastor shares his conviction that sound doctrine and correct behavior go together, the most striking sign of this conviction may well lie in his use of the health metaphor to characterize the traditional teaching which he urges his addressees to maintain. That teaching is described as sound or healthy doctrine (1 Tim 1:10; 6:3; 2 Tim 1:13; 4:3; Titus 1:9, 13; 2:1, 2, 8). With this description the pastor affirms that Paul's teaching is as reasonable as it is useful.

Paul

There is no doubt that Paul is the pastor's great hero. Some modern commentators claim that the pastor may have occasionally misunderstood Paul, as he makes reference to the apostle's words and interprets them here and there throughout his epistles (e.g. Phil 3:12-14 in 1 Tim 6:12 and Rom 8:12-17 in 2 Tim 1:6-9). That may well be true, but there is no doubt that the pastor idealizes, and perhaps even idolizes, Paul. For the pastor, Paul is the model Christian, the paradigm of authentic Christian life.

The pastor's appreciation of Paul comes clearly to the fore at the very beginning of his first epistle to Timothy. There "Paul" says: "I thank him who has given me strength for this, Christ Jesus our Lord, because he judged me faithful by appointing me to his service, though I formerly blasphemed and persecuted and insulted him, but I received mercy because I had acted ignorantly in unbelief and the grace of our Lord overflowed for me with the faith and love that are in Christ Jesus. The saying is sure and worthy of all acceptance, that Christ Jesus came into the world to save sinners. And I am the foremost of sinners; but I received mercy for this reason, that in me, as the foremost, Jesus Christ might display his perfect patience for an example to those who were to believe in him for eternal life" (1 Tim 1:12-16).

This is the only passage in the pastorals where it is explicitly stated that Paul is a model *(hupotupōsis)* for those who believe. Both the temporal and the qualitative meaning of "first" *(prōtos,* translated "foremost" by the RSV in vv. 15c, 16a) must be kept in mind as one reads the pastor's reflection on Paul's conversion. His encomium centers on the theme of faith, as he deftly employs the Greek root *pist*—(from the verb *pisteuō,* "to believe") throughout his portrayal of Paul: faithful *(piston,* v. 12), in unbelief *(en apistia,* v. 13), with the faith *(meta pisteōs,* v. 14), the saying is sure *(pistos ho logos,* v. 15), to believe *(pisteuein,* v. 16). The pastor's words of praise are a brief tale of Paul's before and after, and of the significance of Christ Jesus' coming into the world. His tale is told so that Paul's "life" might serve as an example for those who believe.

Although the pastor idealizes Paul's exemplary life, he also concretizes it. The so-called biographical passages, especially 2 Tim 1:16-18; 3:10-11; 4:6-22; Titus 3:12-15, clearly reveal the pastor's hand at work. Although they fulfill a literary function insofar as they are a continuation of the pseudonymous motif, thereby contributing to the verisimilitude of the pseudonymous attribution, these Pauline passages also fulfill an important role in the pastor's paraenesis. They serve to flesh out the "life" of Paul which is to serve as a model for all Christians. The model which the pastor proposes to his addressees is not some disincarnate myth, but a flesh-and-blood, even if a somewhat idealized, Paul.

What are the traits of the Pauline profile that are particularly highlighted by the pastor? Many of these traits have already been touched upon in passing, but it might be useful to bring some of them together as we try to appreciate the pastor's understanding of Paul. Paul is an example of Christian conversion (1 Tim 1:13-16). He is a model of steadfastness in the midst of suffering (2 Tim 3:10-11; 4:6-7). His entire way of life is exemplary, but one can especially consider his faith and his love (2 Tim 3:10; cf. 1 Tim 1:14). He is also a model of Christian hope (see 1 Tim 1:1; Titus 1:2; 2:13; 3:7), insofar as he expects the crown of righteousness on that Day, that is, at the epiphany of the Lord. Paul is also faithful in his teaching, and in that respect, a model teacher (2 Tim 3:10), an element in the exemplarity of Paul that it is not unimportant for the pastor who has written epistles to pseudonymous teachers called Timothy and Titus (see, for example, 2 Tim 4:2) and has offered instructions for overseers, one of whose qualifications is that they be apt teachers *(didaktikon,* 1 Tim 3:2).

The pastor not only considers Paul as a model for all Christians, especially for those called to a teaching ministry within the church; he also considers Paul to be the ecclesial authority par excellence. Ideally, Paul ought to be able to exercise his authority in person, but given his absence, his authority must be conveyed in the form of a letter. The pastor uses the literary form of the apostolic parousia, as described by Robert Funk, to affirm the authority of the absent Paul. He writes: "I hope to come to you soon, but I am writing these instructions to you so that, if I am delayed, you may know how one ought to behave in the household of God, which is the church of the living God, the pillar and bulwark of truth" (1 Tim 3:14-15).

In what areas does the absent and almost legendary Paul exercise his authority over the church? The pastorals are concerned with the truth of which 1 Tim 3:15 speaks. They are concerned with tradition handed down to Timothy and Titus, who are described in rabbinic-like fashion as the children of Paul because they have been taught by him (1 Tim 1:2; 2 Tim 1:2; Titus 1:4). The pastorals are generally concerned with orthodoxy, to which attention is drawn by such slogans as "sound teaching" and "the saying is sure." Against the horizon of this concern, it is hardly surprising that the pastor presents his hero, Paul, as the one who exercises doctrinal authority over the church. He is, in fact, the principal source of the doctrine of the church, and the ground of its tradition (cf. 2 Tim 2:8).

Timothy is exhorted to continue in what he has learned and firmly believed, knowing from whom he learned it (2 Tim 3:14). If Timothy is to be a good minister of Christ Jesus, he is to teach "these things" (the *tauta* of 1 Tim 4:6 which is a demonstrative pronoun, translated as "these instructions" by the RSV and the NAB, but more accurately by the JB as "all this"). These things are what the Paul of the pastorals has written to Timothy. These things are the words of the faith *(tois logois tēs pisteōs)* and the good doctrine *(kalēs didaskalias)*. In similar fashion, Titus is likewise to declare "these things" (Titus 2:15; 3:8).

Paul is not only the source and guarantee of the church's teaching; he is also the authority for the regulation of church praxis. Every facet of the church's life is related to Paul's authority. In 1 Tim 2, Paul lays out a series of liturgical directives. In many respects these are *ad hoc* liturgical directives. The exhortation that prayers should be offered for all seems to be formulated in the context of a gnosticizing exclusivism and the concrete rules on the role of women in the worshipping community seem to have been formulated as a response to the social and cultic disturbance brought about by the gnostic threat to the church.

A variety of norms for church order are attributed to Paul. It is on his authority that a decree on the qualification of those admitted to the orders of overseers, servants, and widows is promulgated. It is on his authority that Titus appointed elders in Crete (Titus 1:5). The use of a most solemn formula, "I charge you in the presence of God and of Christ Jesus [and of the elect angels]," in 1 Tim 5:21 and 2 Tim 4:1 serves to emphasize the idea that it is Paul's authority which ultimately authorizes Timothy to fulfill his pastoral and teaching ministry.

Yet it is not only the verbal directives of "Paul" which are set out by the pastor as authority for ecclesiastical mores; it is also the way that Paul acted. His way of dealing with opponents and disciples is paradigmatic for the way that church leaders of the pastor's day should keep heretics at a distance and attend to the continuation of ministry within the church. Paul had excommunicated Hymenaeus and Alexander because they had swerved from orthodoxy and disturbed the faith of some members of the community (1 Tim 1:20; 2 Tim 2:17-18). In similar fashion, Titus is exhorted to shun the factious person after having first admonished him once or twice (Titus 3:10-11). Paul is even proposed as the model of the ordaining prelate in 2 Tim 1:6, a passage which, when compared to 1 Tim 4:14, clearly represents an adjustment to apostolic tradition, as Eduard Schwartz proposed as long ago as 1910. This is a clear instance of what I have elsewhere called the "Pauline reductionism" of the pastorals.

A single phrase epitomizes the pastor's vision of Paul. Paul is "the apostle of Christ Jesus." The word "apostle" occurs only five times in the pastoral epistles, but each occurrence is very significant. In 1 Tim 2:7 and 2 Tim 1:11, the pastor offers his addressees a threefold description of Paul. Paul has been appointed preacher, apostle, and teacher. It is almost as if the pastor has consciously multiplied the epithets in order to convey the idea that Paul enjoys the fullness of the apostolate. In 1 Tim 2:7, the pastor even uses the formula of a mild oath ("I am telling the truth, I am not lying") to underscore the accuracy of this titulary description of Paul.

The central position in this threefold description allocated to the title apostle is striking. It is almost as if the pastor wants to explain what he understands the title apostle to mean by joining "herald" (*kērux*) and "teacher" (*didaskalos*) in apposition to the traditional description of Paul. Paul commonly calls himself an apostle and the title is given to him at least once by Luke in the Acts of the Apostles (14:14). Apart from 1 Tim 2:7 and 2 Tim 1:11, however, there is no passage in the New Testament which calls Paul either a herald or a teacher. This makes the pastor's attribution of these titles to Paul all the more significant.

What could the pastor possibly have meant by calling Paul a herald? No other Christian preacher is called by this name in the New Testament. The title obviously suggests Paul's role as a preacher, but more may underlie the pastor's choice of this title than the memory of Paul's activity as a preacher of the gospel. The only other person to be called a herald in the New Testament is Noah when, in 2 Pet 2:5, he is styled "a herald of righteousness." The expression is similar to Qumran's "Teacher of Righteousness" (see 1QH 2:13, 18; 4:27, etc.), according to a suggestion made by Ceslas Spicq. The teacher of righteousness was the interpreter of knowledge, who had a foundational and salvific role to play within the Essene community. To the extent that Spicq's suggestion enjoys merit, the pastor's use of the herald title might well indicate the foundational role attributed to Paul because of his proclamation of the gospel.

Even though teaching is cited within the list of charismatic functions in 1 Cor 12:28 and Eph 4:11, Christian preachers are not generally described as teachers in the New Testament. To the Greek mind, teachers would be expected to make systematic presentations of ideas. Why then is Paul called a teacher in 1 Tim 2:7 and 2 Tim 1:11? The pastor most probably lighted upon this term and cast Paul in the role of *the* teacher of the Gentiles because he wanted to emphasize Paul's doctrinal authority in the face of the heterodox doctrine which was of such great concern to him.

The other context within which the pastor calls Paul an apostle is in the salutation of his epistles. In all three documents Paul is formally identified as "the apostle of Christ Jesus" (1 Tim 1:1; 2 Tim 1:1; Titus 1:1). From the pastor's perspective, there is no other apostle of Christ Jesus; at least he does not give any hint that other apostles might exist. For the pastor, it is simply Paul who is *the* apostle of Christ Jesus par excellence.

The pastor's focus on the identity of Paul as the apostle of Christ Jesus sheds some light on the solemn salutations with which his epistles begin. He wants to underscore the significance of Paul's unique apostolate. Hence, from the perspective of his binary theology, he appends the qualification "by command of God our Savior and of Christ Jesus our hope" to the title in 1 Tim 1:1. In 2 Tim 1:1 he appends a somewhat similar qualification, namely, "by the will of God according to the promise of the life which is in Christ Jesus." This qualification has the particular merit of putting Paul's apostolate within the broad perspective of the divine plan of salvation ("God's will"), but it is contextualized by the idea of the promise in a document which bears so much similarity to a last will and testament of Paul.

A Brief Bibliography

Brown, Raymond E. "The Pauline Heritage in the Pastorals: The Importance of Church Structure," in *The Churches the Apostles Left Behind*. New York: Paulist, 1984, 31-46.

Collins, Raymond F. "The Image of Paul in the Pastorals," *LTP* 31 (1975) 147-173.

Dibelius, Martin—Conzelmann, Hans. *The Pastoral Epistles*. Hermeneia, Philadelphia: Fortress, 1972.

Fiore, Benjamin. *The Function of Personal Example in the Socratic and Pastoral Epistles*. AnBib, 105. Rome: Biblical Institute Press, 1986.

Hanson, Anthony T. *The Pastoral Epistles*. NCB. Grand Rapids, MI: Eerdmans, 1982.

Hanson, Anthony T. "The Domestication of Paul; A Study in the Development of Early Christian Theology," *BJRL* 63 (1981) 402-418.

Karris, Robert J. *The Pastoral Epistles*. NTM 17. Wilmington, DE: Glazier, 1979.

Karris, Robert J. "The Background and the Significance of the Polemic of the Pastoral Epistles," *JBL* 92 (1973) 549-564.

Kelly, J.N.D. *The Pastoral Epistles: I & II Timothy, Titus*. HNTC. New York: Harper and Row, 1963.

Lemaire, André. "Pastoral Epistles: Redaction and Theology," *BTB* 2 (1972) 25-42.

Mott, Stephen Charles. "Greek Ethics and Christian Conversion: the Philonic Background of Titus ii 10-14 and iii 3-7," *NovT* 20 (1978) 22-48.

Rogers, Patrick V. "The Pastoral Epistles as Deutero-Pauline," *ITQ* 45 (1978) 248-260.

Towner, P.H. "The Present Age in the Eschatology of the Pastoral Epistles," *NTS* 32 (1986) 427-448.

Verner, David C. *The Household of God: The Social World of the Pastoral Epistles.* SBLDS 71. Chico, CA: Scholars Press, 1983.

White, R.E.O. *Biblical Ethics*, 1: *The Changing Continuity of Christian Ethics.* Exeter: Paternoster, 1979, 211-215.

4
To the Ephesians

The oldest Greek manuscript of the Pauline epistles is to be found in the Beatty Museum, located just outside of Dublin, Ireland. This extensive text, Papyrus Chester Beatty II, is commonly cited by New Testament scholars under the reference number P^{46}. Dating from about the year 200 A.D., the manuscript does not contain the Pastoral Epistles. With a simple superscription, *Pros Ephesious*, "To the Ephesians," the papyrus manuscript identifies the text known to us as *The Epistle of Paul to the Ephesians*.

The epistle was well known and apparently well read in the early Church. Scholars believe that such early Fathers of the Church as Clement and Ignatius echoed this epistle in their own writings to the churches. It is almost uncontroverted that Ignatius used Ephesians in his letter to Polycarp, the bishop of Smyrna (Pol 5:1), and that Polycarp, in turn, used Ephesians when he wrote to the church at Philippi (*Phil* 1:3; 12:1). By the year 120, the epistle enjoyed a fairly widespread reputation as an epistle of the apostle Paul. Marcion, the Roman heretic of the mid-second century, who had not included the Pastorals within the *Apostolikon,* his canon of Pauline letters, did include the epistle to the Ephesians. Indeed, as the New Testament canon of the great Church began to emerge, it always included, under the name of Paul, the epistle to the Ephesians.

A great fascination with the Greek text of the New Testament developed during the Renaissance. The classical euphoria of the age led a number of humanists to take a serious look at the text of the New Testament in Greek. One of those who did so was Erasmus of Rotterdam (ca. 1466-1536), one of the first scholars to prepare a printed edition of the New Testament in Greek. Erasmus paid special attention to the style of Ephesians, which appeared to him to be quite different from the style of Paul's other epistles. Noting that "it can seem to be by someone else," Erasmus concluded that Paul had expressed himself rather clumsily in this epistle.

Toward the end of the eighteenth century, William Paley had reason to note that the authenticity of Ephesians seemed never to have been doubted. He indicated that the contents of Ephesians came from "a mind revolving a second time the same ideas." That was in 1790. Within two years' time the situation had begun to change. In 1792, Edward Evanson, a Unitarian, was the first scholar to express in print doubts about the Pauline authorship of the epistle. He reasoned that the contents of the letter were not germane to its address and that an epistle in which Paul expressed himself in such a fashion could not be genuine.

Questions about the pedigree of Ephesians remained dormant for the next three decades. Then, in 1824, Leonhard Usteri expressed doubts about the Pauline origins of the epistle on the grounds of its manifest similarity with Colossians. The close connection between these two epistles, along with various considerations on the style and address of Ephesians, led W.M.L. de Wette to question the Pauline authorship of Ephesians in his 1826 Introduction to the New Testament and then to deny Pauline authorship altogether in a short exegetical work published in 1843. Shortly thereafter de Wette's views were echoed by F.C. Baur in his classic work, *Paul the Apostle of Jesus Christ* (Stuttgart, 1845; ET: 2 vols., London, 1875-1876). Baur added to the earlier arguments adduced against Pauline authorship the notion that Ephesians is typical of a situation which he identified as "Early Catholicism" and so, in keeping with his dialectic view of early Christian history, he situated the composition of Ephesians in the early part of the second century.

As the nineteenth century ran its course, other scholars, particularly in Germany, continued to question the Pauline authorship of Ephesians. Its relationship with Colossians was the linchpin of many a critical point of view. In 1868, Sytze Hoekstra advanced the view that Ephesians was a paulinizing corrective of Colossians, a pseudonymous work which the putative corrector thought to have strayed too far from the apostle's thought. In 1870, Ferdinand Hitzig advanced the view that Ephesians was the work of an epigone who subsequently introduced some of his own ideas into the original text of Colossians. In his short 1872 *Critical Study on the Epistles to the Ephesians and the Colossians (Kritik der Epheser und Kolosserbriefe)* and his very influential 1885 *Introduction to the New Testament*, Heinrich Julius Holtzmann proffered the opinion that Ephesians was a revision of Colossians done in the light of other Pauline texts by an editor who subsequently introduced some of the new composition into Colossians.

By the end of the nineteenth century, an ever increasing number of German scholars had come to the conclusion that Ephesians was not authentically Pauline. They were joined in their judgment by some British, French, and American scholars. The emerging view was that Ephesians had been written by an unknown disciple and admirer of Paul, rather than by the apostle himself. Typical of the opinion of many scholars at the beginning of the twentieth century was the judgment expressed by James Moffatt in his 1918 *Introduction to the Literature of the New Testament*. Moffatt held that Ephesians was a "tract for the times," written by a "paulinist imbued with his master's spirit."

Of particular concern to some of the scholars who doubted the Pauline authorship of Ephesians was a plausible reconstruction of the circumstances which gave rise to Ephesians. In 1917, Johannes Weiss suggested as a possibility that Ephesians had been composed by an unknown author who had been compiling a collection of the Pauline correspondence. That kind of approach to Ephesians is often associated with the name of Edgar J. Goodspeed, who published his first significant work on this topic, *The Meaning of Ephesians*, in 1933. Goodspeed suggested that with the publication of Acts in about 90 A.D. there came a renewal of interest in Paul's career and correspondence. At that time, Onesimus, once a runaway slave who had taken refuge with Paul (see Col 4:9; Phlm 10) collected Paul's letters and composed Ephesians as an introduction to the collection. His text would have been "a mosaic of Pauline materials ... almost a Pauline anthology."

Goodspeed's hypothesis labors under the difficulty that none of the extant Greek manuscripts of Ephesians locate Ephesians either at the beginning or at the end of the Pauline corpus, a placement of the text within the Pauline collection which would have been almost unavoidable had Ephesians been composed as an introduction to the entire corpus. Nonetheless, Goodspeed's theory won the approval of John Knox in *Philemon Among the Letters of Paul: A New View of its Place and Importance* (1935), and was generally endorsed by W.L. Knox in *St. Paul and the Church of the Gentiles* (1939) as well as by C. Leslie Mitton in *The Epistle to the Ephesians* (1951), a major work that had a consideration of the authorship of the epistle as one of its main foci. Although these latter two authors did not endorse all the particulars of Goodspeed's hypothesis, particularly the notion of Ephesians' function as an introduction to the Pauline corpus and the specification of Onesimus as the likely author, they generally agree with him that Ephesians was written by someone who was quite familiar with all the Pauline letters and who was particularly well acquainted with Colossians and that its publication was in some way related to the compilation of the Pauline corpus. Moreover, they concur with Goodspeed that the circumstances of about 90 A.D. best illuminate some of the emphases of Ephesians.

At about the same time as Mitton's research, another tack was being taken in Germany by Rudolf Bultmann (see *Das Urchristentum im Rahmen der antiken Religionen*, Zurich, Artemis, 1949) and some of his disciples, particularly Ernst Käsemann and Heinrich Schlier. They studied Ephesians (together with Colossians) in the light of their reconstruction of gnosticism. A conviction that Ephesians not only used the language of gnosticism, but that it also proceeded from gnostic motives was among the reasons which led them to the conclusion that Ephesians was not written by Paul. Later on,

Günther Bornkamm, another of Bultmann's disciples, would also deny the Pauline authorship of Ephesians in a book called *Paul* (1969; ET, 1971).

The issue of the authorship of Ephesians continues to be disputed. Typical of the situation is the fact that the last major commentaries on Ephesians in German take opposite stands on the issue. Schlier, who converted to Roman Catholicism in his later years, vigorously defended the authenticity of Ephesians in his 1957 commentary on the epistle, but Joachim Gnilka, another Roman Catholic, denied Pauline authorship in his 1971 commentary on the epistle. Part of the problem in coming to a judgment as to the authorship of Ephesians is that the epistle is so thoroughly Pauline in its tone. Lucien Cerfaux, for example, once remarked that if Ephesians had not been written by Paul himself, it would have nonetheless had to be written. C.H. Dodd noted that the thought of Ephesians is the "crown of Paulinism," whether or not it was written by Paul, while F.F. Bruce called it "the quintessence of Paulinism," an expression of the dominant themes of Paul's ministry.

A Range of Opinions

Generally speaking, there continue to be four different types of response to the question of the authorship of Ephesians. Many scholars, albeit clearly in the minority today, continue to maintain the tradition of Pauline authorship. Among recent scholars who hold to the tradition are Donald Guthrie in his *Introduction to the New Testament* (1962), Markus Barth, the author of the Anchor Bible commentary on Ephesians (2 vols., 1974), J.B. Polhill, who wrote "An Introduction to Ephesians" for the 1979 issue of *The Review and Expositor* that was devoted to the study of this epistle, and F.D. Howard (1979), who holds that the epistle was written by Paul during his first Roman imprisonment (61-63 A.D.). The Pauline authorship of Ephesians has also been upheld by Aart Van Roon in a significant monograph, *The Authenticity of Ephesians* (1969; ET, 1974), and his 1976 Dutch-language commentary on the epistle.

Other scholars continue to think that Ephesians is Pauline, but only in the sense that it would have been composed by an *amanuensis* writing at Paul's direction or in the sense that the final text results from an unknown interpolator's additions to a letter originally written by Paul. The *amanuensis* hypothesis—deemed totally gratuitous by its critics, for example, Werner Georg Kümmel in his valuable *Introduction to the New Testament*—enjoyed currency among such mid-twentieth century critics such as Maurice Goguel (1935) and Martin Albertz (1952). Particularly notable among the proponents of the amanuensis theory have been a number of Roman Catholic scholars, such as Joseph Grassi, Jerome Murphy-O'Connor, Wilfrid Harrington, Karl Hermann Schelkle, Lucien Cerfaux, Lionel Swain, and Pierre Benoit. Benoit, in a series of articles and his French-language commentary on Ephesians in the Jerusalem Bible series (1949), proposed the view that the apostle had allowed his secretary a great deal of freedom in the composition of Ephesians, even allowing him to use Colossians as an additional source of information for the final draft of Ephesians.

A small group of scholars consider that the entire matter is insoluble. *Non liquet* ("it is not clear")— has been the judgment on the matter by such scholars as Adolf Jülicher, Martin Dibelius, Benjamin Wisner Bacon, Henry J. Cadbury, as well as Alan Hugh McNeile and C.S.C. Williams in their 1965 *Introduction to the Study of the New Testament*.

By far the largest group of contemporary scholars who have pronounced their verdict on this thorny issue believe that Ephesians was not actually composed by Paul. By way of "very broad approximation," Raymond Brown has estimated that about 80% of critical scholarship holds Ephesians to be inauthentic. Brown himself would fall within that category, as would such scholars as Petr Pokorný, H. Langkammer, Peter Trummer, and Helmut Koester. So, too, would Rudolf Schnackenburg (1952) and Josef Pfammatter (1987), German Roman Catholic authors who have written commentaries on the epistle. Some of the scholars who maintain that Ephesians is inauthentic, such as Arthur Patzia and David G. Meade, have done so within the context of a study of the broad phenomenon of Pauline pseudepigraphy. Some authors—for example, Patzia, James Efird, and Patrick Rogers—specifically acknowledge the authenticity of Colossians, all the while maintaining the inauthenticity of Ephesians.

If, following the majority view of contemporary critical scholarship, Ephesians has not been written by Paul, is it possible to suggest some figure in first-century Christianity who might possibly have written the epistle? Goodspeed had suggested Onesimus on the grounds, among other reasons, that Onesimus would have been quite familiar with Colossians and Philemon. The Onesimus suggestion, as has been noted, was not accepted even by some of those who generally agreed with Goodspeed's theorizing about the origins of Ephesians. John G. Gunther (1972), picking up on a suggestion by J.H. Moulton, has identified Timothy as the purported author of Ephesians, but his views have not won support in the scholarly community. On the basis of Eph 6:21-22 (cf. Col 4:7-8), Knox and Mitton proposed an opinion already launched by Schleiermacher and Renan during the nineteenth century. They thought that Tychicus was the most likely author of Ephesians, an hypothesis also supported by G.H.P. Thompson in his 1967 commentary on Ephesians. Because the non-Pauline aspects of Ephesians bear a remarkable affinity to the theology of Luke and because a good portion of the distinctive vocabulary of Ephesians is also to be found in Luke-Acts, Ralph P. Martin (1968), Peter Rhea Jones (1969), and Douglas Rowston (1979) suggest that Luke is the Paulinist responsible for the composition of Ephesians.

Despite their colleagues' options for Onesimus, Timothy, Tychicus, or Luke, most contemporary scholars prefer to respect the real author's chosen anonymity and refuse to propose—since there is so little evidence to cite—a given individual as the author of Ephesians. There is, however, a general consensus that the author of the epistle was a Hellenistic Jewish Christian who truly familiarized himself with Paul's writings. Except for the Pastorals, all the epistles in the canonical Pauline corpus seem to be echoed in Ephesians. When might this anonymous paulinist have composed the epistle to the Ephesians? It is difficult to say, but a plausible suggestion would certainly be the last decade of the first centry, A.D. Nonetheless, a few scholars—Paul D. Hanson, for example—continue to maintain the nineteenth-century view that Ephesians was written during the early part of the second century.

Paul and Ephesus

What are the reasons for suggesting that Ephesians was, most likely, not written by Paul? Initially problematic is the salutation of the letter. The epistle has traditionally been called the epistle to the Ephesians, but the translators of the RSV offer this version of its praescript: "Paul, an apostle of Christ Jesus by the will of God, to the saints who are also faithful in Christ Jesus: Grace to you and peace from God our Father and the Lord Jesus Christ (Eph 1:1-2).

This translation of Eph 1:1-2, like that of the new JB, is based on a Greek text found in P^{46}, the Codex Sinaiticus, and the Codex Vaticanus. Other ancient witnesses, however, especially the Codex Alexandrinus and the Codex Bezae Cantabrigiensis, include *en Ephesō* ("at Ephesus") in the epistolary salutation. The editors of the RSV take note of this fact in a footnote which reads: "other ancient authorities read *who are at Ephesus and faithful.*" Because of the ambiguous evidence of the manuscript tradition, the translators of Ephesians in the NEB and the NIV have included "at Ephesus" in the first verse of the epistle. The editors of the NAB offer a compromise. They include "at Ephesus" in their translation of Eph 1:1, but enclose the expression within brackets. This compromise is also to be found in the popular twenty-sixth edition of Nestle-Aland's *Novum Testamentum Graece.*

Apparently, the text of Ephesians that was available in Rome to Marcion in the middle of the second century did not include the geographical reference because Marcion has provided "To the Laodiceans" (cf. Col 4:16) as a name for the text. Although "at Ephesus" was not to be found in the most ancient texts of the epistle, the tradition was very strong that the epistle had been intended for the church of Ephesus. Thus, "at Ephesus" is found in the overwhelming majority of the Greek manuscripts of Eph 1:1, especially those dating from medieval times. The geographical reference has even been added to the old Sinaiticus and Vaticanus Codices by later correctors of these manuscripts.

The problem is not simply one of textual criticism. Rather it is one whose solution affects the way that the reader looks at the entire epistle. Some commentators have suggested that originally the epistle contained a space, which served as a sort of fill-in-the-blank. Their idea is that the epistle had been intended as a circular or encyclical letter, copies of which were sent to various churches in Asia Minor, of which Ephesus was the principal one. In that case, the name of an individual local church could be inserted as the epistle was being read to the assembly, possibly by Tychicus. Indeed, the name could also be inserted were a copy of the missive to be left behind by the itinerant reader. Although there is no other recorded instance of such a fill-in-the-blank procedure, the hypothesis has enjoyed some popularity among those who hold to the Pauline authorship of Ephesians. If Ephesians was indeed a circular letter, its linguistic and theological peculiarities are somewhat explicable.

On the other hand, the presence of "at Ephesus" in Eph 1:1 is indicative of one of the problematic aspects of Ephesians. Ephesus was not only the site of the chief Christian assembly in Asia Minor, it was also a community well known to Paul. According to Acts, Paul spent more than two years in Ephesus (Acts 19:10; cf. Acts 18:19-19:40; 20:17-38), probably a twenty-seven month period of time which Robert Jewett dates from late 52 A.D. until early 55. It was in Ephesus that Paul's co-workers Priscilla and Aquila (cf. 1 Cor 16:19; Rom 16:3) encountered Apollos, who became so significant in Paul's Corinthian churches (cf. 1 Cor 1:12; 3:4, 5, 6, 22; 4:6; 16:12). It is quite likely that Paul wrote his letters to the churches of Galatia and Corinth from Ephesus. Thus, Paul seems to have had more than a passing acquaintance with the Christian community at Ephesus. Indeed, Paul's relationships with the Christians at Ephesus were such that not a few scholars believe that the problematic long list of greetings found in Rom

16:1-16—problematic, because Paul had not yet visited the church at Rome—was originally part of a short text intended for Ephesus, where Paul surely had many friends and acquaintances.

A troubling feature of Ephesians is the fact that it contains no personal greetings, even though Paul was well known to the Ephesian community. The lack of personal greetings is consistent with the general impersonal tone of Ephesians. Yet this is so unlike Paul's way of writing to communities which he knew and had evangelized—communities in whose faith journey he had shared in a most intimate fashion, communities whose members he called "brothers" *(adelphoi)*, a familiar Pauline usage strangely absent from the epistle to the Ephesians. There seems to be almost nothing in the epistle which suggests that Paul had any personal acquaintance with the Christian community at Ephesus.

Style and Vocabulary

Arguments on the pedigree of texts which are based principally on considerations of style and vocabulary must always be advanced in a somewhat tentative way, especially when the real author may have employed a secretary. Nonetheless, this type of consideration must be carefully evaluated because it is a part of the total gestalt which leads to a judgment as to the authorship of a disputed text.

In the case of Ephesians, particular attention must be paid to its style and vocabulary. These features of the epistle were noticed by Erasmus who was a keen reader of the epistle's Greek text. Translators, however, often hide an author's stylistic and linguistic idiosyncracies. All translations are really a form of interpretation. Moreover, translators are expected to provide readable translations of the texts they have translated. Our modern English idiom prefers short sentences. Thus, the translator of Ephesians into English is almost required to break up the long periodic sentences of the Greek text of Ephesians into shorter English language sentences.

The style of Ephesians is indeed one of its striking features, one that seems to set it over and against the earlier Pauline letters. The style of Ephesians is rhetorical and slow-moving, in contrast to the style of the genuine letters which is rapid, terse, and incisive. Its sentences are lengthy, obscure, and involved (e.g. Eph 1:15-23; 4:11-16), whereas those of the genuine Paulines tend to be sharp and abrupt. The use of *oratio perpetua* (e.g. Eph 2:19-22; 3:1-7, 8-13; 4:11-16) is more common in Ephesians than it is in Paul's own letters. Breaks in the author's thought, indicated by periods and question marks in translations and edited texts, are much less frequent in Ephesians than they are in the authentic epistles. In the epistle to the Ephesians, for example, a question mark is to be found only in Eph 4:9.

Many commentators note that Ephesians seems to reflect a conscious artistic effort, while Paul's own style is looser and free-flowing. The author of Ephesians has, moreover, a tendency to verbosity, piling up synonyms one after another (e.g. "holy and blameless" in 1:4; 5:27; "wisdom and insight," in 1:8 [v.9 in the RSV]). His work contains awkward genitival constructions (e.g. *aphēs tēs epichorēgias*, "every joint with which it is supplied," Eph 4:16; *tasepithumias tēs apatēs*, literally, "lusts of deceit," Eph 4:22). These several features combine to provide the reader with a text which is heavy and ponderous in style and impersonal in tone.

The vocabulary of Ephesians is also somewhat unusual. According to Morgenthaler's count there are 2,425 words in Ephesians, which has a total vocabulary of 529 words. Among these there are forty-two words that appear only in Ephesians within the New Testament. Another thirty-six words appear elsewhere in the New Testament, but are not to be found in any other epistle of Paul. These figures are not unexpected, especially when a significant portion of the special vocabulary of Ephesians is to be found in passages which are a bit unusual, as, for instance, the bridal description in Eph 5:25-27 and the use of the panoply metaphor in Eph 6:13-17. What is more striking is the fact that the paulinist uses other words than does Paul for important concepts. For example, the paulinist generally speaks of "the heavenly places" (*hoi epouranioi*, 1:3, 20; 2:6; 3:10; 6:12), whereas Paul wrote of "the heavens" (*hoi ouranoi*, in the plural, following the Semitic practice, e.g. 1 Thess 1:10). Similarly, the paulinist has written about "bestowing grace" (*charin charitoō*, Eph 1:6) instead of "giving grace" (*charin didōmi*, e.g., Rom 12:3, 6).

A particularly significant feature of the vocabulary and style of Ephesians is its manifest affinity with the language and style of the Qumran texts. In 1960, Karl Georg Kuhn made a comparative study of Ephesians and the recently found scrolls. A few years later Reinhard Deichgräber and Franz Mussner made similar comparative studies. All three authors note that remarkable similarities exist between Ephesians and the Qumran scolls. Kuhn found so much similarity of thought and language among these texts that he came to the conclusion that a semantic universe that is so similar and a vocabulary which is so comparable could not have been developed by the paulinist and the sectarians independently of one another.

Moreover, the hymnic style which gives a liturgical tone to so much of Ephesians is also characteristic of the Hebraic style found in the Qumran texts. Comparing Ephesians to the other epistles in the Pauline corpus, Kuhn noted that instances of Semitic syntax appear in Ephesians four times more frequently than they do in the other Pauline letters. While these and similar considerations on the style and vocabulary of Ephesians do not by themselves totally rule out the possibility of Pauline authorship, they do, in the words of Kümmel, "make extremely difficult the supposition that Paul could have written Ephesians in the form in which it was handed down."

The Relationship with Colossians

The form in which Ephesians has been handed down is the nub of the problematic relationship between Ephesians and Colossians. In many respects, that relationship can be considered as a minor synoptic problem. The comparable structures, content, and vocabulary of the two epistles point to some sort of literary dependency of one upon the other. This thesis was classically proposed in a doctoral dissertation defended at the University of Marburg in 1934 by Werner

Ochel. Ochel basically argued that a paulinist had composed Ephesians on the basis of Colossians, to which was added a previously extant hymn (Eph 1:3-14) as well as some traditional liturgical (Eph 1:19-2:10) and paraenetic (Eph 3:2-7; 5:22-6:9) material.

Some commentators note that more than one third of the 155 verses in Ephesians are parallel to Colossians both in order and content. Among the most striking parallelisms are those between Eph 3:2 and Col 1:25-26; Eph 4:15-16 and Col 2:19; Eph 4:22-24 and Col 3:9-10; Eph 5:22-6:9 and Col 3:18-4:1; Eph 6:21-22 and Col 4:7-8. Moreover, there are verses in Ephesians which seem to have resulted from a conflation of verses in Colossians, for example, Eph 1:7 (= Col 1:13, 14, 20) and 1:19-20 (= Col 1:11; 2:12). Moreover, Eph 3:2-13 seems to have picked up on the theme of Col 1:24-29.

Given the extensive similarity between Ephesians and Colossians, the critic is almost inevitably inclined to conclude that Ephesians is literarily dependent on Colossians. It seems hardly likely that a man of such creativity as Paul would have re-edited an earlier work in such a bland, even if theologically profound, fashion.

On the other hand, a decisive argument against assuming Pauline authorship of both epistles is the consideration that some of the major thematic similarities between Colossians and Ephesians have been developed in a significantly different way in Ephesians from the way they were developed in Colossians. Cases in point would be the epistles' respective presentation of the "mystery" and of the "body of Christ." Such differences in the midst of such striking similarities almost inevitably lead the critic to come to the conclusion that the redactor of Ephesians is quite a different person from the author of Colossians.

Theological Differences

Notwithstanding the doubts that arise with regard to Pauline authorship of Ephesians, virtually everyone who has seriously studied the issue of the epistle's authenticity comes to the recognition that, in the final analysis, it is a consideration of the theological content of Ephesians that proves to be the most telling argument against its having been written by Paul.

We can begin with Ephesians' notion of the mystery, *mustērion*. The term is used six times in Ephesians, particularly in Eph 3:1-13, where it is to be found three times (vv. 3, 4, 9; cf. Eph 1:9; 5:32; 6:19). The Paulinist speaks of "the mystery of Christ" *(en tō mustēriō tou Christou*, v. 4) which is the obvious focus of the gospel as he perceives it. Indeed, he will characterize Paul's ministry as one of proclaiming the mystery of the gospel (Eph 6:19; cf. Eph 3:3). What is the mystery of Christ? It is the union of Jew and Gentile in the same salvation; it is the mystery of Jew and Gentile gathered together in one church, the body of Christ, that is, "how the Gentiles are fellow heirs, members of the same body, and partakers of the promise in Christ Jesus through the gospel" (Eph 3:6).

For the paulinist the notion of the mystery of Christ is an extremely rich and profound theological concept. Knowledge of the mystery comes by way of revelation (Eph 3:3); it has been made known to us (Eph 1:9). This reference to making known the mystery has parallels in the Qumran texts (e.g. lQH 4:27; lQpHab 7:4-5). Kuhn suggests that what ultimately differentiates Ephesians' (which uses the singular, "mystery") notion of mystery from that of Qumran (which tends to use the plural, "mysteries") is the paulinist's christology. In 1:9-10 the paulinist suggests that the mystery is God's plan of salvation, revealed in Jesus Christ. The "mystery" entails not only the unity of Jew and Gentile in the one body of Christ, but also the reconciliation of all things in Christ in the fullness of time. Toward the end of his epistle, the paulinist's use of the term mystery takes on a somewhat unusual turn. In Eph 5:32 "mystery" is used analagously of the relationship between Christ and the Church and of the relationship between Christian husband and Christian wife.

Despite the theological depth of the paulinist's notion of the mystery of Christ and the mystery of God's will, that is, the mystery of God's salvific will revealed in Christ, it is clearly different from anything that we find in the authentic Pauline letters. The term "mystery" appears in the epistle to the

Colossians (Col 1:26, 27; 2:2; 4:3), but there the focus is on the revelation of that which has been hidden, the salvation of the Gentiles in Christ. Missing from Colossians is the key notion of ecclesial and cosmic reconciliation. Still further removed from what the paulinist understands by mystery is the way that Paul uses the term in two of his great letters, Rom and 1 Cor (cf. Rom 11:25; 16:25; 1 Cor 2:1, 7; 4:1; 13:2; 14:2; 15:51). There, especially in the letter to the Corinthians, mystery suggests a secret. It is a matter of hidden divine truths of which the minister of the gospel is the steward.

Not only does Ephesians' notion of mystery differ significantly from the ideas of mystery found in Colossians and the genuine Pauline epistles, it also appears to be a notion somewhat foreign to Paul's own times and ministry. The marvelous reconciliation of Jew and Gentile in the one body of Christ seems far removed from the tensions and struggles between the two cultural groups which so occupied Paul's missionary efforts and required his epistolary care. In Eph 3:5 there is mention of the mystery revealed to the holy apostles and prophets by the Spirit, a notion not only different from that of Col 1:26 which speaks of the revelation to the saints, but one that seems to imply some temporal distance between that revelation and the author's own day. In any case, Paul would not have spoken in terms of the "holy apostles," a bit of phraseology that is foreign to the genuine letters. Finally, the characterization of Paul in the paulinist's presentation of the mystery (Eph 3:8) utterly lacks the spontaneity of Paul's own reflections on his call (e.g. 1 Cor 15:9).

The paulinist's statement about the revelation made to the holy apostles and prophets (Eph 3:5) calls to mind the statement which he had made just a few verses previously, where he concludes a series of thoughts about the two (i.e. Gentile and Jew) being made one in Jesus with the reflection that they (ostensibly the Gentile element) have become "fellow-citizens" *(sumpolitai)* with the saints and members of the household of God, built upon the foundation *(themelion)* of the apostles and saints (Eph 2:20). This statement is quite different not only from what the apostle had said in 1 Cor 3:11 where Jesus Christ is the sole foundation *(themelion)*, but also from what is said in Col 2:7 where Christians are said to be rooted and built up in Christ Jesus the Lord. In sum, the paulinist's thought seems to be characterized by an ecclesial application or expansion not present in Colossians and the authentic writings of the apostle.

The Church is the main theme of Ephesians. This feature so permeates the exposition of the paulinist's thought that Ernst Käsemann has repeatedly claimed that its christology is almost exclusively interpreted from the viewpoint of its ecclesiology, while a more moderate critic like Helmut Merklein acknowledges that the cross has become ecclesiological in Ephesians. The paulinist's specifically ecclesial interest becomes apparent towards the end of the first chapter (Eph 1:22-23), when he uses the term "church" *(ekklēsia)* to refer to Christians who had previously been indicated by the use of the first person plural ("we") and the adjectival noun ("saints").

Within the Pauline corpus the ecclesiology of Ephesians is quite distinctive. Paul writes to and about the church in all of his letters. Ordinarily he uses the term church (*ekklēsia*) to indicate the local community of believers. Most commonly, his usage of this terminology draws attention to the assembly as such (e.g. 1 Cor 11:18; 12:28). Paul can also write about the churches because there are various local gatherings of Christian believers (e.g. Gal 1:2; 1 Thess 2:14). In Ephesians, "church" is never used in the plural. It is always used in the singular (Eph 1:22; 2:10, 21; 5:23, 24, 25, 27, 29, 32) and exclusively designates the universal—and, therefore, somewhat abstract—community of believers.

This shift in emphasis from the local church to the universal church is quite apparent in the way in which the body of Christ is used as a symbol of the church. The image is used in Rom 12 and 1 Cor 12 in reference to the local church. The diversity of members of the human body serves as an analogue to the different charismatic functions within the church. It is, moreover, the entire church which is the body of Christ. In Eph 4:1-16, however, it is the universal church which is described as the body of Christ. Moreover, Christ is described as the head of the body (Eph 4:15; cf. Col 1:18; 2:10, 19), a description which points to his authority over the church and his life-giving role in its regard. The end result, however, is to apply to the church the image of the torso of Christ. The universal church is the body, but Christ is the head. The Church and Christ are not simply to be identified with one another, as the image of Christ as bridegroom and the church as bride in Eph 5:23-32 indicates. Admittedly, many features of Ephesians' ecclesial use of the body image are similar to those of Colossians, but there are significant differences between the two epistles' respective ecclesiologies.

In Eph 5:23 Christ is called the Savior of the body, a striking expression that recalls Phil 3:20. Another aspect of the paulinist's unique profile of the church is his insistence on the holiness of the church (cf. Eph 5:27). Generally, commentators think that the paulinist's emphasis upon the church as an apostolic foundation (Eph 2:20; 3:5) is foreign to Paul's authentic thought. Finally, the paulinist pays virtually no attention to church order (i.e. except for Eph 4:11). In this respect, he is so unlike the pastor, who seems to have regarded the church as a tightly structured institution. In this respect, the paulinist was also rather unlike the apostle who was quite concerned with pastoral care, leadership, and the practical demands of unity within the communities to which he wrote.

The paulinist's unique appreciation of the church deserves further comment, but it can only be touched upon briefly at the present time because it is only one—although a most important one—of the theological differences that set Ephesians apart from the earlier Pauline letters. Another significant difference is Ephesians' complete lack of reference to the Parousia. Some commentators have suggested that, in Ephesians, the expectation of the Parousia has been replaced by the notion of the universal mission of the church. Ephesians introduces a notion of superhuman powers that threaten human existence—"the prince of power of the air" in Eph 2:2 and "the world rulers of this present darkness" in Eph 6:12. Such awesome creatures were apparently unknown to Paul.

Paul rarely writes about the kingdom of God, the terminology that so pervades the Synoptic gospels. On those rare occasions when Paul does write of the kingdom, his language is traditional. He writes about the "kingdom of God" *(hē basileia tou theou;* Rom 14:17; 1 Cor 4:20; 6:9, 10; 15:50; Gal 5:21; cf. Col 4:11; 2 Thess 1:5). In Eph 5:5, the paulinist writes of the "kingdom of Christ and of God" *(hē basileia tou christou kai theou),* an expression that we do not find elsewhere in the New Testament.

Yet another area where commentators occasionally find substantial differences between the views of the paulinist and that of the apostle is that of their respective attitudes towards marriage. The reflection suggests that the positive understanding of marriage found in Eph 5:22-33 is essentially incompatible with the negative views expressed by Paul in 1 Cor 7. It is, of course, true that no other passage in the New Testament, let alone in Paul's genuine letters, speaks of marriage in terms of the mystery (Eph 5:32), but the supposed incompatibility between Paul's views and those of the paulinist may well rest on a misreading of 1 Cor 7:1 (cf. 1 Thess 4:3-5).

An Interlude

The fact that contemporary scholars, a very large percentage of whom do not consider Paul to have been the author of Ephesians, believe that theological considerations are the single most weighty argument against Pauline authorship of the epistle should lead the discerning reader to acknowledge that the issue of Pauline authorship of this epistle—or any other epistle, for that matter—is not simply an introductory question. Consideration of the authorship of a letter is truly an exegetical matter. Conclusions as to authorship result from a careful consideration of the meaning of the text under discussion. To a large extent, the issue of authorship requires a much more in-depth consideration of an author's theology and his thought patterns than do other exegetical approaches to the text.

On the other hand, it sometimes happens that scholars make a judgment as to the inauthenticity of a text without necessarily being consequent with their scholarly judgment. The relative brevity of articles in scholarly journals legitimately dispenses an author from laying out the full range of implications of a text's inauthenticity. Similarly, the summary exposition of the usual introductory issues in the standard Introductions to the New Testament does not allow for a consequent treatment of the position taken on the issue of authorship. Occasionally, however, commentaries and articles are published which are not consequent on the issue of authenticity. A verdict as to an epistle's inauthenticity is rendered, but the text itself is interpreted as if Paul were really the author. Rarely is this legitimate, as it might be, for instance, if the commentator believes that the epigone intended that the readers of the epistle understand the text as if it were written by Paul for the reader of his (i.e. Paul's own) times. It is not legitimate if the commentator believes that the epigone intended that the text be interpreted as a message for Christians of his (i.e. the imitator's) own day.

The Form of the Epistle

In the case of the epistle to the Ephesians, we are certainly dealing with the work of an imitator. Its author had an intimate knowledge of Paul's own letters, at least of all those letters that history has preserved. He has expanded on Paul's own themes so that his work seems to be the diffused echo of the sounds of Paul's own voice. In Eph 2:8-10, for example, he gives an assessment of some of Paul's major themes that would be useful for his own purposes. Such intimacy may serve, in the words of David G. Meade, as indirect testimony to the closeness of the writer to his master. Such intimacy is not found in the third-century epistle to the Laodiceans, which is a none too artistic pastiche of quotations from Paul's genuine letters.

The salutation of that curious text is: "Paul, an apostle not of men and not through man, but through Jesus Christ, to the brethren who are in Laodicea: grace to you and peace from God the Father and the Lord Jesus Christ." In contrast, the salutation of Ephesians is, as has been noted, "Paul, an apostle of Christ Jesus by the will of God, to the saints who are also faithful in Christ Jesus: grace to you and peace from God our

Father and the Lord Jesus Christ" (Eph 1:1-2, RSV). This salutation is a bit unusual insofar as Paul's preferred practice seems to have been to cite the names of other missionaries along with himself as he was writing to the churches which he had evangelized. Romans and Galatians are exceptional in this regard, but Romans was written as a letter of introduction to a community that Paul had not yet visited, and Galatians was an angry letter written to correct a community that had strayed from the gospel of Paul, the apostle. In contrast to these exceptional situations, where Paul alone is the stated author and greeter, Paul, Silvanus, and Timothy are cited as the senders of 1-2 Thessalonians, Paul and Sosthenes are cited in 1 Corinthians, and Paul and Timothy are cited together in the salutations of 2 Corinthians, Philippians, Colossians, and Philemon. In this light, the solitary mention of Paul in Eph 1:1-2 is striking indeed.

In yet another respect Ephesians has "an unusual introduction to a New Testament letter" (Peter T. O'Brien). In Eph 1, we have a salutation (vv. 1-2), followed by a *berakah* or benediction (vv. 3-14), a brief thanksgiving (vv. 15-16), and a prayer report that breaks into a paean of praise (vv. 17-22). Normally, Paul's letters follow the usual Hellenistic epistolary practice, in which a thanksgiving—generally for a specific benefit received—follows immediately upon the salutation. The benediction formulary is more typical of the Jewish world. The epistolary benediction was not foreign to Paul. The apostle employed a benediction rather than a thanksgiving in his second letter to the Corinthians (2 Cor 1:3-4; cf. 1 Pet 1:3-5). What is unusual about the beginning of the epistle to the Ephesians is not the presence of a rather lengthy *berakah*; what is really unusual about this epistle is the presence of both a benediction and a thanksgiving.

A discussion of these features of the first chapter of Ephesians is really a discussion of the form of the text. Is Ephesians really a letter? It is certainly not a letter in the ordinary sense of the term. Raymond Brown considers it to be marginally a letter, while even such a strong defender of the authenticity of Ephesians as Aart Van Roon admits that it is possible that Ephesians is a simulated letter, constructed at a later date. Among English-language interpreters of Ephesians, a fair number of scholars hold that Ephesians was written as a circular or encyclical letter.

On the other hand, Willi Marxsen considers that Ephesians is not at all a letter. He thinks that it is really impossible to identify its literary form because its occasion and purpose cannot be determined with any certainty. Other commentators, equally convinced that Ephesians is not a letter in the proper sense of the term, are a bit more audacious in their judgments. They dare to hazard an opinion as to the text's literary form. At the end of the last century, Holtzmann considered that Ephesians was really a homily. Heinrich Schlier thought that Ephesians was a piece of wisdom literature. More recently, Ernst Käsemann and Wolfgang Schenk have opined that Ephesians is really a tractate or treatise, while John Coutts has considered it to be a discourse on baptism.

William Doty's studies, however, have shown that the epistolary genre was a fairly broad category of ancient Hellenistic writing. It included letters that were truly letters, and texts that only seemed to be like letters. Within this perspective it seems correct to speak of Ephesians as an epistle, but it is not a letter in the ordinary sense of the term. In this regard, Nils Dahl writes that Ephesians "belongs to a type of Greek letters—genuine and spurious—which substitute for a public speech rather than for private conversation. The epistolary purpose is to overcome separation and to establish contact between sender and recipients."

Christology

F.F. Bruce has suggested that the benediction of Eph 1:3-4, "Blessed be the God and Father of our Lord Jesus Christ, who has blessed us in Christ with every spiritual blessing in the heavenly places, even as he chose us in him before the foundation of the world, that we should be holy and blameless before him," provides the reader with the keynote of the epistle. In fact, the benediction comprises only a pair of verses at the beginning of a single long sentence in the Greek text (vv.

3-14 which most modern translations and the editors of the common handbook edition of the Greek New Testament have chosen to break up into smaller units of thought for readability's sake). The paulinist's opening gambit focuses on Jesus Christ, in and through whom God bestows his blessings. The expression "in Christ" *(en Christō)* echoes as a remarkable refrain throughout the introductory paragraph. Three times the paulinist invokes the formula itself (vv. 3, 10, 12). Once he uses a remarkable variant of the traditional Pauline formula, as he writes of the grace freely bestowed on us "in the Beloved" (*en tō ēgapēmenō* v. 6). "In Him" (*en autō*) or "in whom" (*en hō*), syncopated versions of the formula required by the grammatical syntax of the text appears seven times (vv. 4, 7, 9, 10, 11, 13 [twice]) in the paulinist's introductory exposition.

Jules Cambier suggests that the "in Christ" refrain, with its variants, serves to introduce different developments in the divine plan of salvation. God's plan of salvation is the main theme of what he, along with several other scholars, believes to be an ancient Christian hymn, quoted by the author of Ephesians. It is more likely that the paulinist himself composed the benediction in hymnic style than that he adapted an already existing hymn, but there is no doubt that the "in Christ" formula is the leitmotif of his composition. It epitomizes his major christological insights; and those are very rich indeed.

Although the paulinist has composed a text whose main theme is ecclesiology, there is little doubt that he has made one of the most significant christological statements in the entire New Testament. Christology has to do with the significance of Jesus from a theological perspective. Leander Keck suggests that in a developed christology the structure of significance is expressed in terms of three key relationships: to God (the theological correlation), to creation (the cosmological correlation), and to humanity (the anthropological correlation). The depth of the paulinist's appreciation of these three correlations shows that his christological exposition is one of the richest and most developed in the New Testament.

The very fact that the paulinist has chosen the literary form of the *berakah* for his opening christological statement serves to place his christology within a significant theological framework. The *berakah* is essentially a prayer of praise to God for the blessings of his salvation. The paulinist begins his prayer in typical Jewish fashion, "Blessed be God" (*eulogētos ho theos*). Immediately thereafter he identifies the God whom he praises as the Father of our Lord Jesus Christ. The paulinist uses the full christological formula "our Lord Jesus Christ" (*tou Kuriou hēmon Iēsou Christou*, Eph 1:3).

This solemn formula appears in four other places in the epistle (Eph 1:17; 3:11; 5:20; 6:24). In all but one of these instances the full christological formula is explicitly linked to a mention of God. The sole exception is Eph 3:11, where the paulinist departs slightly from his customary usage as he writes about "Christ Jesus our Lord" *(en tō Christō Iēsou tō Kuriō hēmōn)*. Here, the unusual sequence of the words in the paulinist's phrase may well be dictated by the fact that it occurs in the formulation "*in* Christ Jesus our Lord." "In Christ" is his standard formulation. It occurs in the three already cited verses of the opening benediction (vv. 3, 10, 12), and in nine other passages of the epistle (Eph 1:20; 2:6, 7, 10, 13; 3:6, 11, 21; 4:32). In Eph 3:11, when the paulinist writes of "Christ Jesus our Lord" he does not really depart from his normal practice wherein God is his focus as he uses the full christological title. Here, the title occurs in a context in which the paulinist is writing about the role of Paul as one called to make known the mystery of God's salvific plan.

The theological correlation of the paulinist's christology— to which he has given witness by choosing the *berakah* as a literary form and by juxtaposing the mention of God and our Lord Jesus Christ—is further underscored by the paulinist's choice of Father, a relational title, as a divine epithet. The God to be praised is the Father of our Lord Jesus Christ. The paulinist's words are similar to those he will use a little further on when he writes about "the God of our Lord Jesus Christ, the Father of glory" (Eph 1:17). Still further along he will write about "the Son of God" *(tou huiou tou theou*, Eph 4:13, the only time that this title is used in Ephesians). The paulinist is well aware of the nature of the unique relationship that binds the Son of God to the Father.

The *berakah* clearly underscores the initiative of God in the unfolding of the mystery of salvation. It is God who has blessed us (v. 3), chosen us (v. 4), destined us (v. 5), and made known to us the mystery of his will (v. 9). All of this is realized "in Christ." Allan has suggested that here, as throughout the epistle, "in Christ" is used instrumentally, but the expression should not be taken too narrowly. It designates Jesus as the means and mediator of salvation in a very broad sense. It is in Christ that there is grace, redemption, forgiveness, revelation, and the recapitulation of all things.

The broad role attributed to Christ as the mediator of salvation is the high point of the anthropological correlation in the paulinist's christology. His christology borders on a soteriology because the mystery of Christ is the divine plane of salvation for human beings. A particular aspect of the paulinist's christology which ought not to be overlooked is suggested by the opening verses of the *berakah*. Immediately after he wrote "Grace to you and peace from God our Father and the Lord Jesus Christ" (Eph 1:2), the traditional greeting of the Pauline letter, the paulinist wrote about God as the Father of Jesus Christ our Lord. Then he went on to affirm that "he destined us in love to be his sons through Jesus Christ" *(dia Iēsou Christou,* v. 5). Jesus is the mediator of our being sons and daughters of God. In effect, Jesus is the mediator of God being Father to us.

The cosmological correlation of the paulinist's christology also comes to expression in the opening benediction. The paulinist writes of those who are called to be holy and blameless being chosen "before the foundation of the world" *pro katabolēs kosmou,* v. 4). When he first explicitly writes of the mystery of God's will, the content of the mystery is set forth as the recapitulation of all things in Christ (v. 10). This cosmic dimension of the paulinist's christology is frequently highlighted as one of its most significant characteristics. Scholars debate as to whether or not the paulinist affirmed the pre-existence of Christ. Eph 2:12 seems clearly to affirm his pre-existence in Israel, but rabbinic thought attributed a form of pre-existence to the law, paradise, Gehenna, the throne of glory, the heavenly sanctuary, and the Messiah *(Babylonian Talmud, Pesachim* 54a). The paulinist's understanding of the pre-existence of Christ seems, however, to be of a somewhat different order. The paulinist may not have explicitly attributed to Christ a role in creation, but he has strongly suggested the pre-existence of Christ in the *berakah*.

One other element of the christology of the *berakah* which deserves particular mention is its exaltation christology. The paulinist writes of God who "has blessed us in Christ with every spiritual blessing in the heavenly places" (Eph 1:3). His exaltation christology comes to fuller expression in Eph 1:20-23. These verses may well be part of an early Christian liturgical piece which speaks of the resurrection and exaltation of Jesus. "When he raised him from the dead" *(egeiras auton ek nekrōn,* v. 20) preserves the language of what is probably the oldest Christian credal formula (cf. 1 Thess 1:10; Rom 10:9b; 1 Cor 6:14; 15:15). Yet, the paulinist adds to the traditional formula of belief in the resurrection an exaltation schema that reflects Ps 110:1. Together the two formulae reflect different, but related, aspects of the Christ event. The resurrection schema affirms the identity of the one who has been raised with the one who died, while the exaltation schema affirms that resurrection is not mere resuscitation.

The paulinist's exploitation of the exaltation schema in Eph 1:20-23 is likewise not without its theological, cosmological, and anthropological correlations. The paulinist maintains the Pauline tradition and develops the theological correlation as he affirms that it is God who is the agent of the resurrection. The cosmological correlation is considered insofar as he affirms the dominion of the exalted Christ above all superhuman powers. Nonetheless, it is the anthropological correlative which receives particular emphasis. In his linking of resurrection and exaltation schemata, the paulinist wrote about Christ's being raised from the dead *(ek nekrōn,* in the plural, according to the traditional formulation) and his being enthroned in the heavenly places *(en tois epouraniois)*. His subsequent thought turns to the faithful who once were dead *(humas ontas nekrous,* Eph 2:1; cf. v. 5). He proclaims that God's activity on their behalf is similar to his activity on behalf of Christ: he "raised us up with him, and made us sit with him in the heavenly places in Christ Jesus" (Eph 2:6). What God has done for Christ, he has likewise done for us with and in Christ.

The anthropological correlation of the paulinist's use of the exaltation schema is also developed in a specificially ecclesial turn of thought. Ps 8:7 contributes to the image of the enthroned Christ as the paulinist writes that "he [God] has put all things under his [the Christ's] feet and has made him the head over all things for the church, which is his body, the fullness of him who fills all in all" (Eph 1:22-23). The mythical schema of enthronement recurs, once again with an ecclesial referent, in Eph 4:7-16. Here, the paulinist proclaims that the ascension-exaltation of Christ is at the origin of the church. Modifying somewhat the wording of Ps 68:19, he portrays the ascended Christ as one who has given the needed ecclesial gifts to those who have been baptized in order "to equip the saints for the work of ministry, for building up the body of Christ" (Eph 4:12).

The rabbinic-like commentary on the scripture verse, which, in the Hebrew bible, spoke of God, portrays an image of the descent and ascent of Christ. This midrash on Ps 68:19 (vv. 9-10) interprets the scripture in reference to Christ's death and exaltation. Those two realities of the Christ event are foundational for the church, that is, the body of Christ. In Eph 4:9-10 the paulinist's reference to the death of Christ is couched in mythical terms, but there are times when he speaks quite plainly of the death of Christ (see Eph 1:7; 2:13, 16; 5:2, 25).

One of these occasions is Eph 2:13, where the paulinist explains that the death of Christ is the means for the reconciliation of the Gentiles. The paulinist then develops his thoughts by means of an old hymn which he has radically reworked (Eph 2:14-18). A number of hapax legomena ("both," *amphotera*; "dividing wall of hostility," *to mesotoichon tou phragmou*; "enmity," *tēn echthran*; and "flesh," *sarx*, used in reference to the body of Christ) serve as indications that he is using borrowed material. Striking expressions like "the cross" *(dia tou staurou)* and "access to the Father" *(tēn prosagōgēn pros ton patera)*, show just as clearly that he has radically edited the older material which he has used.

The spatial imagery with its metaphor of the dividing wall is striking. Pre-Christian Judaism had a concept of a wall that separated Jew from Gentile. Gnosticism had its image of a redeemer figure knocking down the wall that separates from God those to be redeemed. The thoroughly re-worked imagery gives the reader of Ephesians the paulinist's own image of the reconciliation effected by Christ. Christ has reconciled Jew and Gentile making them one in the household of God. The unity of Jew and Gentile within the church, of which Christ Jesus is the cornerstone, serves almost as a revelatory symbol of that unity between Jew and Gentile which is the content of the mystery which has been revealed. Christ is the eschatological new Adam who gathers together a new, unified humanity in himself. Humanity was divided because of the sin of Adam; now a unified humanity is newly created because of the reconciliation that has taken place in Christ.

The new Adam christology of the reworked hymn is just one, albeit a singularly important one, of the different christological insights offered by the paulinist in Eph 2:14-18. Jerome Neyrey also identifies a new covenant christology insofar as the paulinist speaks of "the covenants of promise" (v. 12) and proclaims that Christ has abolished in his flesh "the law of commandments and ordinances" (v. 15). Neyrey likewise finds in the paulinist's reworked hymn traces of a new temple christology. The wall has been destroyed but "the whole structure is joined together and grows into a holy temple in the Lord" (v. 21). Eph 1:22 serves as the focal point of what Neyrey calls the author's headship christology. Finally, a pentecostal christology can be discerned in Eph 4:4-6, but one must not overlook other passages such as Eph 1:13, 2:18 and 3:16 which speak powerfully of the role of the Spirit. According to this analysis, it is apparent that the author of Ephesians had a very rich and really diversified christology. He has borrowed his material from a variety of sources as well as from the apostle himself.

What's in a name, the modern reader might ask, when it is in "the name of our Lord Jesus Christ" that we always and everywhere give thanks (Eph 5:20). Even a rapid overview of the christology of the epistle to the Ephesians should at least touch upon the paulinist's use of christological titles. "Our Lord Jesus Christ," the full christological title, is found in Eph 5:20 and in four other places in his work, that is, Eph 1:3, 17; 3:11; and 6:24. When the paulinist uses the name of Jesus, it is, with one exception (Eph 4:21), always in conjunction with the "Christ" title ("Christ Jesus," eleven times; "Jesus Christ," seven times).

As the paulinist has used the name of Jesus absolutely just once, so he has used the title "Son of God" just once (Eph 4:13). Other singular titular occurrences are those of Savior (Eph 5:23), head of the Church (Eph 5:23, cf. Eph 1:23), and Beloved (Eph 1:6), a title which Markus Barth considers to be messianic (see the Synoptic accounts of Jesus' baptism and transfiguration, Mark 1:11; 9:7 and par.).

"Lord" *(Kurios)*, Paul's favorite christological title, occurs twenty-six times in Ephesians. Most of the time it appears without further qualification. The paulinist's own preferred christological title is "Christ" *(Christos)*, a title which occurs forty-five times in the epistle. This is a traditional messianic title, but it is clear that the paulinist has used the venerable title to epitomize a christological vision that is uniquely his own.

Paraenesis

A sketch of the paulinist's christology, even one as brief as that just offered, would be radically incomplete if it did not provide at least an opening onto the paulinist's paraenesis. His christology is the foundation of his paraenesis. The paulinist intimated as much in the opening benediction when he proclaimed that God "chose us in him ... that we should be holy and blameless before him" (Eph 1:4) and that "we who first hoped in Christ have been destined and appointed to live for the praise of his glory" (Eph 1:12). Those to whom the epistle is addressed were once dead through their trespasses and sins (Eph 2:1; cf. v. 5). They lived in the passions of the flesh, following the desires of body and mind (Eph 2:3). Now they are made alive together with Christ (Eph 2:5) and are created in Jesus Christ for good works (Eph 2:10), but their salvation is not the result of their works (Eph 2:8-9).

The christological foundation of the paulinist's paraenesis is manifest in the explicitly paraenetical section of this epistle. Only one verb in the imperative mood is to be found in the first three chapters of the work ("remember," *mnēmoneuete*, in Eph 2:11), but imperatives abound in the last three chapters, which contain the epistle's extended paraenesis. There are thirty-six verbs in the imperative mood in Eph 4:25-6:10. This concentration of verbs in the imperative highlights the paulinist's concern to exhort the Ephesian Christians to live a life worthy of the calling to which they had been called (Eph 4:1).

The appearance of "Lord" (*Kurios*) as the dominant christological title in Eph 4-6 highlights the christological foundation of the paulinist's moral exhortation. In the first three chapters of his work, he had used the title "Lord" only six times (Eph 1:2, 3, 15, 17; 2:21; 3:11), all but once (Eph 2:21) in apposition to the personal name, Jesus. In the final three chapters of his work, he uses the "Lord" title twenty times (Eph 4:1, 5, 17; 5:8, 10, 17, 19, 20, 22; 6:1, 4, 5, 7, 8, 9 [twice], 10, 21, 23, 24). Only three times is "Lord" used in apposition to the personal name, and two of those three occurrences are to be found in the final salutation of the epistle (Eph 6:23-24; cf. 5:20). The absolute use of "Lord" as the dominant christological title in the paraenetic section of the epistle is hardly fortuitous. "Lord" is a title which suggests authority (cf. Eph 5:22; 6:1, 7). The presence of this title in a context of moral exhortation is an implicit appeal for compliance.

One prominent feature of the paulinist's ethical exhortation is directly dependent upon his christological insights. In Eph 4:17-24, the paulinist returns to the theme of the new man (the gender inclusive *ho kainos anthrōpos*, Eph 4:24), which he had initially developed in Eph 2:11-22. There, he spoke of the reconciliation of Jew and Gentile, the creation of one new man, and of reconciliation to God. In the paraenesis of Eph 4:17-24, the paulinist urges his addressees to live no longer as Gentiles live, alienated from the life of God (vv. 17-18). "In Christ," they are no longer Gentiles. "In Christ," they are no longer alienated from God. Therefore, they must live according to their new condition. The new condition is that of the new creation. The paulinist develops this theme in an antithetical exhortation: "put off your old nature ... and put on the new nature" (vv. 22-24). He qualifies what he means by "new nature" with a manifest allusion to the biblical story of the creation of humanity (Gen 1:26-27). The new nature is "created after the likeness of God in true righteousness and holiness" 24).

The contrast between light and darkness is a striking and common metaphor. It is often used in religious literature. In Ephesians it serves to contrast the present behavior of the addressees and their prior conduct. The antithesis really functions as a conversion motif in the paulinist's exhortation. Those for whom he writes are "children of light" *(tekna phōtos*, Eph 5:8; cf. "sons of light," *huioi phōtos* in 1 Thess 5:5). Once they were darkness, but now they are light in the Lord (Eph 5:8a)—a striking variant of the "in Christ" formula in a paraenetic context. Hence they must walk as children of light and try to learn what is pleasing to the Lord (Eph 5:8b-10). Of itself, the antithetical metaphor is quite abstract, but the paulinist tries to concretize it by an interpretive parenthesis, "the fruit of light is found in all that is good and right and true" (Eph 5:9). Similar thoughts are found in the Bible (e.g. 1 Sam 15:22; Micah 6:6-8), at Qumran (IQS 1:5), and in various dicta of Hellenistic philosophers.

The concretization of ethical exhortation is a major thrust of the paulinist's paraenesis. After speaking of the new creation in Eph 4:22-24, he writes about working with one's hands and the avoidance of various kinds of evil conversation (Eph 4:25-32). After urging his addressees to imitate God and to walk in love, the paulinist concretizes the ethical demand by naming some of the vices that typically appear on the lists of vices of the Hellenistic ethical tradition. He specifically mentions fornication *(porneia)*, impurity *(akatharsia)*, and covetousness *(pleonexia)*, and adds a word about improper speech (Eph 5:3-4; see v. 5). These things should not even be mentioned among the saints. Those who are guilty of such things share no inheritance in the kingdom of Christ and of God.

Another antithesis occurs in Eph 5:15 as the paulinist

contrasts the ways of the wise and the foolish. He exhorts his readers: "Look carefully then how you walk, not as unwise men but as wise." "To walk" *(peripatein* in Greek, *halak* in Hebrew) is the typical Jewish idiom for behavior. It occurs here for a fifth, and final, time in the paraenetical section of the epistle (Eph 4:1, 17; 5:2, 8, 15), but it is also to be found in the paulinist's exposition on the anthropological significance of God's activity in Christ (Eph 2:1-10; vv. 2, 10). The contrast between the wise and the unwise in Eph 5:15 is one of several indications that the paulinist has been influenced by the Wisdom tradition.

By his use of these different antitheses (old-new, Gentiles-saints, darkness-light, unwise-wise), the paulinist highlights his conviction that Christians truly enjoy a new condition and that their behavior should be consequent upon their condition. Crucial to his understanding of their new condition is the belief that they have been constituted one new person *(kainos anthrōpos)* in Christ. Yet, all that has been effected in Christ is due to God's initiative. Through Jesus Christ, Christians are God's children, the objects of his love (Eph 1:5; 5:1; cf. Eph 4:13; 1:3, 6).

This relationship to God serves as a ground and motivation for the paulinist's paraenesis: "Therefore *(oun)* be imitators of God, as beloved children" (Eph 5:1). The idea of imitating God has its roots in a time-honored Jewish tradition. On the basis of Lev 19:2 (cf. Matt 5:48; Luke 6:36), rabbinic tradition developed a practical morality that was transformed into the idea of God's people collaborating with him in the ongoing recreation of the world. Maimonides listed "imitate God" as the eighth of the mandatory precepts among the 613 commandments revealed to Moses on Sinai.

God's children belong to him. Christianity is heir to a Jewish tradition which holds that whatever belongs to God and serves his purpose is "holy" *(hagios)*. The Greek adjectival noun *hagioi* is usually translated "saints." This is an important notion for the paulinist. Those to whom he writes are "saints" (Eph 1:1; cf. Eph 1:15, 18; 2:19; 3:8, 18; 4:12; 5:3; 6:18). His exhortation that fornication, impurity, and covetousness are not even to be mentioned, "as is fitting among saints" *(kathōs prepei hagiois,* Eph 5:3) recalls the traditional biblical and rabbinic idiom that some forms of conduct are not fitting in Israel. There is a mode of behavior which is appropriate and another which is not appropriate for those who belong to God. Called to be God's very own people, they are to live as saints, as the holy people who truly belong to him (cf. Eph 1:4; 5:27). Thus, we can speak of the paulinist's holiness ethic, which cannot be dissociated from his new covenant christology. This gives rise to a new and important antithesis, that between the children of God (Eph 5:1) and the sons of disobedience with whom these holy ones are not even to associate (Eph 5:6-7; cf. Eph 4:18-19).

Given the christological and theological grounds of the paulinist's ethical exhortation, it is not surprising that the material content of his ethics consists, to a very large extent, of the social virtues and vices which appear in the Hellenistic catalogues of virtues and vices. The paulinist's emphasis is on the cultivation of the social virtues, particularly love (Eph 1:15; 4:2, 15, 16; 5:2; cf. Eph 5:25, 28, 33), and the avoidance of the social vices. Christians are to speak the truth in love (Eph 4:15); they are to walk in love (Eph 5:2). They are to be kind, tender-hearted, and forgiving (Eph 4:32). They are to do honest work, so that they can give to those in need (Eph 4:28). On the other hand, if they have learned from Christ, they are to shun falsehood (Eph 4:25), anger (Eph 4:26), robbery (Eph 4:28), malicious talk (Eph 4:29), bitterness, wrath, anger, clamor, slander, and malice (Eph 4:31). "Living a reconciled life" is the paulinist's ethical mandate.

The use of a household code in Eph 5:22-6:9 provides the paulinist with the opportunity for a singularly significant articulation of his social ethic. The household code was developed in the Stoic ethical tradition, but its roots may lie in the political ethics of such ancient philosophers as Aristotle. In any case, the household code was appropriated by Hellenistic Judaism, and through that medium entered into Hellenistic Jewish Christianity. The paulinist was clearly a Hellenistic Jewish Christian. He borrowed his version of the household code from Col 3:18-4:1, but his rendition of the code has been even more radically Christianized than the one which he had found in his source.

The pericope (Eph 5:22-6:9) contains a mixture of Jewish and Hellenistic themes, but its structure is essentially very simple. The paulinist presents three basic relationships, each in the form of a couplet. Those who were considered inferior according to the social hierarchy of the times are cited in the first member of the couplet; those who were considered superior are presented in the second member. Thus, we have the structure: 1) wives ... husbands; 2) children ... parents; 3) slaves ... masters. The use of this form implies that the paulinist's paraenesis essentially consists of an exhortation to maintain the existing social order. Wives, children, and slaves are exhorted to be subject; husbands, parents, and masters are exhorted to be responsible. While the concrete imperatives may no longer be valid in our society, whose social structures are quite different from those existing in the paulinist's day, the notion that social order is a moral good and the social order is essentially to be respected is as valid today as it was in the paulinist's day.

An exhortation to maintain the existing social order represents a conservative stance in social ethics. Perhaps we should not expect much more, especially if the paulinist was as concerned with the public acceptance of his community as were other New Testament authors (e.g. 1 Thess 4:12). It is, however, important to note that the paulinist has rather thoroughly Christianized the traditional household code which he gives in Eph 5:22-6:9. He introduces the household code by an exhortation to mutual subjection within a context of an eschatological fear of Christ (Eph 5:21). This suggests that traditional social morality must be considered in a new light because of the Christians' new situation in Christ.

Each of the six members of the household code has been expanded in such a way as to provide a specifically Christian motivation for maintaining one's position within the social order. The paulinist introduces much borrowed material into the classic scheme in order to provide a Christian focus for his exhortation. A hymn-like composition that Barth calls "the nuptials of Christ" (vv. 25-27), a proverbial saying (v. 28), a scriptural passage (Gen 2:24; v. 31), and a reflection on the church are introduced into the first couplet (Eph 5:22-33), with the result that it becomes one of the major New Testament statements on marriage. A scriptural citation (Ex 20:12; Deut 5:16; v. 2) and a reflection on the principal responsibility of fathers within the Jewish tradition (that is, training their children in the traditions and mores of their people) fill out the second couplet (Eph 6:1-4). The reflection that slaves *(douloi)* should act as servants of Christ *(douloi Christou)* and that masters *(hoi kurioi)* have a Lord in heaven *(ho Kurios en ouranois)* ironically redefines the social roles of the third couplet (Eph 6:5-9). All of this suggests that there is something radically new about the Christian's commitment to the maintainence of the existing social order.

The paulinist's version of the household code is followed by a relatively long pericope, Eph 6:10-20, which forms the conclusion of the paraenetic section of the epistle. Robert Wild has suggested that v. 12, "for we are not contending against flesh and blood, but against the principalities, against the powers, against the world rulers of this present darkness, against the spiritual hosts of wickedness in the heavenly places," serves as the central element in the pericope. What the verse does is to present the Christian life, in somewhat dualistic terms, as a struggle against hostile astral powers. The cosmic perspective forms a virtual inclusion with the cosmic perspective which the paulinist shared with his addressees as he began his epistle. His horizon is very broad, and he would have his readers know that their behavior is to be understood within that very broad context.

The paulinist exhorts his addressees to be strong in the Lord and in the strength of his might (Eph 6:10), and then uses graphic imagery to state more fully the nature of his exhortation (Eph 6:14-17). The graphic imagery turns on the use of Isa 59:17a, "He put on righteousness as a breastplate, and a helmet of salvation upon his head" (cf. 1 Thess 5:8). In Isa 59, in response to Israel's wretched state before him, God is described as the almighty warrior who girds himself for battle, brings wrath upon his enemies, and turns all impiety away from Zion. By making clear reference to this prophetic passage, the paulinist is urging his readers to remember that no matter what is said about their own role in life, it is ultimately God's struggle. It is God's own armor which is being worn. Consequently Christians can be hopeful because victory will inevitably belong to God. Hence, they are to keep alert with all perseverance and pray in the Spirit (Eph 6:18), which is the power of God.

Paul

An important shift in the focus of the paulinist's exhortation takes place towards the conclusion of his final paraenesis. After a general exhortation to prayer and supplication, the paulinist specifies that the readers should pray for the saints but adds, as a further specification, that they should pray for "Paul." While some commentators might quickly pass over this reference to Paul as a mere literary motif, designed to give a certain amount of verisimilitude to the entire composition (cf. Rom 15:30; 2 Cor 1:11; 1 Thess 5:25; Col 4:3; 2 Thess 3:1), Wild suggests that it is a significant element in the paulinist's "veritable Paulology."

In Ephesians, Paul is clearly given two titulary designations, "apostle" and "prisoner." In Eph 1:1, he is called "an apostle of Christ Jesus *(apostolos Christou Iēsou)* by the will of God," while in Eph 3:1, he is identified as "a prisoner for Christ Jesus *(ho desmios tou Christou)* on behalf of you Gentiles," and in Eph 4:1, as a "prisoner for the Lord *(ho desmios en Kuriō)*." Similar to this identification is the description of the "Paul" who requests prayerful intercession on his own behalf in Eph 6:19. This Paul is ironically called "an ambassador in chains" *(presbeuō en hălusei)*. In fact, there seems to be a touch of irony in all three of the paulinist's portrayals of Paul as a prisoner.

That Paul had been a prisoner is well-attested in the New Testament. In the catalogue of trials, the peristatic catalogue of 2 Cor 11:23-27 (cf. v. 23), Paul attests to his many imprisonments. He wrote at least two letters from prison (cf. Phil 1:13-14; Phlm 1, 10, 23). The post-Pauline epistolary tradition also speaks of Paul's imprisonment(s) (cf. Col 4:18; 2 Tim 1:8;

2:9). The Acts of the Apostles recounts several stories about the apostle's imprisonment (Acts 16:26; 20:23; 23:29; 26:29, 31; 28:16-17). Thus, the paulinist's triple reference to Paul's imprisonment seems well grounded in the memory of the historical events surrounding Paul's preaching of the gospel. Nonetheless, there is something truly ironic about the paulinist's references to Paul, "the prisoner." The use of an articular *desmios* (*the* prisoner) in Eph 3:1 and 4:1 makes it clear that the paulinist intends to portray Paul as a person who in some respects can serve as an ideal prisoner. The way he writes about Paul as a prisoner "of Christ Jesus" (3:1) and as a prisoner "in the Lord" (4:1) seems to imply Paul's real freedom. For the paulinist, it is not some police power which has held Paul as a prisoner. The one who has exercised absolute control over Paul's life and activity is none other than Jesus Christ, the Lord.

It is sometimes suggested that the Dionysian legend of a god who releases himself from the fetters with which he has been bound is the background of the paulinist's presentation of Paul's ironic imprisonment. However, there are other biblical and extrabiblical passages (e.g. Lev 26:13; Wis 5:1) which seem to better elucidate the paulinist's particular configuration of Paul's imprisonment. Paul is, in fact, the freest of the free. He enjoys true *parrēsia*, "freedom," the God-given freedom to speak in his name (Eph 3:12). In the RSV *parrēsia* is translated "boldness" (cf. Eph 6:19, 20). To pagan Hellenists the term *parrēsia* connoted political liberty and freedom of speech. To those familiar with the Greek bible (LXX) it suggested the freedom and boldness with which the biblical prophets proclaimed God's word. Paul is truly "free" because the mystery of the gospel has been boldly proclaimed.

It is significant that the paulinist conveys this final image of Paul, the prisoner, in the context of an exhortation which encourages the readers of the epistle to pray. Luke Johnson considers that a pervasive atmosphere of prayer is the most distinctive feature of the epistle to the Ephesians. "Theology informs the prayer," he writes, "and the prayer itself is the vehicle for theology." Mention has already been made of the hymnic tone of several passages in the epistle. Indeed, many commentators draw attention to the liturgical ring of the text's expression, both in style and in vocabulary.

Ephesians presents the image of a prayerful Paul, not only in the *berakah* of 1:3-14 and the short thanksgiving of 1:15-16, but also in the intercessory prayer of 1:17-19. The paulinist expands upon Paul's intercessory prayer in 3:14-19. This passage concludes with an appropriate and contextualized doxology: "Now to him who by the power at work within us is able to do far more abundantly than all that we ask or think, to him be glory in the church and in Christ Jesus to all generations, for ever and ever, Amen" (Eph 3:20-21). The paulinist's Paul is a man of prayer.

The paulinist's Paul is one who stands in solidarity with the conversion experience of "the saints." Eph 2:1-10 speaks of their passage from death to life. In the story of the saints there is a "then" (*pote*, v. 2) and a "now" (*nuni*, v. 13). Paul is one of the saints. Reflecting on Paul's call to preach the gospel, the paulinist describes Paul not as "the least of the apostles" (see 1 Cor 15:9), but as the "least of the saints" (Eph 3:8). There was also a before and an after in Paul's life. The use of the first person plural in Eph 2:3-7, sandwiched in a context which uses the second person plural (Eph 2:1-2, 8-10) to speak of the change in the "Ephesians" situation, is a subtle but very real indication of the paradigmatic nature of Paul's own coming to be in Christ. With a vision similar to that of the pastor, the paulinist has portrayed the conversion of Paul as a model for all Christians.

The "Paul" who is a model is unique nonetheless. The paulinist speaks of the church's apostolic foundation (Eph 2:20; 3:5; 4:11), yet he mentions only one apostle by name. That is Paul "an apostle of Christ Jesus by the will of God" (Eph 1:1). Proponents of the epistle's authenticity, as well as those who think that the apostle did not write the text, are equally struck by this exclusive mention of Paul. An epistle which highlights the apostolic foundation of the church as a key element in the unfolding of the mystery of salvation cites only the apostle Paul by name. There is no mention of the Jerusalem apostles, and equally no mention of apostles who were Paul's companions and co-workers.

The call and ministry of Paul are interpreted along lines similar to those which indicate the function of the church in the unfolding of the mystery of salvation (Eph 3:1-3; 7-8). Paul's apostolate is a key feature in the unfolding of this mystery, for he is an apostle "by the will of God" *(dia thelēmatos theou)*. God's will is not simply God's moral will (Eph 1:11; 5:17; 6:6), in contrast with "the will of the flesh" (translated "the desires of the body," in Eph 2:3). Rather, God's will has to do with the mystery of salvation itself (Eph 1:5, 9, and 1:1). Paul's call to preach the gospel is integral to the unfolding of the mystery. To him the grace *(charis)* was given "to preach to the Gentiles the unsearchable riches of Christ, and to make all men see what is the plan of the mystery hidden in God who created all things" (Eph 3:9-10). Paul's preaching of the gospel has a universal scope.

In sum, the paulinist has created out of the Pauline tradition an image of Paul who is, uniquely, the apostle of Christ Jesus by the will of God. He is, in the words of Ernst Käsemann, "the apostle per se, for whom the others are merely the foil." Caught up into the unfolding of the mystery of salvation by the very will of God, the Ephesians' "Paul" is a somewhat idealized and mythical figure who serves as the prototype for the proclamation of the gospel of salvation to all human beings called to be saints.

A Brief Bibliography

Barth, M. "Traditions in Ephesians," *NTS* 30 (1984) 3-25.

Black, D.A. "The Peculiarities of Ephesians and the Ephesian Address," *GTJ* 2 (1981) 59-73.

Brown, Raymond E. "The Pauline Heritage in Colossians/ Ephesians: The Church as Christ's Body to Be Loved," in *The Churches the Apostles Left Behind*. New York: Paulist, 1984, 47-60.

Culpepper, R. Alan. "Ethical Dualism and Church Discipline: Ephesians 4:25-5:20," *Rev Exp* 76 (1979) 529-539.

Garland, D.E. "A Life Worthy of the Calling: Unity and Holiness: Ephesians 4:1-24," *Rev Exp* 76 (1979) 517-527.

Lincoln, Andrew T. "Ephesians 2:8-10: A Summary of Paul's Gospel," *CBQ* 45 (1983) 617-630.

Moore, Michael S. "Ephesians 2:14-16: A History of Recent Interpretation," *EvQ* 54 (1982) 163-168.

Neyrey, Jerome H. *Christ Is Community: The Christologies of the New Testament.* GNS, 13. Wilmington, DE: Glazier, 1985, 242-254.

O'Brien, P.T. "Ephesians 1:1: An Unusual Introduction to a New Testament Letter," *NTS* 25 (1978-1979) 504-516.

Rogers, Patrick. "Hopeful, in Spite of Chains: The Indomitable Spirit of Paul in the Captivity Epistles," *BTB* 12 (1982) 77-81.

Rowston, Douglas J. "Changes in Biblical Interpretation Today: The Example of Ephesians," *BTB* 9 (1979) 121-125.

Swain, Lionel. *The People of the Resurrection*, 1: *The Apostolic Letters.* GNS, 15. Wilmington, DE: Glazier, 1986, 210-217.

Van Roon, A. *The Authenticity of Ephesians.* NovTSup, 39 Leiden: Brill, 1974.

Wild, Robert A. "The Warrior and the Prisoner: Some Reflections on Ephesians 6:10-20," *CBQ* 46 (1984) 284-298.

5

The Epistle to the Colossians

The Epistle to the Colossians has occasionally been described as the most puzzling of all of Paul's epistles. No small part of the puzzle is the relationship between this epistle and the epistle to the Ephesians. While many scholars think that the epistle to the Ephesians is based upon Colossians, there is another group of scholars who hold just the opposite opinion, namely that Colossians is dependent upon Ephesians. If that could be proved, and if Ephesians has not been written by Paul, it is virtually impossible to maintain that Paul would have written Colossians. It is quite inconceivable that a thinker and writer as creative as Paul the apostle would have written a letter based on someone else's writing. Fortunately, the number of scholars who hold that Colossians is a revision of the epistle to the Ephesians is rather small. Thus, it is not from this point of view that the Pauline authorship of Colossians has generally been called into question.

Doubts as to the Pauline authorship of Colossians were first expressed by Edward Evanson in 1805, but the first truly systematic attack upon the traditional understanding of the epistle's origins was launched by Ernst Mayerhoff in 1838. In his book, *The Epistle to the Colossians (Der Brief an die Colosser*, Berlin, 1838), Mayerhoff raised a number of issues which in his view militated against the Pauline authorship of the epistle. He believed that Colossians was dependent upon Ephesians, in his view a genuine letter of Paul the apostle. However he thought that the "independent Paul" would not have used one of his earlier compositions in the writing of a new letter.

Mayerhoff also noted a number of differences of style and vocabulary between Colossians and the genuine letters, drawing particular attention to the fact that some of Paul's customary vocabulary is absent from Colossians—for example, to believe *(pisteuō)*, law *(nomos)*, boasting *kauchēma)*, savior *(sōtēr)*, and idol *(eidōlon)*. On the other hand, Mayerhoff indicated that there were a number of terms in the epistle which were not part of Paul's typical vocabulary. In addition, some Pauline terms were used in Colossians, but with a different meaning. As such they served as an indicator of the un-Pauline ideas to be found in Colossians. Finally, Mayerhoff believed that Colossians showed evidence of a controversy with Cerinthus, the gnostic heretic, an idea that necessarily led to a post-Pauline dating of the text.

Mayerhoff's theory was developed by F.C. Baur (1845) and other proponents of the tendency criticism developed in the Tübingen school. Because of their doubts as to the Pauline authorship of Ephesians, with which Colossians was so similar, and their belief that Colossians had been written as a response to the views of the second-century Ebionites, Baur and his disciples raised objections to the Pauline authorship of Colossians. As a non-Pauline text, the epistle was addressed to Colossae, where Paul had not personally evangelized, just as the pseudepigraphical epistle to the Ephesians had been addressed to Laodicea. In 1868 Sytze Hoekstra's article took a quite different approach. Hoekstra, who recognized the interdependence of Ephesians and Colossians, presumed the inauthenticity of Colossians. He argued that Ephesians was an authentic corrective to Colossians, an earlier and inauthentic work.

In the latter part of the nineteenth century the peculiar features of Colossians led some critical scholars to propose a mitigated form of Pauline authorship of the text. In 1857, Heinrich Ewald proposed the view that the text of Colossians, such as we now have it is the work of a scribe. He suggested that Timothy, who had long served as Paul's *amanuensis*, is ultimately responsible for the present text of the epistle.

Similar views had been expressed by J.G. Eichhorn in the third volume of his Introduction to the New Testament (1812). Eichhorn explained that Paul, having already completed Ephesians, dictated a basic draft of Colossians to Timothy who then wrote the text himself.

In 1872, H.J. Holtzmann picked up on a suggestion which had been launched as early as 1855 by Christian Weisse and repeated by Ferdinand Hitzig in 1870. Their idea was that the canonical epistle to the Colossians represents a reworking of an earlier and shorter letter written by Paul. The needs of the polemic against gnosticism provided the occasion for the work. Holtzmann held that the author of Ephesians interpolated various materials into Paul's original letter, thereby assuring for Ephesians a companion piece in the New Testament.

Holtzmann's views, originally expressed in his *Critical Study of the Epistles to the Ephesians and to the Colossians on the Basis of an Analysis of their Compositional Relationships (Kritik der Epheser-und Kolosserbriefe auf Grund einer Analyse ihres Verwandtschaftsverhältnisses,* Leipzig, 1872), were reiterated in his 1885 *Introduction to the New Testament (Einleitung in das Neue Testament).* Some ten years previously Adolf Hilgenfeld's *Historical-critical Introduction to the New Testament (Historisch-kritische Einleitung in das Neue Testament,* Leipzig, 1875) cited the theological differences between Colossians and the earlier letters of the apostle as an argument against the Pauline authorship of the epistle. In this way the idea that Colossians might not have been written by Paul began to appear in the classic Introductions to the New Testament written by critical German scholars towards the end of the nineteenth century.

The arguments against the Pauline authorship of Colossians which were initially expressed in nineteenth-century critical scholarship continued to be echoed throughout the twentieth century. In 1902, Otto Pfleiderer suggested that Colossians was composed on the basis of an earlier draft *(Vorlage)* whose text it is impossible to reconstruct. In 1924, Clayton R. Bowen opined that Colossians resulted from the interpolation of an otherwise unknown Pauline letter. He added that Paul would not have denounced a false teaching of which he could give only such a sparse and vague description as is provided in Col 2. Johannes Weiss, John Knox, and Franz-Josef Steinmetz have also suggested that our extant Colossians represents an interpolation into an earlier work. So, too, did Charles Masson whose 1950 commentary on Colossians (*L'Epître de Saint Paul aux Colossiens*. CNT, 10, Paris, 1950) offered a reconstruction of the hypothetical original. In 1950, P.N. Harrison offered a unique twist on the interpolation hypothesis by suggesting that Onesimus, the author of Ephesians, was likewise the interpolator responsible for the present form of Colossians. Mayerhoff's old idea that Colossians was dependent on canonical Ephesians was taken over by Francis Synge in a 1951 commentary on Colossians *(Philippians and Colossians*, London, 1951).

Rudolf Bultmann and his disciples generally hold to the non-authenticity of Colossians, basing their arguments to a large extent on the theological discrepancies between Colossians and the genuine Pauline correspondence. Günther Bornkamm's study on the notion of hope in Colossians, "Hope in the Epistle to the Colossians: Likewise a Contribution to the Issue of the Authenticity of the Epistle" ("Die Hoffnung im Kolosserbrief: zugleich ein Beitrag zur Frage der Echtheit des Briefes") in the Klostermann *Festschrift* (1961) is representative of this type of argumentation. The theological differences between Colossians and the genuine letters, particularly with regard to eschatology, soteriology, ethics, and ecclesiology, were among the principal arguments cited by Donald Hobson in his 1968 doctoral dissertation (Claremont) which argued against the Pauline authorship of the epistle.

Nonetheless the argument which seems to rise to the surface most commonly in the studies of those who attack the traditional attribution of Colossians to Paul is based on the vocabulary and style of the epistle. Some scholars have included a study of Colossians within a general examination of the linguistic usage of the total Pauline corpus and have concluded that Paul, the apostle, could have written only a very few of the epistles traditionally attributed to him. Thus William Wake (1948) and Andrew Q. Morton and James

McLeman (1964) decided that Colossians could not have been written by Paul. In 1973, Walter Bujard published a significant monograph containing a rather thorough stylistic analysis of Colossians. Bujard's analysis led him to conclude that Paul himself could not have written the epistle. In this opinion he has been followed by a number of subsequent scholars, including Wayne Meeks and Mark Kiley.

A Range of Opinions

The issue of the authenticity of Colossians continues to be hotly debated at the present time. Not only is the evidence evaluated in somewhat different fashion by the authors who address the issue, but the evaluation of the state of extant scholarship also varies remarkably from one author to another. For example, in 1980, Patrick V. Rogers wrote that since the mid-nineteenth century "a small minority of critics has challenged this evidence [for Pauline authorship]." On the other hand, writing in 1984, Brevard Childs cited the "impressive minority voice" which supported Pauline authorship while Raymond Brown estimated that approximately sixty percent of critical scholarship doubted the Pauline authorship of Colossians. In fact, four different judgments on the authorship of the epistle can be identified within contemporary scholarship.

Many authors still hold that the epistle was written by Paul himself. The manifesto of this position is to be found in Ernst Percy's 1946 study, *The Problems of the Epistles to the Colossians and to the Ephesians (Die Probleme der Kolosser- und Epheserbriefe*, Lund, 1946). Martin Dibelius and Ernst Lohmeyer can be numbered among the critical scholars who have opted for Pauline authorship, along with C.F.D. Moule, who did so in his 1955 commentary on the epistle. To their number can be joined a number of moderate and conservative scholars, such as F.F. Bruce, Reginald Fuller, Donald Guthrie, Wilfrid Harrington, Luke T. Johnson, Otto Kuss, and Ernest W. Saunders. Indeed, Rist, who in 1972 advanced the view that only nine of the books in the entire New Testament are authentic, includes Colossians among the authentic writings. In 1983, George E. Cannon reviewed the entire history of the issue. He examined the structure and use of traditional materials in Colossians. Cannon's conclusion was that Paul the apostle was the author of the work.

In recent commentaries on Colossians, Patrick V. Rogers (1980), H.D. McDonald (1980), and Peter T. O'Brien (1982) have defended the Pauline authorship of the epistle. Rogers suggests that the epistle was written by Paul during his Roman imprisonment (ca. 61 A.D.), a position likewise maintained by James Efird (1980). In contrast, Donald Senior, who urged that the arguments advanced against Paul's authorship of the epistle are rather fragile and that the ties of Colossians to the circumstances of Paul's ministry seem too authentic to be the result of literary artifice, believes that the epistle was written during one of Paul's imprisonments in Ephesus.

Since stylistic and linguistic considerations are critical in all discussions of the authorship of Colossians, it is not surprising that many scholars who recognize the stylistic and linguistic differences between Colossians and the earlier Pauline letters believe that these differences are due to a scribe who was responsible for the actual text of Colossians. Ewald noted that this suggestion had been made more than a century ago. He himself proposed Timothy, Paul's longtime companion and chief lieutenant, as the intelligent scribe responsible for Colossians. This position has been revived by Eduard Schweizer ("The Letter to the Colossians Neither Pauline nor Post-pauline?" 1976) who held that Colossians was written by Timothy for Paul at about the time that the letter to Philemon was written. From time to time, other scholars, going back to Albert Klöpper in 1882, have proposed Epaphras as the secretary responsible for Colossians. In 1963, Pierre Benoit once again proposed the *amanuensis* theory, but he did not make any concrete suggestion as to the identity of the scribe.

Somewhat akin to the idea that Colossians was actually written on Paul's behalf by a secretary working for him is the view that Colossians arose within a "Pauline school." In his 1968 commentary on the epistle Eduard Lohse proposed that the author of Colossians was thoroughly acquainted with the principal themes of Pauline theology and that he acquired this familiarity by "an exacting study of the Pauline school tradition." In an article published in *New Testament Studies* in 1974-75, Hans-Martin Schenke proposed that an anonymous editor working at Ephesus produced Colossians from fragments of various Pauline letters left behind in the capital of Asia Minor. Alexander Sand (1981) judged that this editor must have been one of Paul's former co-workers. A 1974 doctoral dissertation presented to the University of Göttingen by Helga Ludwige proposed that Colossians is the result of the combination of a series of reminiscences about Paul's genuine letters and some notes taken by one of Paul's co-workers during his stay in Ephesus.

Mark Kiley, in a doctoral dissertation presented at Harvard University in 1983 and published in 1986, also suggested that Colossians originated within a Pauline school. Because of the prominence given to Epaphras in the epistle (Col 1:7; 4:12), Kiley claims that it is Epaphras who actually wrote the text. Epaphras is described in terms reminiscent of those traditionally used of Paul. According to Kiley, the author's glowing positive self-characterization served to undergird his own authority.

Helmut Merklein (1981) believes that the long list of greetings to be found in Col 4:10-14 is an indication of the existence of a Pauline school, most probably located in Ephesus, a site likewise suggested by Lohse in his commentary. According to Merklein, Aristarchus, Mark, Jesus Justus, Epaphras, Luke, and Demas were probably leaders of the school. In his 1986 communication to the thirty-sixth annual Louvain Biblical Colloquium, Jean Giblet also maintained that Colossians is the result of a Pauline school at work.

Finally, there is considerable contemporary scholarly opinion which holds that Paul was not the author of Colossians. One of the first Roman Catholic authors to opt for the non-Pauline authorship of Colossians was Gerhard Dautzenberg who did so in a general work on the New Testament published in 1969. The non-Pauline authorship of the epistle is maintained in the latest major German-language commentaries on the epistle, namely, those by Eduard Lohse

(1968; ET: *Colossians and Philemon*. Hermeneia. Philadelphia, 1971), Eduard Schweizer (1976, in the EKK series), Joachim Gnilka (1980), and Josef Pfammatter (1987). Other authors have examined the issue of the authorship of the epistle in various scholarly articles and have come to a similar conclusion. Among those who have reached the conclusion that Paul could not have been the author of Colossians, after an explicit study of the issue, are Helmut Merklein (1981), Andreas Lindemann (1981), Wolfgang Schenk (1983), and Charles M. Nielsen (1985).

Style and Vocabulary

My own study of the recent scholarship on the epistle to the Colossians indicates that the majority—granted, not a strong majority, but a majority nonetheless—of contemporary authors think that Colossians was written by someone other than the apostle Paul. The reasons which lead these scholars to this conclusion vary from one to another, but they inevitably include a variety of considerations on the vocabulary and style of the document.

While acknowledging the manifest linguistic similarity between Colossians and the earlier epistles of Paul, Eduard Lohse has identified thirty-four hapax legomena in Colossians, beginning with "heard previously" *(proakouein)* in 1:5 and ending with "comfort" *(parēgoria)* in 4:11. To these words which do not occur elsewhere in the New Testament can be added another forty-three words which do not appear in the seven letters generally recognized as Paul's very own by contemporary scholarship. These seventy-seven words represent an unusually high percentage of the vocabulary of Colossians, but the percentage is not totally without parallel in the letters belonging to the genuine Pauline corpus. The epistle to the Philippians, for example, roughly equivalent in length to Colossians, contains some thirty-six hapax legomena and an additional forty-three words that are not cited in the remaining six letters almost universally recognized as Pauline.

Linguistic considerations are further complicated by the fact that, of the forty-three words found in Colossians, but not in the Pauline homologoumena, fifteen are to be read in the epistle to the Ephesians, and an additional ten words would be peculiar to the epistle to the Colossians were it not for the fact that they are also found in Ephesians. Thus, while contemporary scholarship is constrained to recognize the special vocabulary of Colossians, it must also recognize the linguistic affinity that exists between Colossians and Ephesians.

Even more striking than the special vocabulary of Colossians is the fact that some of the most common and most significant Pauline terminology is absent from the epistle. Lohse cites some fifteen terms, with their cognates, in this category. Among these, the most important appear to be the following: "sin" *(hamartia*, in the singular), "justification" *(dikaiosunē)*, "freedom" *(eleutheria)*, "promise" *(epaggelia)*, "boasting" *(kauchēma)*, "law" *(nomos)*, "to believe" *(pisteuein)*, and "salvation" *(sōtēria)*. This absence of characteristic Pauline expressions is remarkable, notwithstanding the fact that not all of Paul's common terms are to be found in each one of the letters which he wrote.

The stylistic features of Colossians seem to set it even more sharply apart from the genuine letters of Paul than does its somewhat special vocabulary. Walter Bujard's extensive 1973 study of the style of Colossians is still the most important tool for a consideration of this aspect of the distinctiveness of Colossians. The style of Colossians is unusually heavy and full. It is, in the words of Werner Georg Kümmel, "cumbersome, wordy, overloaded almost to opaqueness with dependent clauses, participial and infinitive constructions, or substantives with *en.*" Whereas Paul's own style makes abundant use of conjunctions and short, pithy statements, Colossians makes far less use of conjunctions and is marked by unusually long sentences (e.g. Col 1:3-8, 9-20; 2:11-13). In its use of participial and relative clauses, the epistle smacks of the *oratio continua* of Hellenistic rhetoric and lacks, as Bujard has shown, not only the articular infinitive (especially to denote purpose), but also those adversative, causal, consecutive, recitative, copulative, and disjunctive conjunctions so characteristic of Paul's personal style.

Contributing substantially to the heaviness of Colossians is the author's tendency to pile up synonyms, for example, "praying and asking" *(proseuchomenoi kai aitoumenoi)* and "wisdom and understanding" *(sophia kai sunesei)* in Col 1:9. Bujard notes that there are some thirty cases of amassed synonyms in Colossians. In addition, the author has strung together five unnecessary series of genitives, for example, "in the word of the truth of the gospel" *(en tō logō tēs alētheias tou euaggeliou)* in Col 1:5, but Paul uses this construction only eight times in all of the genuine letters combined. In his correspondence, Paul occasionally (thirteen times altogether) locates a circumstantial definition with an *en* clause in the middle of a sentence, but this construction is to be found some eleven times in Colossians (e.g. "in truth," Col 1:6). Unknown to the authentic Paul is the use of *ho estin*, a functional "i.e.," which occurs some four or five times in Colossians (e.g. Col 1:24). Along with all of these stylistic idiosyncracies, Bujard also cites an unusual occurrence of constructions with *pas* ("all") and *plēr* ("full") to suggest abundance or superabundance whereas Paul uses *perisse-*, *pleon-*, or *huper-* with the same purpose.

The Opponents

Some nineteenth-century critics deemed the epistle to the Colossians to be inauthentic because it seemed to attack heresies which arose after Paul's death. Mayerhoff thought that Colossians was directed against the errors of Cerinthus, whereas Baur and his disciples judged that the epistle sustained a polemical argument against the views of the Ebionites. Scholars who have supported the Pauline authorship of the letter have also sought to identify "Paul's opponents." Toward the end of the nineteenth century, for example, the British scholar J.B. Lightfoot, who did not want to "place any weapon in the hands of those who would assail the early date and Apostolic authorship of the epistle," held that "the view that the writer of this epistle is combating a gnostic heresy seems free from all objections." In this century, Martin Dibelius suggested that Paul was combating a mystery cult, of which the rites of Isis initiation provide a good example. Other commentators have spoken about some form of Jewish mysticism or Hellenistic syncretism. The discovery of Essene manuscripts at Qumran and of gnostic texts at Nag Hammadi after the Second World War have provided new food for thought in the effort to identify the opponents under attack in the epistle to the Colossians. Every commentator on the epistle must take up this issue because it is important that the text be interpreted within its historical context. The matter is also important from a linguistic point of view, since not a few interpreters have suggested that one of the factors contributing to the special vocabulary of the epistle is the fact that its author has borrowed the language of his opponents.

Unfortunately, however, there is no scholarly consensus as to the identity of the heretics or opponents envisioned in the epistle. Part of the problem is the fact that the author of the epistle is unusually reticent in his description of those with whom he is taking issue. Two verses epitomize the problem with which he is dealing. They are Col 2:8, "See to it that no one makes a prey of you by philosophy and empty deceit, according to human tradition, according to the elemental spirits of the universe, and not according to Christ," and Col 2:18, "Let no one disqualify you, insisting on self-abasement and worship of angels, taking his stand on visions, puffed up without reason by his sensuous mind."

The ambiguity of these verses has led various scholars to seek after a Hellenistic, Jewish, or syncretistic background against which to understand the epistle. While many have thought that the author was taking issue with some form of angel worship, a significant trend in current interpretation is the suggestion that the author has in mind some form of apocalyptic visionary experience or an ecstatic participation in angelic liturgy (thus Fred O. Francis, Christopher Rowland, and Roy Yates). It is, moreover, the ambiguity of these verses which led Charles Nielsen to suggest, in 1985, that the author of Colossians had no particular heresy in mind. Rather, he was intent on proposing his personal christological vision as a corrective to a whole host of errors.

This very ambiguity may well be a significant indicator of the non-Pauline origin of the epistle to the Colossians. In the genuine epistles, Paul characterizes the problem at hand with considerably more detail than does the author of the epistle to the Colossians. The problem or problems addressed in Paul's genuine letters are real problems, not hypothetical deviations that may occur some day. Paul writes with passion about those who propose another gospel or who would make his work in vain. He identifies his opponents and sometimes calls them names. In contrast, the opponents taken to task in Colossians are identified simply as "someone" *(tis)*, much in the fashion of the opponents of the pastorals. Deviations seem, for the most part, to be potential or hypothetical and there is none of the passion which fairly shouts from, for example, the pages of the letter to the Galatians.

In sum, although it is impossible to state that the opponents envisioned in Colossians represent a post-Pauline heretical development within the church, it is accurate to affirm that the author's way of characterizing and dealing with the problem at hand is quite unlike that of Paul. In the words of Mark Kiley, "Col is inauthentic... not because it portrays a specific heresy developed after Paul's death..., but more accurately said, Col is inauthentic because it depicts a heresy whose personnel is an indefinite 'someone' (as in 1 Tim). This situation differs from that of Paul who opposes more sharply delineated characters. In addition, Paul fights real heresies, whereas the present state of research prevents us from saying the same thing of Col."

Paul's Financial Transactions

Kiley has also made a unique contribution to the ongoing discussion about the authorship of Colossians by suggesting that the epistle is remarkably silent with respect to Paul's financial activity on behalf of his mission of evangelization. Kiley grants that his argument is truly an argument from silence and that arguments from silence are notoriously weak. They presume that the circumstances were such that an author should have written about such a topic. Notwithstanding the inherent weakness of arguments from silence, Kiley believes that his own argument is "worth observing."

In point of fact, all seven epistles in the canonical corpus which contemporary scholarship unanimously deems to be the genuine work of Paul somehow address themselves to financial considerations related to the Pauline mission. This type of financial consideration is quite different from the paraenesis on financial integrity such as we find in the pastorals. Rather, it is concerned with monetary support of the work of evangelization.

One major concern was the collection on behalf of the poor in Jerusalem. This collection is cited in Rom 15:26, 1 Cor 16:1-4; 2 Cor 8-9, and Gal 2:10. Virtually all commentators on the pertinent passages draw attention to the fact that the collection served to legitimize the Pauline mission, particularly in the eyes of the members of the mother church in Jerusalem. The collection also served as an important theological symbol, for a variety of reasons systematically rehearsed by Keith F. Nickle *(The Collection: A Study in Paul's Strategy.* SBT, 48, London, SCM, 1966). Nickle cites the value of the collection as an act of Christian charity, a sign of Christian unity, and a proleptic realization of Christian eschatology. At the very least, it served as a concrete expression of gratitude on the part of the younger, Gentile, churches toward the Christian community of Jerusalem within which the gospel was first proclaimed.

In the earliest of his works, Paul wrote to his beloved Christians at Thessalonica: "You remember our labor and toil, brethren; we worked night and day, that we might not burden any of you, while we preached to you the gospel of God" (1 Thess 2:9). While it is clear that Paul mentions that he earned his own keep so as not to be a burden on those to whom he preached, this passage might derive from Paul's rabbinic background insofar as the teachers of the law were expected to exercise a trade. Then again, the passage might allude to the possibility that an artisan's workshop served as the site of his evangelization in a way similar to that in which Cynic philosophers made use of artisans' locales as they philosophized.

Each of the genuine captivity epistles also talks about money matters and Paul's mission. Paul expressed his gratitude to the Philippian Christians who, by their generosity, participated in his mission (Phil 4:10-19). Kiley suggests that there might also be an allusion to the financial support of Paul's work in Phil 2:17's reference to an "offering" (see 2 Cor 9:12 and Phil 2:30 where this word recurs). Even the short personal note to Philemon and his household takes up fiscal matters when it includes a pledge by the apostle to pay off Onesimus' indebtedness (Phlm 18-19).

According to Kiley, concern with "mission finances" is characteristic of the genuine letters, whereas it is absent from the inauthentic letters. Since Colossians does not make mention of financial transactions related to the Pauline mission of evangelization, this silence can serve as one weapon in the arsenal used in the attack upon the Pauline authorship of the text. All arguments from silence are weak, and perhaps this one is even picayune, yet it might well serve as a piece of corroborative evidence in the general case against Pauline authorship of the epistle to the Colossians.

Pauline Creativity

Critical scholarship has long considered that Paul was both a creative author and a creative theologian. Thus, it does not easily abide the notion that Paul would have slavishly followed some of his own earlier work in his later writings. The conviction of Paul's creativity was at the root of Mayerhoff's suggestion that Colossians represents a reworking of Ephesians and, therefore, must be inauthentic. Critical scholarship has long since abandoned any fascination that it might have entertained for Mayerhoff's views, just as it has also abandoned Weisse-Hitzig-Holtzmann's nineteenth-century suggestion that the present text of Colossians is an expansion of an earlier text with material taken from the inauthentic Ephesians. Contemporary scholars do not believe that Colossians is dependent upon Ephesians, but they do hold to the view that Paul was a creative author and theologian and so they are inclined to the view that any suggestion of the dependence of Colossians upon earlier Pauline texts should be taken as an indication of its inauthenticity.

Having compared Philippians and Colossians in this regard, Ed Sanders (1966) concluded "that there are at least two separate passages in Colossians (Col 1:26-27 [cf. 1 Cor 2:7; Rom 16:25-26; 9:23-24] and Col 2:13-14 [cf. Rom 6:4; 4:24; Gal 1:1; Rom 6:11; 8:32]) which very clearly evidence conflation or serial quotation of three or more passages from Paul's letters, in which the extent and type of verbatim agreement make it almost incredible that Paul himself did it." Sanders also noted that there are a few sentences and phrases in Colossians (esp. 1:10 [cf. 1 Thess 2:12]; 2:10 [cf. 1 Cor 15:24]; 3:2[cf. Phil 3:19]; and 3:15 [cf. Phil 4:7]) which are taken verbatim from Paul but with one or two theological or stylistic changes which show evidence of an adaptation of Paul's words to a later situation, style, and theology.

Another proponent of the view that Colossians is dependent upon the genuine Pauline epistles is Eduard Lohse. In his view Colossians is a clear example of the degree to which the letter to the Romans, in particular, influenced the Pauline school tradition. He especially insists on the similarity between the epistolary sequence of instruction and exhortation found in Colossians and Romans (Col 1-2 and 3-4; Rom 1-11 and 12-15) and that both Rom 6:1-11 and Col 2:11-13 take up the theme of the Christian's union with the death and resurrection of Jesus as grounded in baptism. In addition to this preponderant influence of Romans on Colossians, Lohse finds that the author of Colossians has also been influenced by his reading of Galatians, 1-2 Corinthians, and Philippians.

While rejecting the pseudepigrapher's dependence on the major letters of Paul, Mark Kiley has forcefully argued the claim that the author of Colossians has written his composition in dependence upon Philippians and Philemon, the two genuine captivity epistles. Between Philippians and Colossians he has noted a similar prayer for the community's increased "knowledge" (Phil 1:9; Col 1:9), a christological, doxological passage mentioning "the cross," used as a didactic passage (Phil 2:6-11; Col 1:15-20), a description of the community as blameless (Phil 2:15; Col 1:22), a discourse on a "circumcision," linked to Christ and accompanied by a negative portrayal of the "flesh" and a polemic against certain practices (Phil 3:3-4; Col 2:11, 13, 18, 23), a description of the community's heavenly status with a negative portrayal of participation in "the earthly" (Phil 3:19-20; Col 3:1-5), and a presentation of Epaphras [Epaphroditus] as a link between Paul and the community (Phil 4:18; Col 4:12). Between Philemon and Colossians, Kiley notes the similarity of Phlm 5 with Col 1:4 and of Phlm 13 with Col 4:9 as well as the list of greeters in Phlm 23-24, Epaphras, Mark, Aristarchus, Demas, and Luke, to which Colossians adds only the name of Jesus Justus (Col 4:10; cf. Col 4:10-13).

Theological Considerations

Although each of the foregoing considerations, particularly the stylistic analysis of the epistle, carries its own weight in the argument against the non-Pauline composition of Colossians, it is the theological content of the epistle which most often comes to the fore as the single most significant reason for judging Colossians to have been written by an author other than Paul. Commentators almost unanimously draw attention to the significant differences of thought that exist between Colossians and the genuine Pauline letters with regard to christology, ecclesiology, eschatology, the portrait of the apostle, and the understanding of baptism. Even scholars who maintain the Pauline authorship of the letter must deal with those theological points of view which seem to set Colossians apart from the other Pauline letters. For those who maintain that the epistle is non-Pauline, these theological differences are particularly significant factors leading to a conclusion of non-Pauline authorship.

Since the plan of the present work calls for an independent treatment of the christology and of the image of Paul in each of the epistles of which it treats, these important topics will be temporarily passed over. Likewise we shall omit, for the time being, an overview of the paraenesis of Colossians, which not a few critical scholars estimate to lack at least the distinctive Pauline eschatological edge.

It is in its understanding of eschatology that the epistle to the Colossians is most often considered to be theologically inconsistent with the genuine Pauline letters. The charge of inconsistency is epitomized in the idea that the temporal categories of Paul have given way to spatial categories. Although there are a few traces of consequent eschatology in Colossians (cf. 3:4, 6, 24; 4:11), the "already" but "not yet" schema typical of Paul is absent from Colossians. In its place we find the language of "recognizing" and of "growing" (cf. 1:9-10; 2:2-3, 19; 3:10). Spatial concepts come to the fore in 1:26-27, and 3:1-4. Passages such as 2:12, 2:13 and 3:1 seem almost to suggest that the pseudepigrapher's eschatological schema belongs to the category of realized eschatology. In Col 1:5, 23, 27, hope appears to be an objective and other-worldly reality rather than a subjective expectancy of the salvific future. Moreover, such notions as the Parousia of the Lord, the resurrection of the dead, and the judgment, so central to Paul's own eschatological thinking, are absent from Colossians.

The pseudepigrapher's eschatological ideas impinge upon his view of baptism. By baptism, the Christian has been raised with Christ (Col 2:12; 3:1), and has been made alive again with him. By baptism, Christians are already in heaven, or at least in the sphere of salvation, which is the church. That soteriology is a function of the church is especially apparent in the pseudepigrapher's use of the "body of Christ" concept. The metaphor does not suggest the difference of responsibilities and activities on the part of the various members of the church as it does in Romans and 1 Corinthians. Rather it implies that those who belong to the body are saved. From this perspective, the idea that Christ is the "head of the body" (Col 1:18; 2:10, 19) is all important, but the idea of the body's head played no role at all in the ecclesiological use of this metaphor in the genuine Pauline letters. The cosmic christology associated with the body of Christ notion in Colossians suggests that by "church" *(ekklēsia)* in Col 1:18, 24 (cf. Col 4:15, 16) the pseudepigrapher was referring to the world-body of believers *(pace* Peter O'Brien who sees in "church" a reference to the heavenly assembly around the risen and exalted Christ). The pseudepigrapher's ecclesiology focused on the universal church, whereas that of Paul emphasized the local community of believers. Moreover, Colossians supposes no specific church order. Apart from greeting Nympha, in whose house the local community met (Col 4:15) and commanding Archippus to fulfill his ministry (Col 4:17), the epistle makes no reference to the structure of the community.

The Epistolary Form of Colossians

Col 4:15-16 suggests that the church at Colossae was, in fact, a domestic church. Nonetheless, the epistle was not addressed to a church as such. The praescript reads: "Paul, an apostle of Christ Jesus by the will of God, and Timothy our brother, to the saints and faithful brethren in Christ at Colossae. Grace to you and peace from God our Father" (Col 1:1-2). This greeting resembles those found in the Pauline letters. In some respects it is most similar to the prescript of the first letter to the Corinthians. On the other hand, Col 1:1-2 shares with 2 Cor 1:1, Phil 1:1, and Phlm 1 the identification of Timothy as the co-sender of the epistle (see also 1 Thess 1:1 and 2 Thess 1:2 where Timothy is mentioned along with Silvanus). By itself, the appearance of Timothy's name in the prescript of the epistle to the Colossians is not unusual, but it takes on a different allure when considered within the total gestalt of the epistolary features of Colossians.

Farewell greetings are typical of the Pauline letter. The farewell greetings of Colossians are a bit unusual in that they lack the typical formula "The grace of our Lord Jesus Christ be with you [or "your spirit"]," an expression that occurs in all of the indisputably genuine Pauline letters (Rom 16:20; 1 Cor 16:23; 2 Cor 13:14; Gal 6:18; Phil 4:23; 1 Thess 5:28; Phlm 25; cf. 2 Thess 3:18). Instead of this typical formula, Colossians uses the brief "grace be with you" as a farewell greeting.

Colossians, moreover, includes a list of people associated with Paul in the sending of greetings. Of itself, the list is not unusual because Paul often associates others with himself in sending greetings. He did so as he brought to a close his letters to the Corinthians (1 Cor 16:19-20), the Philippians (Phil 4:21-22), the Romans (a somewhat unusual case, see Rom 16:21-23; cf. Rom 16:3-23), and Philemon (Phlm 23-24). What is striking about the farewell greetings in Colossians is that its list of co-greeters (Col 4:10-14) is quite similar to that found in the letter to Philemon. Since it is quite likely that the pseudepigrapher "borrowed" his list of co-greeters from the letter to Philemon, it is not impossible that the appearance of the mention of Timothy as a co-sender in Col 1:1 also represents an imitation of the epistolary style of Philemon.

The epistle to the Colossians was addressed to a community that Paul himself did not evangelize (Col 1:7-8; 4:12-13). Colossae was a well-known city in the upper Lycus valley (in modern Turkey), which had lost its prominence to the advantage of the nearby city of Laodicea by the time of Paul. Colossae was probably destroyed, along with Laodicea, in the earthquake of 60-61 A.D. (see Tacitus, *Annals*, XIV, 27 and Orosius, *Historiae adversum paganos*, VII, 7, 12), but whereas the citizens of Laodicea had sufficient resources to rebuild their city, Colossae was not rebuilt. Thus, at the time that Colossians was written, Colossae was probably an uninhabited site. Because of this likelihood, and given the many references to Laodicea in the epistle (Col 2:1; 4:13, 15-16), Lindemann has suggested that the text was actually addressed to Christians in Laodicea. Hence, it is quite possible that the mention of Colossae in the prescript of the epistle is just one of its pseudepigraphical features.

According to Lindemann, the pseudepigrapher projected tendencies present in the church with which he was concerned onto a fictive situation in the life of the Christian community at Colossae, formulating "Paul's" position as a response to those tendencies. The theology of the epistle is blatantly un-Pauline. It has, however, been given a Pauline color by its selective use of Pauline language and concepts. Among the epistle's principal new theological formulations are the views which it presents on Christ and the representation of the apostle which it offers.

Christology

Any study on the Christology of the epistle to the Colossians should begin with the Christ hymn of Col 1:15-20. The hymn is a major christological statement which the pseudepigrapher has strategically placed at the very beginning of his work. Hence the hymn probably articulated the leitmotif of the christology of Colossians. There are authors who consider the epistle's subsequent christological statements to be only an elaboration of the ideas seminally expressed in the hymn. According to Craig Evans, the hymn is a non-polemical piece introduced by the author of the epistle in order to state a common ground, on the basis of which he can correct certain erroneous practices. If it can be said that the hymn dominates the exposition of Colossians in this fashion, it is even more clear that the hymn is the distinctive feature which sets the christology of Colossians apart from the christology of the genuine Pauline letters.

Verses 15-20 of Colossians 1 are not a hymn in the sense that they would have been sung by a congregation raising its voice in harmonious melody. The "hymn," as New Testament interpreters use the term, is a fairly broad category. It encompasses a variety of materials which are essentially separable from the literary contexts within which they are found and which are characterized by their distinctive vocabulary and rhythmical cadence.

The centrality and the distinctiveness of the christological hymn found in Col 1:15-20 are such that it has attracted a perhaps undue share of scholarly attention. The scholarly literature devoted to it is quite extensive. The issues most frequently studied are those which concern the hymn's form and structure, its background and its authorship. While a few demurrers have been raised in recent years—notably by Wayne McCown, L.R. Heyler, John F. Balchin, and Mary Ann Getty—most scholars are convinced that the parallelism, the introductory formulae, the unusual vocabulary, the contextual dislocation, the strophic arrangement, the syllabic balance, the chiastic structure, and the christological argumentation of the verses coalesce to indicate that the hymn had existed prior to the composition of Colossians.

A strong argument in support of the pre-existence of the hymn is to be found in what are apparently two significant interpolations into the text. According to Ernst Käsemann and Eduard Lohse, the added phrases are "the church" in v. 18 and "by the blood of the cross" in v. 20. These additions serve to reinterpret the traditional material in a very Pauline manner.

In its present formulation, the hymn consists of two strophes as follows:

> He is the image of the invisible God,
> the first-born of all creation;
> for in him all things were created,
> in heaven and on earth,
> visible and invisible,
> whether thrones or dominions
> or principalities or authorities—
> all things were created through him and for him.

> He is before all things,
> and in him all things hold together.
> He is the head of the body, the church;

> he is the beginning, the first-born from the dead,
> that in everything he might be pre-eminent.
> For in him all the fulness of God was pleased to dwell,
> and through him to reconcile to himself all things,
> whether on earth or in heaven,
> making peace by the blood of his cross.

This translation of the hymn (the RSV, presented according to my own arrangement) clarifies the meaning of the Greek text which is only part of one long, very complicated sentence (vv. 12-20). One might note that the hymn does not include any christological titles as such, but that it celebrates the one who has been identified as "the beloved Son (literally, "the son of his love," v. 13). Each stanza of the hymn begins with a statement of the exalted status of the Son, keying on the idea that he is "the first-born." This description does not so much designate the Son as the first of a series; rather it is a biblical epithet which indicates the uniqueness and pre-eminence of the one who is first-born.

In its present form the hymn clearly offers a cosmological perspective, but the author's point of reference is just as clearly the fact of redemption. The hymn chosen by the pseudepigrapher presently celebrates the beloved Son, "in whom we have redemption, the forgiveness of sins" (v. 14). A redemptive point of view dominates the entire construction. The notions highlighted by the explanatory additions are those of the church and the reconciliation of all things. It is as if the church, vivified by its head, functions as the symbol of the reconciliation of all things in the Son. In contrast to the epistle to the Ephesians, where the reconciliation of Jew and Gentile in Christ serves as a focus of the author's interest, the emphasis in Colossians is upon universal reconciliation.

It is impossible to read this christological hymn without catching allusions to the wisdom tradition, but allusions to the Genesis story of creation are just as patent. "The image of the invisible God" (v. 15) recalls the "image and likeness of God" in which humankind is made (Gen 1:26) and "the beginning" recalls the very first verse of Genesis. The phraseology suggests that the prototypical humans were in fact a kind of antitype for Christ. God was thinking of the humanity of Christ when he formed Adam. It is not so much Adam who is the summit of creation as it is the beloved Son. Indeed, v. 16 affirms that the Son is both the agent and the goal of creation.

While there are similarities between Colossians' christological hymn and other christological hymns in the New Testament, particularly the prologue of the gospel of John (John 1:1-18), there are specific nuances in the Colossians' hymn which are noteworthy. These are especially significant because they are important for the pseudepigrapher's argumentation. Major emphasis is placed upon the universal perspective. The use of effective contrasts (in heaven and on earth ... visible and invisible ... on earth and in heaven), the frequency of "all" (vv. 15, 16 [twice], 17 [twice], 18, 19, 20), and the notion of creation (vv. 16, 17) provide the perspective. The beloved Son is Lord of all; there is nothing that escapes his dominion. In addition, there is a manifest emphasis upon the humanity of Jesus. The entire hymn is encompassed between the idea that the beloved Son is the image of the invisible God and the idea that he made peace by the blood of his cross. Creation is culminated in the reconciliation achieved through the cross.

Since everything was created in Christ, that is, through him and for him, everything is subservient to him. The hymn affirms that the thrones and dominions, the principalities and the powers, were created in him. Most probably, these categories represent some form of superhuman beings. Perhaps the "Colossians," living in the midst of the Hellenistic, syncretistic world, were tempted to worship them (see Col 2:18). By his cross, Christ deprived these forces of whatever power they might have enjoyed (Col 2:15). Thus, it would be out of character for those who have been incorporated into Christ to remain beholden to them. With Christ, Christians have died to the elemental spirits of the universe (an expression that probably has reference to some form of astral deities [see Col 2:8, 20]).

The hymn's emphasis on the creation and reconciliation of all that exists in the Son effectively valorizes all of creation. There is nothing that results from the activity of some demiurge or other. The positive evaluation of creation, in Christ, precludes all forms of dualism. There is nothing which escapes the dominion of the Son. Effectively, the pseudepigrapher has ruled out of court any undue asceticism which would avoid some forms of creation because they are presumed to be evil. The hymn's christology provides an important foundation for his paraenetic exhortation: "Whatever you do, in word or deed, do everything in the name of the Lord Jesus, giving thanks to God the Father through him" (Col 3:17).

The fact that the pseudepigrapher's christology is essentially soteriological and that it serves as the essential basis for his moral exhortation is one of the salient features of the christology found in Colossians. The soteriological emphasis of the epistle's christology comes to clear expression in Col 2:9-15, the pseudepigrapher's second major christological statement. The language of this statement recalls that of the christological hymn. Particularly striking is the notion that "the fullness of the deity dwells bodily in him" (Col 2:9), a phrase that recalls Col 1:19. The phraseology is as distinctive as it is striking. Many commentators claim that the pseudepigrapher has taken over the language of his opponents at this point in order to affirm that the fullness of diety resides in Christ. In him the essence and power of God are realized.

As the fullness of deity dwells in Christ, Christians who have received Christ Jesus as Lord live in him and are fulfilled in him (Col 2:10). Allusive references to the "circumcision made without hands" and the "circumcision of Christ" point to the fact that, by virtue of their baptism, Christians share in the Christ event. By baptism, Christians are buried with Christ and are raised with him from the dead (Col 2:12). In sum, they have been made alive with him. The pseudepigrapher's use of compound verbs with *sun*-("with")—buried with, raised with, made alive with, and so forth—recalls Paul's own predilection for this type of neologism to express the reality of the Christian's participation in the redemptive mystery, but his ideas on the baptismal appropriation of salvation are uniquely his own. Expressed in Col 2:9-15, they give evidence of the pseudepigrapher's pastoral concern and show that his christology is essentially soteriological. His teaching about Christ is an attempt to understand redemption.

In the pseudepigrapher's understanding of redemption, the death, resurrection, exaltation, and appearance of Jesus are significant events. On at least five different occasions he calls to mind the death of Christ. The death of Christ is first mentioned in 1:20, the climax of the christological hymn. There, in a remarkable phrase, "making peace by the blood of his cross," which Eduard Schweizer believes to be one of the interpretive additions to the older composition, the pseudepigrapher reminds his readers that reconciliation has not occurred in some esoteric, other-worldly drama. Rather it has taken place by means of a historical event, the death of Christ on the cross (cf. Col 2:14). Use of the phrase was probably polemical insofar as the author of the epistle was opposed to a gnosticizing interpretation which passed over the death of Jesus as if it were unreal. A similar polemical intent can be discerned in 1:22, where the pseudepigrapher writes that "he has now reconciled in his body of flesh by his death" *(en tō sōmati tēs sarkos autou dia tou thanatou)*. This somewhat awkward expression includes a Hebraism ("body of flesh," cf. 1QpHab 9:2; Col 2:11) and underscores the reality of the physical death of Christ.

The death of Christ upon the cross is the decisive event in reconciliation. It is the focal point of the pseudepigrapher's soteriological reflection and serves as a point of departure for much of his reflection on Christian existence. He speaks of Christ's afflictions for the sake of his body, the church, as he seeks to interpret the sufferings of Paul (Col 1:24). He alludes to Christ's death and burial in his reflections on baptism (Col 2:12-13; cf. 2:20). Within the context of that reflection, he makes reference to the "circumcision of Christ" (Col 2:11), which may well be a metaphor for the death of Christ and the cross (thus Moule and O'Brien; *e contrario*, Sahlin and Lohse who interpret the phrase as a reference to the circumcision of the week-old Jesus of Nazareth).

Whereas the pseudepigrapher exploits the physical death of Christ on the cross as the linchpin of his teaching on redemption, thereby developing his own particular appreciation of that death, his references to the resurrection of Jesus are more traditional. In Col 2:12, he has cited a traditional credal formula, "God, who raised him from the dead" *(tou theou tou egeirantos auton ek nekrōn*, cf. 1 Thess 1:10; Acts 3:15). Then, on two occasions, he argues that Christians have been raised with Christ *sunēgerthēte*, (Col 2:12; 3:1) as he reflects on baptism and urges his readership to lead the Christian life.

Early tradition also lies behind our author's references to the exaltation and parousia of Christ. The cosmic vision of Christ, *pantokratōr*, is that of the exalted Christ. The pseudepigrapher's insistence on the humanity of Christ and the reality of his physical death link Christ's sovereign supremacy to the death on the cross. In Col 3:1, the pseudepigrapher presents a vision of Christ "seated at the right hand of God," an allusion to Ps 110:1, the traditional reference so dear to the homilist who composed Hebrews. Almost immediately thereafter, the pseudepigrapher makes his only reference to the parousia of

Christ. Echoing a formula of primitive Christian eschatology (see 1 John 2:28; 3:2), to which he has joined a short interpretive confession ("who is our life"), the epigone has written: "When Christ who is our life appears, then you also will appear with him in glory." When Christ, who is now enthroned at the right hand of God, appears at the end of days, then it will be manifest that those who are his own are indeed "with him" *(sun autō)*.

Four times within this brief passage (Col 3:1-4), the author refers to Christ, each time introducing the title by means of the article. The articular and absolute use of the Christ title is characteristic of the epistle to the Colossians. "Christ" is the author's favorite way of designating the mediator of salvation. The title occurs twenty-five times in the epistle (Col 1:1, 2, 3, 4, 7, 24, 27, 28; 2:2, 5, 6, 8, 11, 17, 20; 3:1 [twice], 3, 4, 11, 15, 16, 24; 4:3, 12), most often without the use of Jesus and without any other title in apposition. Christ is the name which appears in the formula "in Christ" (Col 1:2, 28; cf. 1:4) and the expression "with Christ" (Col 2:20; 3:3; cf. 2:13; 3:4). In Col 3:24, Christ is called "Lord" in contrast to other lords. The frequency of the anarthrous and absolute use of the Christ title (eight times, i.e., in Col 1:2, 27, 28; 2:2, 5, 8, 20; 3:4) would seem to indicate that "Christ" is the name by which the pseudepigrapher really knew the mediator. His use of the Christ title indicates that, for him, "Christ" is a conventional title. The pseudepigrapher's epistle does take advantage of the formal messianic significance of the title.

Apart from 4:12, where it is the name of the one called Justus, the name of Jesus occurs only five times in Colossians, and never by itself. Four times it is used with the Christ title, namely, in Col 1:1, 3, 4 and 2:6, and once it is used in the formulaic expression "in the name of the Lord Jesus" (Col 3:17). This formulaic expression is rather striking because two of the author's other uses of the name of Jesus are also to be found in solemn formulae, namely, the full "our Lord Jesus Christ" of Col 1:3 and the shorter "Christ Jesus the Lord" of Col 2:6.

The Christ hymn celebrates, as has already been mentioned, "his beloved Son" (Col 1:13), a Semitic expression that highlights the uniqueness of the one to be praised. This form of titling is unique in the epistle to the Colossians and is not to be found otherwise in the New Testament. Almost by itself it raises the issue of the sources of the pseudepigrapher's christology. That is an issue too broad to be treated here. One must note, however, that the pseudepigrapher did occasionally make use of the title Lord, Paul's own favorite designation of Jesus. Apart from the use of this title in the formulaic expressions of Col 1:3; 2:6; and 3:17, and a significant contextual reference to Christ the Lord in Col 3:24, the author of Colossians uses the title Lord absolutely, but always in a paraenetic context (Col 1:10; 3:13, 16, 18, 20, 22, 23, 24; 4:1, 7, 17).

Paraenesis

Almost from the very beginning of his work, the author of the epistle to the Colossians shows that he has a real interest in moral exhortation. The emphasis placed upon the knowledge of God's will and the consequent obligation to lead a life "worthy of the Lord, fully pleasing to him" (Col 1:10) indicates that the pseudepigrapher has a pastor's interest in the good behavior of those with whom he is concerned. His concern is that those for whom the epistle is intended should not live as if they still belonged to the world (Col 2:20). That world, the cosmos, is one in which human precepts and doctrines *(ta entalmata kai didaskalias tōn anthrōpōn*, Col 2:22) serve as regulatory principles. These principles have the allure of wisdom, but in the author's view, they are of no value *(ouk en timē tini*, literally, "not of honor to any one," Col 2:23).

It is the manifest intention of the author of Colossians to set the Christian way of life which he proposes over and against the way of a rigid asceticism with its list of "thou shalt not's." "Do not handle, Do not taste, Do not touch" (Col 2:21) sums up the moral teaching of the encratists. "Rigor of devotion, self-abasement, and bodily severity" (Col 2:23) are generally recognized to be slogans of the false teachers. They had regulations on food and drink (Col 2:16). So it would seem that the moral error combatted by the author of Colossians is some form of depreciation of matter, such as was associated with dualistic gnostic thought.

Seduced by the elemental spirits of the universe, the addressees of the epistle had formerly been estranged. Their life was one of evil deeds (Col 1:21); in them they had lived and walked (Col 3:7). Now, there is a new situation, for Christians have been delivered from the dominion of darkness and share in the inheritance of the saints in light (Col 1:12-13). Light characterizes the domain in which God has placed these Christians because of the mediatorial action of Christ. There can be absolutely no doubt that the most characteristic feature of the ethical exhortation of the epistle to the Colossians is its christological reference.

In the domain of ethics and moral behavior, four elements of this christological reference seem to be most important. First of all, the new situation of Christians, because of their baptismal association with Christ, is such they must no longer live as if they belonged to the world. Rather they must "lead a life worthy of the Lord, fully pleasing to him, bearing fruit in every good work" (Col 1:10). There is an ethical demand that is consequent upon the fact of redemption. The ethical imperative follows upon the redemptive indicative.

Secondly, there is a new nature to be put on "after the image of its creator." Accordingly, there cannot be Greek and Jew, circumcised and uncircumcised, barbarian, Scythian, slave and freeman, because Christ is all and in all (cf. Col 3:11). The author's formulation recalls Gal 3:28 and indicates that the differences which separate human beings from one another are abolished. At the very least, the pseudepigrapher has ruled out the type of exclusivism associated with gnosticism.

Thirdly, the universal domain of Christ implies that Christ, who is all and in all, reigns over all creation. There is nothing that escapes his dominion. Accordingly, all ethical dualism is ruled out in principle. There is nothing from which the Christian must abstain merely because of its material nature. An asceticism which deprecates the value of creation has no place in the Christian vision of things.

Finally, the Christian's being with Christ provides motivation for the concrete ethical exhortations which are to be found in the epistle to the Colossians.

It is generally admitted that the pseudepigrapher has borrowed generously from traditional materials for the practical contents of his moral exhortation. This is immediately apparent in the first great ethical section of the epistle (Col 3:5-17), with its contrasting negative (vv. 5-11) and positive (vv. 12-17) paraenesis. Each of these subsections is characterized by the use of an ethical catalog. Catalogs of vice appear in verses 5 and 8, while a catalog of virtues appears in verse 12.

These ethical catalogs are similar to the catalogs of virtues and vices that are found in the Pauline writings and other early Christian literature (e.g. Rom 1:29-31; 2 Cor 6:6; 12:20; Gal 5:19-21; 5:22-23; Eph 4:31; 5:3-5; Phil 4:8; 1 Tim 1:9-10; 3:2, 3, 8 ; 6:4-5, 11; 2 Tim 3:2-5; Titus 1:7, 8; 3:3; Jas 3:17; 1 Pet 2:1; 4:3, 4; 2 Pet 1:5-7; Jude 8, 16; Rev 9:20, 21; 21:8; 22:15; *Did.* 5:1; *1 Clem.* 35:45; Polycarp, *Phil.* 2:2; 4:3; 5:2; 6:1). These Christian ethical lists are akin to similar lists found in the writings of the Stoics and some Jewish writings of the Hellenistic period. Thus, there is little possibility of doubt about their conventional character.

Ethical writings of the period frequently contained catalogs of virtues and vices, but there was no standard list as such. The specific listing of a given set of virtues or vices is particular to the text in which it appears, even though the lists are usually quite general and may have little to do with the context in which they appear.

Thus, the author of the epistle to the Colossians has appealed to a *topos* of conventional ethical wisdom as he lists vices in vv. 5 and 8 and virtues in verse 12. The device serves to set one's way of life before conversion apart from the way of life after conversion. In context, the catalogs concretize the general exhortation found in the introduction to the epistle's paraenesis: "... seek the things that are above ... set your minds on things that are above, not on things that are on earth" (Col 3:1-2). The incorporation of the catalogs into the epistle indicates that the way of life promoted by its author is not one of ethereal meditation; life with Christ is reflected in concrete action.

The pseudepigrapher has chosen to invoke a bit of conventional wisdom in order to advance this point of view and to establish a contrast between life with Christ and life in the world. There are, however, some particular features of his use of the ethical catalogs that are striking. First of all, each of his lists consists of five items. This is in keeping with his predilection for series of five, which some commentators consider to be a stylistic feature of the entire epistle. The catalogs of vices are placed in apposition (to "what is earthly" in v. 5; to "all" in v. 8), and the last of the five is given a specific interpretation ("which is idolatry," v. 5; "from your mouth," v. 8).

Secondly, each of the lists seems to have a central focus. The catalog of vices in verse 5 is concerned with sexual sins, much in the manner of the Holiness Code (Lev 18), while the catalog in v. 8 focuses on antisocial conduct. The list of virtues in verse 12 promotes a subdued, yet outreaching, way of life which George Cannon thinks to be so Christlike in character that the list may reflect the ways in which the early church remembered Jesus.

The third distinctive feature of these lists is their hortatory nature. Frequently, lists of vices are used, even by New Testament authors (e.g. Rom 1:29-31; Titus 3:3), to create a derogatory profile, but the author of Colossians offers his lists of vices in the context of an exhortation to turn from these evils. Put them to death, put them away, he writes. In contrast, he urges his readers to lead a truly Christian way of life when he writes "put on, then, as God's chosen ones...." The metaphor of clothing suggests that these virtues and vices were linked with the baptismal catechesis of the early church. Reference to baptismal catechesis would be contextually well situated in a document which highlights the importance of Christian baptism as much as does the epistle to the Colossians.

In addition to their use of various ethical catalogs, the ethical writings of the Stoics and Hellenistic Jews were frequently characterized by the use of so-called household codes *(Haustafeln)*. Household codes are to be found in the writings of Seneca, Epictetus, and Plutarch, as well as in Philo, Josephus, and the book of Tobit (Tob 4:3-19). Scholars debate among themselves as to the precise orgin and the specific characteristics of the literary genre, but they are of one mind in affirming that Col 3:18-4:1 is a household code. This is probably the oldest example of the use of a household code by a Christian author. Shortly afterwards the use of this ethical device would become commonplace in early Christian literature (see, for example, 1 Tim 2:8-3:13; 5:1-22; Titus 2:1-10; *Did.* 4:9-11; *Barn.* 19:5-8; *1 Clem.* 1:3; 21:6-9; Polycarp, *Phil* 4:1-6:2). Some scholars have suggested that the use of the household code in early Christianity was a way of dealing with the problem of the delayed Parousia. From this point of view, the Christian use of the genre would represent a post-Pauline development.

Examination of the pre- and early Christian use of the genre shows that it was easily adapted according to the purposes of the author who was using it. Bearing in mind the pseudepigrapher's freedom of expression in this regard, we can look at some of the conspicuous features of the version of the household code that he offers in Col 3:18-4:1. It is a self-contained paraenetic unit, essentially separable from its present context, and consisting of three pairs of reciprocal exhortations. Tightly structured, it is most comparable to the household codes found in Eph 5:22-6:9 and 1 Pet 2:13-3:8, and may well have served as the inspiration for these later codes.

Among the conspicuous features of the household code in Colossians is its use of direct address. Rather than reflecting on the mutual responsibilities of wives and husbands, children and parents, slaves and masters, it is addressed to the members of each of these groups. Although the principle of reciprocity is clearly operative in the pseudepigrapher's exhortation, one of the special features of his household code is the emphasis placed on the duties of the subordinate members of the household, particularly the slaves (Col 3:22-25). While the use of the middle voice in verse 18 *(hupotassesthe,* "be subject") invites the voluntary submission of wives to their husbands, the use of the active imperative in verses 20 and 22 *(hupakouete,* "obey") demands absolute obedience.

Another striking feature of this particular household code appears in the address to slaves, specifically, in the motivational clause of verse 24, where there is to be found one of Colossians's rare references to future eschatology. Indeed, the pseudepigrapher's use of explicitly Christian motivation in his exhortation to all three groups of subordinates, as well to masters, is perhaps the most striking feature of his version of the household code. "As is fitting in the Lord" (v. 18) sums up the situation. There is a new attitude and a new behavior expected from those who now acknowlege Christ as Lord.

The fact that the pseudepigrapher has made his own the household code of Col 3:18-4:1 and has made it a key part of his paraenesis shows that the principle of essential Christian equality enunciated in Col 3:11 does not mean the elimination of social differences and specific social responsibilities. The pseudepigrapher's balance of the principle of social order with the principle of Christian equality may well provide the key to his adoption and adaption of the household code. It is quite likely that those for whom his composition was intended were prone to the form of social disorder typically associated with the "enthusiasm" of the gnostic movement. While the negative and positive paraenesis of Col 3:5-17 urges his readers to respond to the demands of their new life with Christ, the household code of Col 3:18-4:1 reminds them that this new life is to be lived in the real world of social relationships.

Patriarchal structures characterized the social world of post-Pauline times. The pseudepigrapher's use of a household code in which women were urged to be obedient to their husbands serves as an indication of the patriarchalism of those times. Yet another sign might be the absence of the male-female pair from Col 3:11, so obviously dependent on Gal 3:28. The patriarchalism of Colossians and other post-Pauline literature makes it rather unlikely that it was a female author who hid her personal identity, and her gender, by resorting to the device of Pauline pseudepigraphy. My present willingness to cite the truly anonymous pseudepigrapher as a "he" is based on this exegetical judgment.

Paul

The epistle to the Colossians does not make the claim that Paul the apostle had founded the Christian community in that city of the Lycus valley. Indeed, it clearly recognizes that the church of Colossae was founded by someone other than Paul (Col 1:7). Nevertheless, the epistle seems to make some claims about Paul the apostle, and it is to these claims, albeit somewhat implicit, that we must turn our attention as we bring this brief study of the epistle to a close.

Perhaps the most striking affirmation made about Paul in the epistle is found in its opening words. Paul is called "apostle of Christ Jesus by the will of God" (Col 1:1). At first sight the description is innocent enough. Paul is called "apostle" in Rom 1:1; 1 Cor 1:1; 2 Cor 1:1; and Gal 1:1 (cf. Eph 1:1). Indeed, the expression "apostle of Christ Jesus by the will of God" *(apostolos Christou Iēsou dia thelēmatos theou)* seems to have been taken over verbatim from the Corinthian correspondence. Yet, in Colossians, the expression seems to ring with an uncalled for solemnity, especially in an epistle addressed to a community in which Paul's authority has not been opposed.

The pseudepigrapher's concern seems to focus on Paul's office. The formal significance of the term apostle (meaning "one who has been sent") is absent from his perspective—and necessarily so. He has made no pretense of Paul's having been sent to the Colossians. In Colossians, there is no mention of other apostles—neither Peter nor the Twelve, neither Epaphroditus (see Phil 2:25) nor any other of the historical Paul's companions and co-workers (see Rom 16:7; Gal 1:19; 1 Thess 2:7 [v. 6 in the RSV]). In the pseudepigrapher's eyes, Paul is the only apostle. "Paul is, as *the* Apostle to the nations, the one and only apostle," says Eduard Lohse in his commentary on Colossians.

Two elements of the pseudepigrapher's understanding of Paul's apostolic office stand out immediately and sharply distinguish what the pseudepigrapher understood Paul to be as an apostle from what the historical Paul understood himself to be as an apostle. These features are the singularity and the universality of the apostolic office as it is portrayed by the author of Colossians. Both of these characteristics come to sharp focus in a passage in which the pseudepigrapher reflects on Paul's mission and his pastoral care (Col 1:24-2:5). The uniqueness of Paul as the apostle is not only highlighted by the author's silence as to the existence and mission of other apostles, it is also underscored by the use of the emphatic clause "of which I, Paul, became a minister" *(ou egenomēn egō Paulos diakonos)* in Col 1:23. This is one of the rare citations of the name of Paul in the body of a New Testament epistle (see also Col 4:18; cf. 1 Cor 16:21; 2 Thess 3:17; Gal 5:2; Phlm 19). Otherwise, apart from its appearance in the epistolary salutation, the name of Paul is only cited in 1 Cor 1:12, 13; 3:4, 5, 22; 2 Cor 10:1; Eph 3:1; 1 Thess 2:18; Phlm 9. Stylistically the presence of an emphatic, and otherwise unnecessary (in Greek), "I" *(egō)* suggests that the author is focusing his interest sharply on the figure of Paul. With this "I," Paul is distinguished from other members of the church. Previously the epigone had imitated Paul's epistolary style as he used the first person plural, "we," in the thanksgiving (Col 1:3) and prayer report (Col 1:9). The author of the epistle to the Colossians further highlights his focus on Paul in 1:25, where he again uses an emphatic "I" as well as an explicit term for Paul's office: "of which I *(egō)* became a minister according to the divine office which was given to me, for you."

The universal import of Paul's apostolic office is expressed in various ways in the Pauline reflection found in Col 1:24-2:5. Paul is called a "minister of the gospel" (v. 23, *diakonos tou euaggeliou)* and a "minister of the church" (v. 25, *diakonos tēs ekklēsias).* Of itself this description is not unusual. Paul is called a "minister" in 1 Cor 3:5; 2 Cor 3:6; 6:4; and 11:15. What is a bit unusual is that "minister" is used in the singular. In the Corinthian correspondence, the term is used in the plural; Paul includes himself among the ministers. One of these ministers is Apollos (1 Cor 3:5). Timothy is another (1 Thess 3:2; cf. 1 Tim 4:6). In Colossians, to be sure, Epaphras is called a faithful minister of Christ in Col 1:7 (cf. Eph 3:7;), as are Tychicus and Archippus (see Col 4:7 [cf. Eph 6:21]; Col 4:17). Nonetheless, the singularity of the description of Paul as a minister of the gospel and of the church is particularly striking.

Neither of these characterizations of the apostle Paul appears in the genuine Pauline letters. The gospel of which Paul is a minister is the gospel for the whole world. It has "been preached to every creature under heaven" (Col 1:23), a bit of hyperbole which is consistent with the universal perspective of the pseudepigrapher's composition, of which consistency of thought is a characteristic feature. Because Paul is the minister of the universal gospel he can be described as a minister of the church, for the church is the symbol of universal salvation. That church is composed of Greek and Jew (Col 3:11, where the reversal of the normal Pauline order, Jew and Greek, is noteworthy). The church of which Paul is the minister is the universal church. Hence, Paul's ministry has relevance for "the Colossians," even though the apostle Paul did not evangelize their community. The office that was given to him was for them: ". . . the church of which I became a minister according to the divine office which was given *to me for you (moi eis humas)*" (Col 1:24-25).

In the exercise of his apostolic office Paul enjoys authority over the community of "the Colossians." Paul's apostolic office is important for those whom he has not met personally (Col 2:1-3). Retrospectively, perhaps, Paul's authority ratifies the ministry of Epaphras (Col 1:7, where the RSV, along with the JB, NEB, and NAB, reads "he is a faithful minister of Christ on our behalf," but the ambiguity of the manuscript evidence leads some editors, especially those of *The Greek New Testament*, to read "on *your* behalf.") Commenting on the paradigmatic character of Paul's apostolic office, Lohse has commented that "the emphasis is that the gospel has binding validity because of its apostolic character. . . . The church lives from the apostolic word and is thereby bound to the apostolic office."

One of the most striking features of the pseudepigrapher's profile of Paul is his affirmation of the apostle's vicarious suffering (Col 1:24). Rather than come to the community, the apostle is to suffer on its behalf. This type of affirmation is without parallel in the rest of the New Testament (see, however, 2 Cor 1:4-7) and has been a *crux interpretum* since the earliest times. It is difficult to comprehend the author's understanding of the relationship between Paul's sufferings and those of Christ. The use of the first person singular ("I rejoice," ... "I complete") places an emphasis on Paul, the individual, while "for your sake" (*huper humōn*) points to the vicarious nature of Paul's sufferings. They are of benefit to those whom he had never met, let alone evangelized. The choice of the noun *panthēmasin* ("sufferings") seems to imply, following customary Greek usage, the necessity and inevitability of these sufferings. Paul's portrait has been painted in the light of his martyrdom. His vicarious sufferings belong to this apostolic office.

In sum, the author of the epistle to the Colossians seems to have been one of the first Christian writers to have a vision of Paul, "the apostle and martyr." Lohse has explained that "the image of the apostle which was formed by the second Christian generation was essentially characterized by the exhibition of his sufferings, much like the image which post-biblical Judaism developed of the prophets. Without exception, they were pictured as persecuted and suffering, and martyrdom was the very reason they were raised to their position of honor."

Two additional aspects of the epistle's projected image of Paul deserve at least a passing mention. One is the use of the athletic metaphor in Col 2:1, "For I want you to know how greatly I strive for you, and for those at Laodicea, and for all who have not seen my face." The apostle had used the imagery of the isthmian games to speak of his energetic activity in the Thessalonian community (1 Thess 2:2); now the pseudepigrapher uses the *agōn* motif ("the strife") to describe the broader relationship between the apostle and the communities to which his apostolate relates.

The other aspect of the Pauline image to be mentioned is the use of the prayer motif. Thanksgiving, prayer reports, prayers, and intercession are characteristic of the Pauline letters. So, in Colossians, we find a thanksgiving (Col 1:3-8), a prayer report (Col 1:9-10; cf. 1:3, "when we pray for you"), and a brief intercessory prayer (Col 1:11-12). Since the thanksgiving is a characteristic feature of the beginning of a Hellenistic letter, the presence of a thanksgiving in Col 1 represents, therefore, a feature of the pseudepigrapher's choice of the epistolary form for his composition. The presence of this intercessory prayer expresses the specific conviction that God's power is at work in the unfolding of the mystery about which the author writes in his letter. More generally, however, it can be affirmed that the prayer motif of the epistle to the Colossians is part and parcel of its imitative character. The reproduction of this feature in Colossians shows that the pseudepigrapher appreciated Paul not only as an apostle and as one who suffered, but also as a man of prayer.

The pseudepigraphical nature of his composition gave rise to other features of his work which touch upon the figure of Paul. Just as the farewell greetings of Col 4:10-14 give a certain degree of verisimilitude to the work, so, too, does the biographical note found in Col 4:7-9. Reference to the apostle's signature (which would not have been recognized in a community which he had never visited and with whom he, presumably, had not previously corresponded) is an implicit plea for the recognition of the authority of the work (Col 4:18a). "Remember my fetters" (Col 4:18b) is unique among the final greetings of the New Testament epistles. Might it not be a literary affirmation of the absence of Paul? As a matter of fact, Tychicus and Onesimus are presumably to speak about the absent Paul. Indeed, the absence of Paul seems to be a factor with which the epigone has had to deal. His work does not contain what Robert Funk calls the "apostolic parousia," the expression of a desire to be present which is so typical of the genuine Pauline letters (Rom 15:30-32; 1 Cor 16:5-9; 2 Cor 13:10; Phil 2:24; 1 Thess 2:17-20; Phlm 22). As far as the epistle to the Colossians is concerned, the epistle itself stands in for the absent Paul. Paul could not possibly come in person, because he is the apostolic figure from the past.

A Brief Bibliography

Cannon, George E. *The Use of Traditional Materials in Colossians,* Macon, GA: Mercer University Press, 1983.

Francis, Fred O. and Meeks, Wayne A. *Conflict at Colossae: A Problem in the Interpretation of Early Christianity Illustrated by Selected Modern Studies.* Sources for Biblical Study, 4. Rev. ed.: Missoula, MT, Scholars Press, 1975.

Kiley, Mark. *Colossians as Pseudepigraphy.* The Biblical Seminar. Sheffield: JSOT, 1986.

Mullins, T.Y. "The Thanksgivings of Philemon and Colossians," *NTS* 30 (1984) 288-293.

O'Neill, J. "The Source of the Christology in Colossians," *NTS* 26 (1979-1980) 87-100.

Pollard, T.E. "Colossians 1. 12-20: A Reconsideration," *NTS* 27 (1980-1981) 572-575.

Sanders, Ed Parish. "Literary Dependence in Colossians," *JBL* 85 (1966) 28-45.

Senior, Donald. "Letter to the Colossians," *TBT* 23 (1985) 11-17.

Vawter, Bruce. "The Colossians Hymn and the Principle of Redaction," *CBQ* 33 (1971) 62-81.

Weiss, Herold. "The Law in the Epistle to the Colossians," *CBQ* 34 (1972) 294-314.

Yates, Roy, "'The Worship of Angels,' (Col 2:18)," *Exp Tim* 77 (1985) 12-15.

6

The Second Epistle to the Thessalonians

In recent years it has often been said that the problem with 2 Thessalonians is 1 Thessalonians. Those who say such things are reflecting the common view that there really would be no serious reason to call into question the Pauline authorship of 2 Thessalonians were it not for the existence of 1 Thessalonians. As it is, 1 Thessalonians does exist. As a matter of fact, it is generally considered to be the first of the New Testament letters and the oldest extant Christian text. The relationship between this letter and 2 Thessalonians constitutes the heart of the matter in the discussion of the latter's authenticity.

It was in 1798 that serious discussions began to be entertained as to the authenticity of 2 Thessalonians. Johann Ernst Christian Schmidt focused his attention on 2 Thess 2:1-12. Because of the apparent contradictions between this passage, the apocalyptic section of 2 Thessalonians, and 1 Thess 4:13-5:11, the twofold apocalyptic disclosure of 1 Thessalonians, Schmidt proposed that 2 Thess 2:1-12 had not been written by Paul. Schmidt's views were initially supported by W.M.L. de Wette in his 1826 Introduction to the New Testament, but de Wette had changed his mind by the time of the appearance of the fourth edition of the Introduction and the publication of his short commentary on the Thessalonian Correspondence in 1841.

In 1839, the discussion of 2 Thess 2:1-12 broadened considerably with the publication of F.H. Kern's seminal article on the pericope. Kern focused his attention on the language and content of 2 Thessalonians rather than on the comparison between the eschatological sections of 1 and 2 Thessalonians. Kern suggested that the apocalyptic scenario portrayed in 2 Thessalonians is similar to that found in Rev 13:3-10 and 17:8-14. Kern also claimed that the description of the man of lawlessness in 2 Thess 2 was dependent upon the legend of Nero redivivus. Since Nero died in 68 A.D., reliance upon a myth which circulated after his death would have precluded the composition of 2 Thessalonians during Paul's lifetime, let alone by his own hand.

Kern estimated that the epistle was written between 68 and 70 A.D. by a "paulinist" who "paulinized" the apocalyptic material as he incorporated it into a text based on 1 Thessalonians. Kern was thus the first author to use the methodology of comparative literature in his study of 2 Thessalonians, but he also insisted upon the idea that 2 Thessalonians was essentially an imitation of 1 Thessalonians. In his judgment 2 Thess 3:17 provided a clear indication that 2 Thessalonians was the work of an epigone.

Views similar to those of Kern were advanced by Karl Schrader in the fifth volume of his 1836 study on *Paul the Apostle (Der Apostel Paulus, 5,* Leipzig, Kollmann, *1836)* and by Richard Adalbert Lipsius in an 1854 article on the epistle. However it was Kern's work which had the greatest influence on German scholarship during the second half of the nineteenth century.

In his 1845 book, *Paul the Apostle of Jesus Christ* (ET, 1875), Ferdinand Christian Baur capitalized on the comparison between 2 Thess 2 and Revelation. He thought that the author of 2 Thessalonians had adopted and adapted Revelation's image of the Antichrist. He also drew attention to the inconsistencies that exist between the eschatology of 2 Thessalonians and the eschatology of 1 Cor 15. The inconsistencies between 2 and 1 Thessalonians were, however, of little concern to Baur since he also claimed that 1 Thessalonians was inauthentic. The lack of anti-Judaic polemic in both 1 and 2 Thessalonians served to convince him that each of these epistles derived from post-Pauline times.

By way of reaction to Baur's book on Paul, K.L.W. Grimm (1850) defended the Pauline authorship of 1 Thessalonians, but conceded that 2 Thessalonians might well be the work of a pseudepigrapher. The members of the Tübingen school, however, generally continued to think along the same lines as did Baur, the founder of the school. Thus, in his 1875 *Introduction to the New Testament (Historisch-kritische Einleitung in das Neue Testament*, Leipzig, Fues, 1875), Adolf Hilgenfeld could cite 2 Thessalonians' apparent dependence on Revelation, along with the inconsistencies between 1 and 2 Thessalonians, as the principal reasons for denying Pauline authorship of 2 Thessalonians. Then, in 1898, in a work on *The Gospel of Paul (Das Evangelium des Paulus*, 2, Berlin, Reimer, 1898), Carl Johann Holsten argued for the inauthenticity of 2 Thessalonians on the grounds of its lack of anti-Judaic polemic.

In 1865, the Dutch scholar, W.C. van Manen rejected the authenticity of 2 Thessalonians in a study explicitly devoted to the authenticity of the Thessalonian Correspondence *(De Echtheit van Paulusbrieven aan de Thessalonicenses*, Utrecht, 1865). In Germany, while the affinities between 2 Thessalonians and Revelation continued to be highlighted, it was being suggested that 2 Thess 2's profile of the man of lawlessness smacked of gnosticism. The tendency to identify this mysterious figure with gnosis and, therefore, deny the authenticity of the epistle was found in a series of scholarly studies, especially those by W. Bahnsen (1880), Hans von Soden (1885), Karl von Weizsäcker (1886), and Otto Pfleiderer (1887).

In his popular 1891 commentary on 2 Thessalonians *(Die Briefe an die Thessalonicher und an die Korinther*. HKNT 2, 1 [Freiburg, Mohr, 1891]), Paul Wilhelm Schmiedl used the apparent contradiction between the eschatologies of 1 and 2 Thessalonians as a major reason for denying the Pauline authorship of the latter. Similarly, Friedrich Spitta (1893) denied the Pauline provenance of 2 Thessalonians. He held that it had been written by Timothy who had used a Jewish apocalypse from the time of Caligula for the second chapter. In the third edition of his influential Introduction to the New Testament (1892), as well as in his *New Testament Theology*

(Neutestamentliche Theologie, 3rd. ed., Tübingen, 1911), but most especially in an important 1901 article in the *ZNW,* Heinrich Julius Holtzmann used the comparison with Revelation as a basis for denying the authenticity of 2 Thessalonians, but he had begun to move away from affirming the immediate literary dependency of 2 Thessalonians on Revelation. He thought that 2 Thessalonians was essentially a summary and paraphrase of 1 Thessalonians, with new material contained in the apocalyptic sections (2 Thess 1:5-12; 2:1-12) and biographical references (2 Thess 2:15; 3:2, 10, 14, 17).

In 1903, the discussion of the authenticity of 2 Thessalonians took a sharp turn away from the approach of comparative religion when William Wrede published his important monograph on the topic, *The Authenticity of the Second Epistle to the Thessalonians (Die Echtheit des zweiten Thessalonicherbriefs,* Leipzig, Hinrichs, 1903). Rather than focus on comparative eschatology, Wrede concentrated his attention on the literary relationship between 2 Thessalonians and 1 Thessalonians. Having arranged 1 and 2 Thessalonians in parallel columns, Wrede noted remarkable similarities of sequence and themes between the two texts. On the other hand, there were significant differences of wording in the texts' exposition of similar themes. In effect, the relationship between 1 and 2 Thessalonians constituted something of a synoptic problem. Wrede concluded that 2 Thessalonians was an imitation of 1 Thessalonians, written sometime during the first decade of the second century.

Since 1903 the apparent literary dependence of 2 Thessalonians upon 1 Thessalonians has been a key issue in the discussion of the authenticity of 2 Thessalonians. Wrede's contention was already endorsed by Georg Hollmann in a 1904 article in the *ZNW.* In addition to the argument based on literary dependency, Hollmann added arguments based on the contradictions between 2 Thess 1:1-12 and 1 Thess 5:1-11, the lack of personal references in 2 Thessalonians, and the references to forgery in 2 Thess 2:2; 3:17.

In 1952, Herbert Braun published a study "On the Post-Pauline Origin of the Second Epistle to the Thessalonians"

("Zur nachpaulinischen Herkunft des zweiten Thessalonicherbriefes, *ZNW* 44 [1952-1953] 152-156), in which he suggested that the text's tendency towards postapostolic moralism was a significant reason to judge it to be inauthentic. According to Braun, another argument in favor of the post-Pauline origin of 2 Thessalonians was its presentation of a delayed parousia. In his 1957 French-language commentary on the epistle, Charles Masson argued that the eschatological teaching of 2 Thess 2:1-12 was a "decisive argument" against the epistle's authenticity. Somewhat curiously, he then made an exegesis of the text as if it had been written by Paul (see his commentary, p. 84, note 1).

In 1960, a statistical analysis of the vocabulary of the entire Pauline corpus apart from Hebrews led Kenneth Grayston and G. Herdan to suggest not only that 1 and 2 Thessalonians do not necessarily come from the same hand, but also that the author of 2 Thessalonians might well have copied part of 1 Thessalonians. Then, in 1963, Peter Day used financial considerations as a basis for denying the authenticity of 2 Thessalonians. He argued that 1 Thessalonians appears to consider ministers worthy of support from their flock, while 2 Thess 3:6-15 seems to plead that ministers of the gospel should work for their livelihood. Day concluded that 2 Thessalonians was a post-Pauline composition, written to oppose the establishment of a paid clergy, but the specificity of his conclusion has not garnered much support within the exegetical community.

In the same year (1963), Willi Marxsen published his important *Introduction to the New Testament: An Approach to its Problems (Einleitung in das Neue Testament: eine Einführung in ihre Probleme,* Gütersloh, Mohn, 1963; ET, of the third edition [1964]: Oxford, Blackwell, 1968). Marxsen claimed that 2 Thessalonians was written to counter gnostic enthusiasm (see 2 Thess 2:1-2) and perfectionism. He further argued that the epistle's exclusively future eschatology is non-Pauline, as is its emphasis on apostolic authority (2 Thess 2:15). That spurious letters were already in circulation at the time of composition of 2 Thessalonians (see 2:2 and 3:17) would also be an indication of the epistle's post-Pauline origin.

In 1972 the publication of Wolfgang Trilling's *Research on the Second Epistle to the Thessalonians (Untersuchungen zum zweiten Thessalonicherbrief,* Erfurter theologische Studien, 27, Leipzig, St. Benno-Verlag, 1972) was a high-water mark in discussions on the authenticity of 2 Thessalonians. Trilling devoted his attention to the epistle's vocabulary and style, a variety of form-critical considerations, and the theology of the text. While noting the ambiguity of the evidence, Trilling cited seventeen hapax expressions, a general poverty of expression, a "full" (*plerophorisch*) and "official" (*amtlich*) style, and the absence of typical characteristics of Pauline style. A comparison of 2 Thessalonians with 1 Thessalonians led him to consider that the two works could not have come from the same hand and to classify 2 Thessalonians as a general didactic and exhortative tract rather than a letter addressed to a specific community. Trilling's theological comparison focused principally on the epistle's eschatology and its notion of tradition. The study concluded that the theological development found in 2 Thessalonians is such that the text must have originated in post-Pauline times.

In a 1977 article in the *ZNW,* Andreas Lindemann took up where Trilling had left off. He introduced a new twist into the discussion by arguing that the purpose of 2 Thessalonians was to discredit the authority of 1 Thessalonians (see 2 Thess 2:2) and to replace it by a later, pseudepigraphal, letter (see 2 Thess 3:17). This would have been done in order to refute the eschatological teaching of the earlier text, specifically the expectation of an imminent Parousia. Similar thoughts have been expressed by Willi Marxsen and Gerhard Krodel.

Equally radical, but totally different, is the opinion of Andrew Q. Morton and S. Michaelson. Their computer analysis of both 1 and 2 Thessalonians led them to the conviction that the two epistles were written by the same person, a person different from the apostle Paul. While the work of Morton and Michaelson has been generally criticized by responsible scholarship, their computer analysis does serve to underscore the general similarity of expression in 1 and 2 Thessalonians.

A Range of Opinions

This brief historical survey clearly shows that it is the relationship between 1 Thessalonians and 2 Thessalonians which really does lie at the heart of the discussion about the authorship of 2 Thessalonians. The authors cited in the survey have evaluated various aspects of that relationship in such a way that they have concluded that 2 Thessalonians is a non-Pauline composition.

Other analyses of the problematic relationship have led to other conclusions. As long ago as 1640, Hugo Grotius attempted to resolve the appearance of the problematic signature in 2 Thess 3:17 with the suggestion that 2 Thessalonians antedated 1 Thessalonians. This ingenious solution to some of the strange features of 2 Thessalonians recurs from time to time in the interpretation of 2 Thessalonians. Some of the more notable proponents of this approach have been Johannes Weiss, Wilhelm Michaelis, and T.W. Manson. More recently, R. Gregson (1966) and Robert Thurston (1973) have similarly argued that 2 Thessalonians was written before 1 Thessalonians. According to this view, the canonical sequence of the two epistles does not reflect the chronological order of their composition.

Another approach to the problematic relationship between the two epistles is the suggestion that the two texts had been intended for different addressees. While 1 Thessalonians was written for the general church community at Thessalonica, 2 Thessalonians was written for its Jewish Christian minority (so, Adolf von Harnack and Martin Albertz), its leaders (Martin Dibelius), or to a church in a different locale (Beroea for Maurice Goguel, Philippi for Eduard Schweizer). Yet another approach is to suggest that neither of the canonical epistles is the original composition. What we have is a compilation of earlier texts by a later editor. In 1964, Walther Schmithals proposed, for example, that the present text is a composite of two letters, 1:1-12 + 3:6-16 and 2:13-14 + 2:1-12 + 2:15–3:5 + 3:17-18.

The use of different secretaries can partially account for some differences of style and vocabulary between documents which come from the same author. The *amanuensis* hypothesis has been invoked quite often in the discussions on the authorship of Ephesians, but it rarely occurs in discussions on 2 Thessalonians. Occasionally, however, a suggestion is advanced to the effect that Timothy might have functioned as Paul's secretary in the composition of 1 Thessalonians while Silvanus performed this service for the apostle while he was writing 2 Thessalonians. Quite exceptional in this regard was the opinion of Robert Scott (1909). Scott held that Timothy was the scribe who actually wrote 2 Thess 1-2 and that Silvanus was responsible for the writing of 2 Thess 3.

By and large, however, when the authorship of 2 Thessalonians is the topic under discussion, most scholars belong to either one of two camps. There are those who hold that the epistle has been written by Paul the apostle and those who do not. Among those who have held that Paul wrote the epistle are two authors who attacked Wrede in short monographs, *The Authenticity of the Second Epistle to the Thessalonians*. These were Josef Wrzol (1916) and J. Graafen (1930). The authors of many of the classic critical commentaries on 2 Thessalonians have also been vigorous defenders of the Pauline authorship of the letters, especially Wilhelm Bornemann (1894), Ernst von Dobschütz (1909), Martin Dibelius (1911), and Béda Rigaux (1956).

In recent years some of the most important English-language commentaries on 2 Thessalonians have strongly endorsed the traditional view that Paul the apostle was indeed the author of the epistle. The list of so-minded commentators would include the names of A.L. Moore (1969), Ernest Best (1972), James M. Reese (1979), F.F. Bruce (1982), Leon Morris (1983), I. Howard Marshall (1983), and Roger Aus (1984). Reese noted that those who argue for the non-Pauline origin of 2 Thessalonians have not provided a satisfactory motive for its existence and suggested that it was imprudent to fill in the gaps by conjecture and then interpret the letter in terms of such proposals. Charles Homer Giblin's 1967 detailed commentary on 2 Thess 2 also confirmed—at least to his own satisfaction—the Pauline authorship of the epistle.

In 1986, Robert Jewett criticized the salient points in the

argumentation of both Wrede and Marxsen. Admitting that 2 Thessalonians is "both an abbreviation and an expansion" of 1 Thessalonians, Jewett proposed that 2 Thessalonians "must be placed in a category of 'probably' Pauline". This stance represents something of a mediating position between the two camps. Nonetheless, Jewett thought it useful to cite Marshall's remark to the effect that since the early 1970s "the tide of critical opinion has shifted decisively in favor of inauthenticity."

To a large extent, this shift of tide is due to the gravitational pull of Trilling's work. The four major German-language commentaries to appear in the 1980s hold that the epistle is not authentic. In their commentaries, Wolfgang Trilling (1980) and Willi Marxsen (1982) maintained the cogency of their earlier arguments for the non-Pauline authorship of the text. Gerhard Friedrich (1981) and Franz Laub (1985) have also written commentaries from the point of view that the epistle has not been written by Paul. The idea that 2 Thessalonians is to be considered an inauthentic work is also maintained by Philipp Vielhauer (1978), Hans-Martin Schenke (1978), and Helmut Koester (1980; ET, 1982) in their respective Introductions to the New Testament. Rudolf Pesch, who discerned a clear reference to 1 Thessalonians in 2 Thess 2:15, concluded his 1984 study of the first epistle with the verdict that "2 Thessalonians does not come from Paul."

In the English language, Gerhard Krodel's 1978 commentary on 2 Thessalonians in the Proclamation Commentary series stands as a beacon of the new trend. Krodel took a radical stance, similar to that of Lindemann, by suggesting that, in order to have his own writing accepted as apostolic, the author of 2 Thessalonians resorted to a trick in 2 Thess 3:17. Nonetheless, as of 1986, a major commentary on 2 Thessalonians from the standpoint of the non-Pauline authorship had not yet been written in English. Nevertheless, even within the English-speaking world, a scholarly trend in favor of the non-Pauline authorship of 2 Thessalonians clearly exists. A significant indicator of the new trend can be found in the fact that the second edition of Calvin J. Roetzel's popular book, *The Letters of Paul: Conversations in Context* (Atlanta, John Knox, 1982) cited 2 Thessalonians in a new chapter entitled "the first interpreters of Paul."

In 1978, John A. Bailey's important article, "Who Wrote II Thessalonians?," developed four arguments against Pauline authorship of the epistle. In papers presented to the Society of Biblical Literature in 1978 and 1983 Daryl Schmidt unearthed features of the style and language of 2 Thessalonians which are not typical of Paul, noting that many of these uncommon traits are also to be found in Ephesians and Colossians. In "A Stone that Will Not Fit," a communication prepared for the 1984 Society of Biblical Literature Seminar on the Thessalonian Correspondence, Edgar Krentz added to his rehearsal of the earlier arguments of Wrede and Marxsen various arguments based on stylistic and rhetorical considerations.

The doctoral dissertations presented by Frank W. Hughes, *Second Thessalonians as a Document of Early Christian Rhetoric* (Northwestern University, 1984), and Glenn S. Holland, *The Tradition that You Received from Us: 2 Thessalonians in the Pauline Tradition* (University of Chicago, 1986) have also argued the case for the non-Pauline origin of 2 Thessalonians. Holland, in a paper prepared for the 1985 meeting of the SBL, had presupposed the non-Pauline authorship of 2 Thessalonians when he argued that the epistle offered a reformulation of Paul's eschatology.

The Literary Evidence

If the tide has indeed turned against the traditional postulation of Pauline authorship, what are the principal reasons which can be cited as indicators that 2 Thessalonians was probably not written by the apostle himself?

Bailey's essay provides a good entry into the discussion. Following the lead of Wrede, as is the wont of virtually all commentators since then, Bailey highlights the remarkable structural similarity of 1 and 2 Thessalonians, by offering the following table:

	2 Thess	1 Thess
A. Letter Opening	1:1-12	1:1-10
1. Prescript	1:1-2	1:1
2. Thanksgiving	1:3-12	1:2-10
B. Letter Body	2:1-16	2:1-3:13
1. Second Thanksgiving	2:13	2:13
2. Benediction	2:16	3:11-13
C. Letter Closing	3:1-18	4:1-5:28
1. Paraenesis	3:1-15	4:1-5:22
2. Peace Wish	3:16	5:23-24
3. Greetings	3:17	5:26
4. Benediction	3:18	5:28

The presence of a second thanksgiving is particularly remarkable since this feature is not found in the other letters of the Pauline corpus. The structural similarity between the two epistles is the strongest element in the literary argument, but it does not stand by itself. There is also a virtual identity of theme between the two writings. 2 Thessalonians contains no theme not found in 1 Thessalonians, and both texts have the same central theme, namely, eschatology. Granted that the eschatology of 2 Thessalonians is different from that of 1 Thessalonians, it is obvious that the choice of a central theme is the same in both of the epistles.

There are, moreover, remarkable similarities of vocabulary scattered here and there throughout the epistles. The linguistic similarities are obvious from the very beginning of a comparative reading. Each of the two epistles begins "Paul, Silvanus, and Timothy, to the church of the Thessalonians in God our [the] Father and the Lord Jesus Christ: Grace to you and peace" (1 Thess 1:1 = 2 Thess 1:1-2a). No two other epistles in the New Testament begin in exactly the same manner, not even the two letters to the Corinthians. The greeting of 2 Thessalonians is additionally problematic in that a binary mention of God and of Jesus occurs in both the address and the greeting ("grace to you and peace from God the Father and the Lord Jesus Christ;" 2 Thess 1:2b) of the epistle. This phenomenon occurs in no other Pauline epistle and seems best explained as the work of a copyist who is copying the greeting of 1 Thessalonians but making use of the typical salutation.

"With toil and labor we worked night and day, that we might not burden any of you" (2 Thess 3:8) is strikingly similar to 1 Thess 2:9. 2 Thess 2:13b-14 and 1 Thess 4:7 are the only Pauline passages where "call" *(kalein)* and "holiness" *(hagiasmos)* are found together. "Idlers" *(ataktoi)* occurs as a New Testament hapax in 1 Thess 5:14. Its cognates, the adverb "idly" *(ataktos)* and the verb "to be idle" *(ataktein)* occur in 2 Thessalonians (2 Thess 3:6, 11; 3:7) but are to be found nowhere else in the New Testament. In the benedictions of 2 Thess 2:16-17 and 1 Thess 3:11-13, Christ and God are jointly cited as the source of the blessing but, in both instances, the verb is remarkably in the singular.

Examples of similar vocabulary and striking expression could continue to be multiplied, yet it should be noted that 2 Thessalonians contains some linguistic usage that represents a notable departure from Paul's normal way of writing. Greek particles and conjunctions often reflect the imprint of an author's hand, yet many of Paul's favorites (e.g. "for," *gar*) are hardly represented in 2 Thessalonians. The different turns of phrase found in 2 Thessalonians seem to indicate another hand at work, especially since several of the non-Pauline expressions occur in the writings of the early Fathers of the Church. Within the distinctively non-Pauline phraseology of 2 Thessalonians there is the twice-repeated "we are bound to give thanks" *(eucharistein opheilomen,* 2 Thess 1:3; 2:13; cf. *1 Clem* 38:4) in place of the more familiar "we give thanks" *(eucharistoumen)*; "boast" with *egkauchasthai* (2 Thess 1:4) instead of with Paul's typical *kauchasthai*; and "be made worthy of the kingdom of God" *(eis to kataxiōthēnai humas tēs basileias tou theou,* 2 Thess 1:5) in place of Paul's usual "inherit the kingdom of God."

Moreover some Pauline phrases seem to be used in a non-Pauline fashion in 2 Thessalonians. As a case in point, one can consider "work of faith" *(ergon pisteōs)* a rather unusual phrase. The phrase is not found in the canonical Pauline correspondence other than its occurrences in 1 Thess 1:3 and 2 Thess 1:11. Nonetheless, the meaning of the expression varies from one letter to the next. In 1 Thessalonians, it signifies the dynamism of the believer's faith whereas, in 2 Thessalonians, it identifies faith as a work of God. More generally, expressions derived from the linguistic roots *doxa* (glory), *axios* (worthy), *dik-*(just or righteous), and *tass-*(order) seem to be employed in a non-Pauline sense. Indeed, the whole matter of the literary affinity between the two epistles takes on the allure of a small synoptic problem. In this case, the resolution of the problem seems to point to a person other than Paul as the real author of 2 Thessalonians.

The Eschatological Factor

The main points of the twofold apocalyptic disclosure of 1 Thessalonians are: 1) that there is no need to grieve for those who have died because those who believe that God raised Jesus from the dead are convinced that he will also raise those who have died in Christ so that they can meet the Lord Jesus at the Parousia (1 Thess 4:13-18), and 2) that the day of the Lord will come suddenly and unexpectedly (1 Thess 5:1-11).

The main thrust of the eschatology of 2 Thessalonians is quite different. Its purpose is to contradict the erroneous teaching that the day of the Lord has already come (2 Thess 2:2; cf. 3:6-13). In contrast, it was the fact that the day of the Lord had not yet come which was proving so troublesome to the recipients of 1 Thessalonians. To counter the erroneous belief that the day of the Lord had come, the author of 2 Thessalonians cites a number of apocalyptic events which must take place in the eschatological drama *before* the day of the Lord occurs. It is difficult to decipher with certitude the esoteric language employed by the author as he writes about the scenario yet to unfold. He speaks of the rebellion and the revelation of the man of lawlessness, the mysterious restrainer and the equally mysterious restraining force, and the mystery of lawlessness. His readers should appreciate that the day of the Lord has not yet come. Indeed, one should not even begin to speak about its potentially sudden appearance for the preliminary eschatological scenario has not yet been played out.

Lack of Personal Warmth

Whereas 1 Thessalonians is a warm and very personal letter, the tone of 2 Thessalonians is quite formal. It gives the impression of being an "official" text. 2 Thessalonians lacks the apostolic parousia, a statement of Paul's desire to be physically present to the community, which is so characteristic not only of 1 Thessalonians but also generally of all Paul's letters. Moreover, hardly anything in 2 Thessalonians corresponds to the first forty verses of 1 Thessalonians (1 Thess 1:1-3:10) where Paul recalls his welcome by the Thessalonians. Even the very brief personal remarks of 2 Thess 3:7-9 seem to be based on 1 Thessalonians.

The very language of 2 Thessalonians contributes to the impression of formality which it evinces. Paul's favorite vocative, "brethren" *(adelphoi)* is used eighteen times in 1 Thessalonians, but it is found in 2 Thessalonians only when it is part of a structural formula or when it is taken over from 1 Thessalonians (see 2 Thess 1:3; 2:1, 13, 15; 3:1, 6, 13). The presence of emphatic pronouns, "we" *(hēmeis)* and "you" *(humeis),* provides 1 Thessalonians with a character of being an epistolary element in an interpersonal dialogue, but these pronouns are relatively absent from 2 Thessalonians, where they occur only three times (2 Thess 1:12; 2:13; 3:13).

Whereas 1 Thess 1:2 and 2:13 spontaneously employ the traditional "we give thanks" *(eucharistein)* of the Hellenistic letter, 2 Thess 1:3 and 2:13 employ the somewhat officious expression "we are bound to give thanks" *(eucharistein opheilein).* The paraenesis of 1 Thessalonians is introduced by the diplomatic "we exhort you" *(parakalein,* 1 Thess 4:1; cf. 1 Thess 4:10; 5:11, 14; 2:12; 3:2, 7; 4:18 [cf. 2 Thess 2:17]). In its stead, 2 Thessalonians has the peremptory "we command" *(paraggelein,* 2 Thess 3:4, 6, 10, 12). 2 Thess 1:5 and 2:12 affect a moralizing tone, which is generally absent from 1 Thessalonians. In sum, while the readers of 1 Thessalonians are inevitably struck by the note of solidarity between author and recipients which is sounded at virtually every turn, 2 Thessalonians is patently more authoritarian in its tone.

This difference in tone points to a different quality of

relationship between the respective authors of 1 and 2 Thessalonians and the community at Thessalonica. Were the two letters to have been written by the apostle himself, he would have had to change his attitude toward the Thessalonian Christians rather radically in a very short space of time—a few months at most. The hypothesis of the pseudepigraphal origin of 2 Thessalonians, however, clearly explains why there is a different relationship between the community and the authors of 1 and 2 Thessalonians. The relationships are different because the authors are different.

Epistolary Comments

Two verses in 2 Thessalonians are highly problematic for those who maintain the traditional position of the Pauline authorship of the epistle. These verses are 2 Thess 3:17, "I, Paul, write this greeting with my own hand. This is the mark in every letter of mine; it is the way I write," and 2 Thess 2:2, ". . . we beg you brethren not to be shaken in mind or excited, either by spirit or by word, or by letter purporting to be from us, to the effect that the day of the Lord has come."

Initially, 2 Thess 3:17 appears to be quite like Gal 6:11, 1 Cor 16:21, and Phlm 19. In these verses, Paul similarly refers to his own handwriting. In all three of these instances, the letters were probably composed by a scribe with Paul adding a postscript to the text composed by his secretary. 2 Thess 3:17 differs from these other verses insofar as it alone adds a note to the effect that the postscript has been added as a guarantee of the epistle's authenticity. The modern reader has the impression that the author of 2 Thessalonians, as Hamlet's queen, protests too much.

Moreover, if 2 Thessalonians was really composed by Paul it had to have been written, as has been noted, within a very short period of time after 1 Thessalonians. So far as it can be determined, 1 Thessalonians is the first of Paul's apostolic letters to have been written. Given these circumstances, the Pauline authorship of 2 Thessalonians would require that, almost immediately after Paul had written his first letter to a community which he had evangelized, forgeries bearing his name had already begun to circulate. The situation is theoretically possible, but hardly likely.

It is, in fact, the necessary proximity of the composition of 2 Thessalonians to 1 Thessalonians in the event of Pauline authorship of both letters which constitutes the problem of 2 Thess 2:2. Not only has the eschatological understanding of the Thessalonians changed radically within a few months' time, but also within that same short span of time forgeries had begun to circulate in Paul's name. It is true that the phrase *di'epistolē hōs di'hēmon,* rendered "by letter purporting to be from us" in the RSV, is sufficiently ambiguous in Greek to allow for the possibility that Paul was referring to his own earlier letter to the Thessalonians. Yet, such a reading would require that the Thessalonians had almost totally misconstrued the clear message of his earlier letter. Thus, it is much more likely that the Greek really does mean a "letter purporting to be from us." In which case, 2 Thessalonians is suggesting that forged Pauline letters were already circulating at the time that 2 Thessalonians was composed. Such a circumstance requires that 2 Thessalonians be written at a time after Paul himself could have written it.

Thus, the temporal distance between the composition of 2 Thessalonians and 1 Thessalonians required for a plausible understanding of 2 Thess 2:2 makes it quite logical to cite this verse as an argument in favor of the post-Pauline composition of the text. However, a commentator on 2 Thessalonians must also reflect on the function of the author's mention of a "letter purporting to be from us." The phrase may serve as a prelude to 2 Thess 3:17 and indicate that the author is well aware of the emergence of Pauline pseudepigraphal writings and wants to make sure that his own work is accepted as authoritative. On the other hand, as Lindemann and Krodel have suggested, the phrase may well have been used to undermine somewhat the authority of 1 Thessalonians at the time that 2 Thessalonians was written. If so, the phrase serves as a clear indication that Paul the apostle was not the author of 2 Thessalonians.

Theological Differences

In evaluating the question of the authorship of the various epistles appearing in the New Testament canon under the name of Paul, scholars are wont to consider with special care the theology of the texts. Frequently theological differences between these texts and the letters deemed to be authentic lead to the conclusion that the texts under study could not have been written by Paul the apostle. The situation is somewhat different in the case of the second epistle to the Thessalonians.

In the hypothesis of the pseudepigraphal origin of 2 Thessalonians, the epistle is clearly an imitative text. Because of this, the theological differences between 2 Thessalonians and the genuine letters of Paul are not as apparent as they are in the case of the other disputed letters of the Pauline corpus. Nonetheless, I. Howard Marshall, a staunch proponent of the Pauline authorship of 2 Thessalonians, has written that "there is admittedly less of Paul's theology in 2 Thessalonians." He opines that a satisfactory explanation is to be found in the suggestion that 2 Thessalonians is to be regarded as a kind of explanatory appendix to 1 Thessalonians. Marshall's opinion represents an accurate assessment of the theological situation, but the crucial questions are by whom and for what purpose is an additional explanation offered in 2 Thessalonians.

Would not the interpretation of 2 Thessalonians be enhanced if it were considered to have been written by someone other than the apostle himself? As a case in point one might consider Jouette Bassler's opinion that the hitherto prevalent exegesis of the moralistic 2 Thess 1:5 is a bit skewed because it was too much influenced by the presupposition of Pauline authorship and consequent reference to Phil 1:28. If 2 Thessalonians was not written by Paul, which seems to be the most likely hypothesis, then the interpretation of 2 Thessalonians is freed, as it were, from the shackles of Paul, even if it is dependent upon Paul. In this hypothesis, 2 Thessalonians must be interpreted in its own right and its theology evaluated in its own light.

Because of the imitative character of 2 Thessalonians, the theological differences between it and 1 Thessalonians are minimal. Since 1 Thessalonians is certainly a genuine letter, this implies that there are relatively few major theological differences between 2 Thessalonians and the body of genuine letters. Nonetheless, as Trilling has indicated, the differences between the use of some word groups in 2 Thessalonians and 1 Thessalonians and the obvious predilection for "Lord" *(Kurios)* as a christological title in 2 Thessalonians imply a specific way of thinking and conceptualizing which is proper to 2 Thessalonians. The specificity of the author's thought seems to focus upon his understanding of Christ, the Christian life, and the apostle Paul himself.

Christology

A study of the christology of 2 Thessalonians might well begin with the observation that there are twenty-three explicitly christological references in this relatively short epistle (2 Thess 1:1, 2, 7, 8, 9, 12 [twice]; 2:1, 2, 8, 13, 14, 16; 3:1, 3, 4, 5 [twice], 6, 12, 16 [twice], 18). With but one exception, each of these references employs the *Kurios* title.

The exception is to be found in the wish prayer of 2 Thess 3:5, but that may not prove to be a real exception since the verse is one of only three verses in 2 Thessalonians to cite two explicitly christological references in a single verse. The prayer itself is phrased somewhat curiously, to wit, "May the Lord direct your hearts to the love of God and to the steadfastness of Christ." Within the context of a short pericope on prayer (2 Thess 3:1-5), it is clear that the prayer is addressed to Jesus (see vv. 1, 4). Yet, for some reason, Jesus as Lord seems to be distinguished from Jesus as Christ. The apparent distinction is all the more intriguing in that this is the only unqualified use of the Christ title in the entire epistle.

Although this wish prayer does not mention Jesus by name, the author of the epistle is obviously not unfamiliar with the name of the man Jesus. He cites the name of Jesus thirteen times within his epistle, nine times in conjunction with both the Lord and Christ titles in the full christological formulation, "[our] Lord Jesus Christ" (2 Thess 1:1, 2, 12; 2:1, 14, 16; 3:6, 12,

16), and four times in conjunction with the title Lord (2 Thess 1:7, 8, 12; 2:8). Nonetheless, the author of 2 Thessalonians, unlike Paul (see 1 Thess 4:14), never uses the name of Jesus in an absolute, unqualified fashion.

The author's avoidance of an independent use of the name of Jesus and his reluctance to use the Christ title in an unqualified fashion may provide some insight into the basic structure of his christology. The apostle Paul used the Christ title with particular reference to the death and/or resurrection of Jesus. Following tradition, he used the name of Jesus when he wanted to make reference to the historical person, Jesus of Nazareth. In 2 Thessalonians there is little, if any, reference to the life, death, and resurrection of Jesus. Apart from 2 Thess 3:5 where "the steadfastness of Christ" might suggest that the author's prayer is that the Thessalonian Christians follow the example of the patient endurance of the suffering Christ by virtue of a gift of Christ himself, there is no reference to his suffering or to his cross, no intimation of an imitation of Jesus, nor any suggestion that by baptism the Christian participates in the death and resurrection of Jesus. The christology of 2 Thessalonians seems to be almost exclusively oriented towards the future.

This orientation is manifest in 2 Thessalonians' preference for *Kurios* as the christological title par excellence. The title occurs twenty-two times in the epistle, nine times associated with "Jesus Christ" (2 Thess 1:1, 2, 12; 2:1, 14, 16; 3:6, 12, 16), four times with "Jesus" (2 Thess 1:7, 8, 12; 2:8), eight times by itself (2 Thess 1:9; 2:2, 13; 3:1, 3, 4, 5, 16), and once in the expression "the Lord of peace" (2 Thess 3:16).

The context of the first absolute appearance of Lord as a christological title in 2 Thessalonians is the epistle's first thanksgiving period (2 Thess 1:3-12). Verses 3-10 constitute but a single sentence in Greek, yet there is a marked shift in thought and tone from the expression of gratitude with which the pericope opens (vv. 3-4) and the peroration on judgment which dominates (vv. 5-10). In verse 9, the punishment of "exclusion from the presence of the Lord and his might" conveys an impression of the Lord as judge in awesome majesty. The notion of punishment by means of exclusion from the Lord's presence is remarkably similar to the idea of banishment found in the Matthean apocalypse (Matt 25:41, 46), that is, in a gospel which may well be contemporary with the pseudepigraphal 2 Thessalonians. The language of 2 Thess 1:9, however, echoes that of the Bible. It recalls words found in the book of Isaiah the prophet to describe the terrifying flight from Yahweh on the Day of the Lord (Isa 2:10, 19, 21).

Within this context, the author of 2 Thessalonians interprets the kingdom of God (2 Thess 1:5) in markedly apocalyptic fashion. 2 Thess 1:7 places the focus of Christian hope on "the revelation of the Lord Jesus" *(en tē apokalupsei tou Kuriou Iēsou)*. The expression does not have quite the same connotation as "the coming *(parousia)* of the Lord Jesus" (see 2 Thess 2:1, 8; cf. 1 Thess 2:19; 3:13; 4:15; 5:23); with "revelation" *(apokalupsis)*, it is the apocalyptic schema which dominates the thought. The presence of the mighty angels (cf. Zech 14:5) indicates the power of the Lord Jesus. When he is manifest in power, then the sufferings of the Thessalonian Christians will come to an end.

On the other hand, vengeance also is to be meted out by the Lord Jesus. Within the biblical tradition, it is Yahweh who exercises vengeance; now it is affirmed that Jesus exercises vengeance. In 2 Thess 1:5, judgment belongs to God, but according to verse 8 it is clearly Jesus the Lord who is designated as the one to exercise judgment. The flaming fire of verse 7 suggests his divine character (Exod 3:2) and his punitive function (cf. Dan 7:9). As God's vicegerent, Jesus is to repay those who have afflicted the Christian community. His vengeance is to be directed towards those "who do not know God and upon those who do not obey the gospel of our Lord Jesus" (2 Thess 1:8). Most probably, the double description identifies but a single group, non-believers as a whole. These do not obey "the gospel of our Lord Jesus." The expression is unusual; Paul himself normally wrote about "the gospel of Christ." If the author of 2 Thessalonians writes of "the gospel of our Lord Jesus," it is probably because apocalyptic patterns have dominated and will continue to dominate his thought.

"The coming of our Lord Jesus Christ" is formally indicated as the subject of the apocalyptic topos which is introduced at 2

Thess 2:1. The formula itself is similar to that employed by the apostle himself in 1 Thess 2:19, but it is to be distinguished from Pauline usage by reason of the addition of "Christ." This difference confirms the formulaic nature of the full christological title in 2 Thessalonians as well as the fact that "Christ" is virtually without formal significance in the epistle.

According to the author of 2 Thessalonians, the day of the Lord will be made manifest by the presence of Jesus Christ as Lord. Whereas the "day of the Lord" is traditional, prophetic language, previously used by Paul in 1 Thess 5:2, the thought that there occurs a false anticipation of that day is similar to an idea found in the Markan apocalypse (Mark 13:3-6; par Matt 24:4-5). Both 2 Thessalonians and the Markan text express the conviction that the appearance of apocalyptic prodigies will indicate the coming of Jesus as eschatological Lord. According to 2 Thessalonians, it is only after the apocalyptic timetable has been completed that the Lord Jesus will appear (2 Thess 2:8, where the language of "coming," *parousia*, is complemented by the language of "appearing," *epiphaneia*). Then, he will appear as judge and vindicator. By the breath of his mouth he will slay the mysterious Lawless One (2 Thess 2:8). This picture of the warrior Lord has biblical precedents (cf. Isa 11:4; 66:15-16; Mal 4:1) and similarly occurs in Jewish apocalyptic (cf. *Asc. Isa.* 4:14).

The apocalyptic scenario in which Jesus appears as *Kurios*, as the agent of ultimate, divine judgment, fleshes out the epistle's understanding of Jesus as Lord. The *Kurios* title has been filled with a specific, apocalyptic, content by means of allusions to the Jewish biblical tradition in a way similar to that in which other Jewish apocalyptic texts made use of the biblical, and especially the prophetic, tradition. Within this process of filling out *Kurios* as a christological title, the author of 2 Thessalonians has applied to Jesus as Lord motifs that had been traditionally applied to Yahweh.

The phenomenon of the attribution to Jesus of functions and epithets that traditionally belong to God is one of the most characteristic features of the christology of 2 Thessalonians. As the author begins his second thanksgiving, he appeals to the Thessalonians as "brethren beloved by the Lord" (2 Thess

2:13). In context, this is an affirmation of the Thessalonians' being loved by Jesus. The expression has biblical overtones and recalls Paul's description of the Thessalonians as "brethren beloved by God" (1 Thess 1:4). In his letter to the Thessalonians the apostle had proclaimed the fidelity of God (1 Thess 5:24; cf. 1 Cor 1:9; 10:13; 2 Cor 1:18), but the pseudepigrapher has declared that "the Lord is faithful" (2 Thess 3:3).

This tendency is also to be seen in the prayer formularies of 2 Thessalonians. "Now may the Lord of peace himself give you peace at all times in all ways" (2 Thess 3:16) is the final wish prayer of 2 Thessalonians. It seems to be patterned after the wish prayer of 1 Thess 5:23, where it is "the God of peace himself" who is invoked (cf. 1 Cor 14:33; 2 Cor 13:11; Rom 15:33; 16:20; Phil 4:9). The earlier wish prayer, "May the Lord direct your hearts to the love of God and to the steadfastness of Christ" (2 Thess 3:5), reflects Semitic anthropology in which the heart functions metonymously for the core of the person. In the Jewish scriptures, it is Yahweh, the sole scrutinizer of the human heart, who is in relationship with humans at the very depth of their being. Now, it is the Lord who is perceived as directing hearts. Even in the blessing of 2 Thess 2:16, our Lord Jesus Christ himself is mentioned before God our Father in apparent dependence on, but in striking contrast to 1 Thess 3:11, where God is mentioned before our Lord Jesus.

This brings us to the problematic expression of 2 Thess 1:12, "the grace of our God and the Lord Jesus Christ" *(tēn charin tou theou hēmon kai kuriou Iēsou Christou)*. Although similar to the formula of 2 Thess 1:2, the expression has long been a crux for interpreters insofar as it seems to call Jesus God. Such a description would be contrary to Pauline usage. So unusual would be the description that Bailey has noted that, as it stands, 2 Thess 1:12 constitutes evidence against Pauline authorship of the epistle. It must, however, be acknowledged that the Greek text itself is somewhat ambiguous.

In my judgment, weighty arguments can be cited in support of the position that the Lord Jesus Christ is not called God in 2 Thess 1:12. Among these considerations are the parallelism with 1:2, the fact that "our" *(hēmon)* separates the two titles in the Greek text, and that "our God" *(tou theou hēmon)* enjoys a formulaic character. While the ambiguity of the present text may well be due to scribal difficulties, the reason for the expression may well be to unite God and the Lord within a single frame of reference. In any event, the final christological formulation of 2 Thessalonians, appropriately enough a blessing, looks to our Lord Jesus Christ almost exclusively as the source of grace: "The grace of our Lord Jesus Christ be with you all" (2 Thess 3:18).

One other feature of the christology of 2 Thessalonians which must not be overlooked is its emphasis on the "name of the Lord Jesus" (2 Thess 1:12; 3:6). Within the categories of biblical and Semitic thought, the power of the name is well attested. A name is closely associated with its bearer; it discloses something of the bearer's nature and function.

When mention of the name of the Lord Jesus is first made in 2 Thessalonians, it occurs within the context of the thanksgiving period, where the emphasis is on the judgment to be meted out to those who have afflicted the community. Yet, there is also attested the idea that the destruction of the afflicters means rest for the afflicted (2 Thess 1:7). At the revelation of the Lord Jesus from heaven, he will be glorified in his saints and marvelled at in all who believe (2 Thess 1:10). The two expressions most likely indicate a single group (cf. 2 Thess 1:8), as the author identifies the holy ones as believers and affirms that the apocalyptic glory of the Lord Jesus will appear among them.

The notion that the coming of Jesus as "our Lord" is to be awaited by Christians as a salvific event is essentially recapitulated in the formula on the name in 2 Thess 1:12, "so that the name of our Lord Jesus Christ may be glorified in you, and you in him" *(hopōs endoxasthē to onoma tou kuriou hēmon Iēsou en humin kai humeis en autō*; see also 2 Thess 1:10). This passage adds the notion of reciprocity in glorification (see John 13:31; 17:22) to the formulation of v. 10. As such it points to the importance of the name as that of *our* Lord Jesus Christ. While some commentators (Cerfaux, Rigaux, Bruce, etc.) think that the phrase refers to Jesus' glorification within the Christian community, it is more likely that the author's thought continues to focus on the revelation of the Lord Jesus from heaven as he writes about the actual glorification of the Lord Jesus and those who believe in him. In any event, the phraseology of 2 Thess 1:12 is ultimately based on Isa 66:5, where it is said that the name of Yahweh is glorified.

Mention of the name of our Lord Jesus Christ recurs in 2 Thess 3:6, where the Lord Jesus is invoked as the real authority in a matter of discipline. The command to shun those whose mode of life is not in conformity with the received traditions recalls the disciplinary ban of the incestuous man in 1 Cor 5:1-5. There, Paul had written of judgment made "in the name of the Lord Jesus" *(en tō onomati tou kuriou Iēsou)*. The pseudepigrapher's formulation adds a formulaic "our" *(hēmon)* and "Christ" *(Christou)* to the Pauline expression. Given his earlier emphasis upon Jesus as parousiac Lord, it would seem that his words at this point subtly point to the authority of Jesus as eschatological Lord and judge, as well as his present authority over the community which recognizes him as "our Lord."

The pseudepigrapher's emphasis upon the name of the Lord Jesus Christ undoubtedly points to the significance of the *Kurios* title for the Christian community. To a reader familiar with the Pauline correspondence, his onomatology may well recall Phil 2:9-11 which proclaims that *Kurios* is the title by which the exalted one is designated. Nonetheless, there are manifest differences between the pseudepigrapher's understanding of the title, and Paul's own reflections on the name. Most significantly, one might note the absence of that theocentric perspective which so dominates Paul's own reflection.

Paraenesis

Since the christological emphasis of 2 Thessalonians falls on the future and since Jesus as eschatological Lord is "our Lord" (2 Thess 1:8, 12; 2:1, 14, 16; 3:18), that is, the Lord of the believing community, with some degree of accuracy it can be said that Jesus' significance for the community also really lies in the future. His future role as Lord is the basis for the paraenetic appeal of 2 Thessalonians. Although the explicitly paraenetic section of 2 Thessalonians is relatively brief (2 Thess 3:6-15), there is a significant element of exhortation present in the earlier part of the epistle. This is in keeping with the apocalyptic style which the pseudepigrapher has adopted. One of the features of apocalyptic literature is that it is often a literature of consolation. It seeks to encourage those who are afflicted, urging them to remain steadfast because of the conviction that, in the end, God will conquer evil and vindicate those who have remained faithful to him. Clearly, the community to which 2 Thessalonians is addressed is afflicted (2 Thess 1:4-7). Like many a beseiged community, it is in danger of wavering in its belief (2 Thess 2:2-3). Given this set of circumstances, the pseudepigrapher exhorts his addressees to remain unshaken in their belief (2 Thess 2:3, 15) and steadfast in their way of life (2 Thess 1:4; 3:5). If they do so, they will obtain the glory of the Lord Jesus Christ for which the author prays (2 Thess 2:14; cf. 1:11-12).

The paraenetic period of the epistle consists of two sections, an exhortation on unruliness within the community (vv. 6-13) and an order for church discipline (vv. 14-15). The tone of the paraenesis is most obvious in the longer, first section. Three features of its tone provide it with a distinctive ring.

First, there is the mandatory and authoritarian character of the section. Its peremptory tone is such that Trilling believes that the pericope should not even be categorized as paraenesis. Indicative of the tone is the use of the verb "command" *paraggellein*, 2 Thess 3:6, 10, 12) which encompasses the passage (vv. 6, 12). By means of the literary device of *inclusio*, the entire unit of material is promulgated as an authoritative order.

The second characteristic feature of the tone is also highlighted by means of the technique of ring construction. The section opens with a mention of the name of our Lord Jesus Christ (v. 6) and closes with a command and exhortation in the Lord Jesus (v. 12). Mention of the name of the Lord Jesus Christ (cf. 1 Cor 5:4) highlights the character of the person of the Lord Jesus and indicates that apostolic authority is essentially the authority of the same Lord Jesus. It is in the name and by the authority of the parousiac Lord that the paraenesis is promulgated.

Yet there is more present here than a mere invocation of the ground of apostolic authority. There is also an intimation of the present situation of the Thessalonian believers who anticipate the appearance of the Lord Jesus as judge and source of glory. For F.F. Bruce, "in the Lord Jesus Christ" may imply Christ's personal involvement in the situation.

A third quality of the paraenesis of this section is its insistence on apostolic imitation. The apostolic example *(tupos)* is twice cited (vv. 7, 9) as an example to be imitated. The imitation *(mimēsis)* of the apostles is really not an option. The Thessalonians ought to *(dei)* imitate the apostle and his companions. An infinitive of purpose ("to imitate," *eis to mimeisthai hūmas)* is used in v. 9 to emphasize the aim of the apostles' behavior (cf. 1 Thess 1:6). "To give ourselves as an example in order that you imitate us" is a somewhat cumbersome, but literally accurate reading of the Greek text. In any event, the apostolic example is presented antithetically. The apostles' pattern of conduct stands in sharp contrast to the conduct of those who are unruly in the community.

Who are these unruly ones? A common exegesis of vv. 6-13 identifies them as idle persons who have abandoned their secular responsibilities because of the expectation of an imminent parousia. However, there is no specific mention of the parousia in the discussion at hand and there seems to be no formal connection between the eschatological and paraenetic sections of the epistle. Moreover, Ceslas Spicq has shown that on the basis of its usage in popular, koine, Greek the root *atakt—*was used in general of disorderly, antisocial behavior rather than mere idleness. Spicq has suggested that within the context of a Christian community, disorderly behavior covers sins against Christian charity, activities that promote disharmony, and the refusal to accept various ecclesiastical customs or church discipline.

It is, therefore, various antisocial forms of conduct that the pseudepigrapher has in mind in vv. 6, 7, and 11 of his exhortation. Who is responsible for this disruptive behavior?

More than one commentator has suggested that the unruly ones are, in fact, various Christian workers. The suggestion would explain why the paraenesis lays so much emphasis on the example of Paul. Far from disturbing or burdening the community, Paul and his companions worked day and night so as not to be a burden (2 Thess 3:8; cf. 1 Thess 2:9). In the hypothesis of the pseudepigraphal origin of 2 Thessalonians, the citation of the example of Paul in this regard might be an indication of the text's post-apostolic provenance.

The proverbial saying of v. 10, "if any one will not work, let him not eat," is quite similar to a rabbinic adage, "If I do not work, I have nothing to eat," based on Gen 3:19 (see *Gen. Rab.* 2:2 on Gen 1:2). The importance of gainful employment and of providing for oneself recurs in vv. 11-12. In the Greek text a skillful play on words summarizes the reported situation, "some of you are living in idleness, mere busybodies, not doing any work (*mē den ergazomenous alla periergazomenous*). This leads to the exhortation of v. 12 to do their work in quietness and to earn their own living *(ton heautōn arton esthiōsin*, literally, to eat one's own bread). While the thought reflects that of 1 Thess 4:11, the emphasis on the quiet, respectable life is consistent with the ideal of a bourgeois mentality which Trilling and others have identified as typical of post-apostolic paraenesis.

The second topos in the paraenesis of 2 Thessalonians is a disciplinary regulation (2 Thess 3:14-15). It requires that those who refuse to obey the putative author's injunction are to be shunned. In the casuistic protasis, we can again note an emphasis upon apostolic authority: "If any one refuses to *obey* what *we* say in this letter *(ei de tis ouch hupakouei tō logō hēmōn dia tēs epistolēs*, literally, "obey our word in the letter"). In fact, only the injunctions of 2 Thess 2:15 and 3:6 have thus far really called for obedience. The regulation requires that those who trouble the community be shunned. Its purpose is not to punish, but to shame in order that the offender reform. The administrative procedure enjoined is somewhat similar to those reflected in 1 Cor 5:9-11 and Matt 18:15-17, yet the offender is not banished altogether from the community. He is still to be treated as a brother. The offender is still to be regarded as a member of the Christian community. Some would suggest that the less severe dissociation from others envisioned by 2 Thess 3:14-15 is due to the offense itself being less severe. In this view, the passage is dealing only with second degree offenders, that is, it deals with shunning (v. 14) those who have associated with the unruly (v. 6). According to this interpretation, neither the unruly nor their immediate associates are to be treated mildly; leniency is reserved to those who associate with the companions of the unruly. To the extent that this reading represents an accurate interpretation of the text, the whole procedure is rather complicated and perhaps warrants the epithet of impracticality with which Trilling labels it, since he sees it not as a real practice, but as a pseudepigraphal motif.

Paul

The image of Paul that emerges from a reading of 2 Thessalonians within the hypothesis of its pseudepigraphal origin is remarkably simple, yet it is also in some ways considerably different from the portraits of Paul offered by the authors of the pastorals, Colossians, and Ephesians. The simplicity of the portrait is a function of both the length of the epistle and the fact that it is an imitation of 1 Thessalonians. The absence of biographical notes and the generally impersonal tone of the epistle contribute to the poverty of its portrayal of the apostle. Except within the radical parameters of the Lindemann-Marxsen-Krodel hypothesis that 2 Thessalonians was intended as a replacement for 1 Thessalonians, it can be suggested that the author of 2 Thessalonians presumed that his readers were familiar with the autobiographical traits of Paul cited in the earlier, authentic letter.

2 Thessalonians shares with the earlier letter the tendency to use the first person plural. Apart from the reference to the authenticating apostolic postscript in 2 Thess 3:17, the use of the first person singular is absent from 2 Thessalonians. A form of Pauline reductionism is generally characteristic of the deutero-Pauline epistles. They view Paul, not only as the

apostle par excellence, but also—at least for all practical purposes—as the only apostle. This kind of Pauline reductionism is absent from 2 Thessalonians. As a matter of fact, 2 Thessalonians does not even attribute the title of apostle to Paul (cf. 1 Thess 2:7, according to the division of verses in Greek).

What is, nonetheless, distinctive of the image of Paul in 2 Thessalonians is the nature of his exemplarity. No other New Testament text presents the manual labor of Paul (and his companions) as having been done *in order that* example be given. Elsewhere, we have the impression that Paul exercised his trade in order that the preaching of the gospel be unimpeded by economic concerns, or in order that no economic burden be placed on those newly evangelized, or in order that his artisan's workshop serve as a locale for evangelization. Indeed, any combination of these motives might well characterize Paul's attitude towards self-employment. Yet, 2 Thess 3:9 suggests that the very purpose of Paul's exercise of his trade was that Paul give a personal example of the value of work for a Christian.

Although no titular usage fills out the pseudepigrapher's projected image of Paul, his Paul has a definite profile. One of its most characteristic features is that Paul is a letter writer. No other book in the New Testament stresses the identity of the text as a letter so much as does 2 Thessalonians. 2 Cor 10:9-11 contains a brief apology for Paul's letters, but 2 Thess 3:17 proclaims that the letter itself enjoys the guarantee of Paul's authority. As such, it demands obedience (2 Thess 3:14). Indeed, a comparison can be made between the binding authority of the spoken work and the binding authority of the epistolary word (2 Thess 2:15). Indeed, the authority of the apostolic letter is such that it enjoys the faint praise of fraudulent imitation (2 Thess 2:2). The pseudepigrapher's Paul is clearly an epistolographer, a man renowned as a writer of letters.

Nonetheless, the single most characteristic feature of the pseudepigrapher's portrait of Paul is that Paul is an authority for the church of the Thessalonians. The major linguistic and stylistic elements which contribute to this aspect of the Pauline profile have already been cited. They are the significance of the Pauline example (2 Thess 3:7, 9), the use of the verb "command" *(paraggellein)* in the paraenesis of 2 Thess 3:6-12 (vv. 6, 10, 12), and the importance of obedience to what is written in the letter—a call for obedience which is unparalleled in the genuine Pauline letters.

If the pseudepigrapher's Paul is an authority figure, some passages in the letter try to bridge the gap between the projection of Pauline authority and the memory of the one who, with his companions, had ministered among the Thessalonians in warm and humane fashion (cf. 1 Thess 2:7, 11). Such a mediating verse is 2 Thess 3:4, "We have confidence in the Lord about you, that you are doing and will do the things which we command." Despite its pastoral allure, the verse recalls the word of one who commands.

There seems almost to be something forced about the memory of the apostle. Twice the epistle speaks of traditions taught by Paul and received by the community. These traditions are authoritative. The Thessalonians are exhorted to "stand firm and hold on to the traditions *(krateite tas paradoseis)* which you were taught by us, either by word of mouth or by letter" (2 Thess 2:15). There is a pattern of unruly conduct which is "not in accord with the tradition *(mē kata tēn paradosin)* that you received from us" (2 Thess 3:6).

The emphasis on tradition is different from the occasional mention of tradition in the genuine Pauline correspondence (1 Cor 11:2; Gal 1:14). There the matrix of thought appears to be Jewish. The notion is that of traditions passed along from one generation of teachers to the next. In 2 Thessalonians the idea that appears to be most stressed in the notion of tradition is that of Paul as the source and authority of apostolic tradition. In this regard, it might be interesting to note, that 2 Thessalonians lacks the credal formulae which Paul had adopted and passed along to the community (cf. 1 Thess 1:10; 4:14; 5:9-10). Rather than portraying Paul as a medium of tradition, the pseudepigrapher presents him as a source of tradition.

This notion may well be present in two other passages of the epistle, where the reader encounters somewhat unusual expressions, namely, 2 Thess 1:10 and 2:14. 2 Thess 1:10 mentions the fact that Paul's testimony was the object of the Thessalonians' faith. The point is underscored by a redundant reference to the belief of the Thessalonians. While the commentators note that "our testimony" *(to marturion hēmōn)* is akin to the common Pauline phrase, "our gospel" *(to euaggelion hēmōn)*, few note that the expression is not otherwise found in the Pauline corpus. Moreover, whereas "our gospel" frequently suggests an active sense, that is, the act of proclamation by Paul, "our testimony" has more of an objective sense. It refers to the content of the testimony. "Our gospel" is to be found in 2 Thess 2:14. The expression is indeed Pauline (see 1 Thess 1:5; 2 Cor 4:3; cf. Rom 2:16; 16:25). The notion that the gospel of Paul is the means of the divine call is, however, a notion that is peculiar to 2 Thess 1:10.

The links between Paul and the community over which the author proclaims Pauline authority are affirmed in a series of passages which are but a faint echo of the expression of strong bonds between Paul and the Thessalonians which so characterize 1 Thessalonians. In 2 Thessalonians the expression of their common faith is virtually reduced to the occasional use of "our" *(hēmōn)* in the formulaic "our God" (2 Thess 1:11, 12), "God our Father" (2 Thess 1:1, 2 [in the Greek text]; 2:16), and, especially, "our Lord Jesus Christ" (2 Thess 1:8; 2:1, 14, 16; 3:6; cf. 2 Thess 1:12). The exhortation to "pray for us" (2 Thess 3:1) is apparently very personal. The request is, however, taken over from 1 Thess 5:25 (cf. Rom 15:30) and may function principally as an element of the pseudepigraphal schema (cf. Eph 6:19; Col 4:3).

In sum, it seems quite plausible to suggest that the author of 2 Thessalonians presents Paul and his companions as noble figures from the past. It is the witness of their testimony which lies at the source of the Thessalonians' belief. They continue to exercise authority over the community. That authority is embodied not only in the teaching which has been transmitted but also in the memory of their way of life. Our author also knows of the significance of Paul as an author of letters. At the time in which he lived Paul's letters were not only recognized as authoritative, there was also some dispute as to which of the letters written in his name were genuinely his and truly authoritative.

The Paul about whom our author writes is, however, not only a figure from the past. He is also an eschatological figure. Indeed the author's Paul is an eschatological figure within the perspective of a consequent or futuristic eschatology. The author of 2 Thessalonians can write about Paul and the Thessalonian Christians coming together at the parousia of the Lord Jesus Christ (2 Thess 2:1, *hēmōn episunagōgēs ep'auton*). Addressing himself to the Thessalonians' hope for delivery from their afflictions, the author describes their salvation by means of the image of resting with Paul and his companions *(anesin meth'hēmōn,* 2 Thess 1:7). His portrait of Paul is a sketch of Saint Paul.

A Brief Bibliography

Bailey, John A. "Who Wrote II Thessalonians?" *NTS* 25 (1978-1979) 131-145.

Holland, Glenn S. "Let No One Deceive You in Any Way: 2 Thessalonians as a Reformulation of the Apocalyptic Tradition," in K.H. Richards, ed., *Society of Biblical Literature 1985 Seminar Papers.* Atlanta, GA: Scholars Press, 1985, 329-341.

Jewett, Robert. *The Thessalonian Correspondence: Pauline Rhetoric and Millenarian Piety.* Foundations & Facets: New Testament. Philadelphia: Fortress, 1986.

Kaye, B.N., "Eschatology and Ethics in 1 and 2 Thessalonians," *NovT* 17 (1975) 47-57.

Krodel, Gerhard. "The 2nd Letter to the Thessalonians," in J. Paul Sampley, Joseph Burgess, and Gerhard Krodel, *Ephesians, Colossians, 2 Thessalonians, the Pastoral Epistles.* Proclamation Commentaries. Philadelphia: Fortress, 1978, 73-96.

Reese, James M. *1 and 2 Thessalonians.* NTM, 16. Wilmington, DE: Glazier, 1979.

Schmidt, Daryl. "The Authenticity of 2 Thessalonians: Linguistic Arguments," in Kent Harold Richards, ed., *Society of Biblical Literature 1983 Seminar Papers.* Chico, CA: Scholars Press, 1983, 289-296.

7

The Pauline Pseudepigrapha

Our study of ancient writers (chapter two) led to the conclusion that the confluence of the Jewish religious tradition, by which Christianity was influenced and to which it was heir, and the Hellenistic environment, in which Christianity took shape, was such as to make the production of Pauline pseudepigrapha a likely possibility. These historical circumstances make it rather plausible that there existed an epistolary literature attributed to Paul, but not written by him. The existence of spurious Pauline letters in the third and the fourth centuries of Christian history proves that the phenomenon of Pauline pseudepigrapha is more than a mere possibility. At least from that time on, the existence of Pauline pseudepigrapha is a demonstrable fact.

For the serious student of the New Testament, the real issue is not whether fictive Pauline writings were written two or three hundred years after the death of the apostle. For the student of the New Testament the issue is whether or not some of the Pauline pseudepigrapha were written so soon after the death of the apostle that they enjoyed wide currency in early Christianity and were eventually incorporated into the classic Christian canon of the New Testament. Are some of the New Testament epistles pseudepigraphal? That is the exegete's question. The methods which he or she uses to come up with an answer to the question are historical and literary.

An exegete's response to the question posed is not one which easily wins the acceptance of all. The reasons are partially historical and literary. Interpreters do not weigh and evaluate the available data in exactly the same manner. Indeed, it has been suggested that exegesis, the science of textual interpretation, is as much an art as it is a science. That this is true is clear when we see how different exegetes disagree among themselves on the issue of the existence (and extent) of Pauline pseudepigrapha within the New Testament.

There are, however, other reasons for disagreement as to the validity of the exegete's scholarly conclusions. These reasons come from areas of discourse beyond the merely historical and the merely literary. They derive from theology, from an understanding of the church and the Christian tradition. The concerns touch upon the nature of the biblical canon and the authority of the New Testament.

Some Christians think that a verdict of inauthenticity of any New Testament text is to deprive it of its authority within the Christian faith community. There are also those who are aware that the popular conviction that certain ancient texts were apostolic in origin was one of the primary factors leading to the acceptance of these books into the Christian biblical canon at the end of the fourth and in the early fifth century. Thus, members of the biblically based churches as well as members of those churches which have a strong reverence for tradition are a bit uneasy when a scholar says that one or another book of the New Testament, which seems to have been written by Paul, was, in fact, not written by him.

Indeed, since most exegetes belong to one of the churches it occasionally happens that ecclesial traditions and theological positions often enter into the presentation of scholarly conclusions. If it can be said that all of the books of the New Testament were written by authors who were pastorally engaged, it is almost as true to say that most of the commentaries on the books of the New Testament have been written by authors who are pastorally engaged. At the very least, it must be acknowledged that New Testament exegetes are not immune to bias. Their theological and ideological questions and answers serve to configure their exegesis.

Within the parameters of these ancient and modern circumstances it is, nonetheless, apparent that an increasing number of biblical scholars are coming to the conclusion that one or more of the New Testament's epistles of Paul were not written by Paul the apostle. Our own study has suggested that discussion of the issue of the authenticity of the Pauline epistles began in earnest almost two hundred years ago and that the discussion has continued until the present day. As the years have passed, not only has the number of scholars who admit the existence of Pauline pseudepigrapha within the New Testament increased, but the number of New Testament texts that are judged to be Pauline pseudepigrapha has also increased.

Our study has also indicated that there are weighty reasons, generally based on a consideration of the documents themselves, which have led to the historical-literary judgment that the pastoral epistles, the epistle to the Ephesians, the epistle to the Colossians, and the second epistle to the Thessalonians were not written by Paul. By and large, judgments as to the inauthenticity of these texts were originally expressed in occasional journal articles and in scholarly monographs, but similar thoughts are now appearing in a more popular literature.

Moreover, the science of exegesis is becoming more consequent with regard to the consensus judgment on the authorship of these texts. More and more commentaries are being written from the standpoint that these epistles were not written by Paul. Thus, there is an increasing consistency of approach to these texts. Points of view expressed in the introductions and independent literature are now being carried through to the commentaries themselves.

The previous chapters have certainly not attempted to provide detailed commentary upon the epistles which have been passed in review. However, the brief remarks that have been offered apropos their insights into christology and ethics, as well as their understanding of the person and mission of Paul, have, hopefully, served to show that there is a consistent way of reading these epistles under the umbrella of the pseudepigraphal hypothesis. Even if not written by Paul, 1-2 Timothy, Titus, Ephesians, Colossians, and 2 Thessalonians make sense in and of themselves.

In sum, from an exegetical standpoint, the hypothesis of the existence of pseudepigraphal Pauline writings within the New Testament is workable. The category would seem to encompass six texts. Acceptance of the hypothesis has significant ramifications, as does a specific judgment that any one of the six texts was not written by the apostle himself.

Terminology

If it appears reasonable to state that the majority of exegetes, no matter their ecclesial confession, have concluded that 1 Timothy, 2 Timothy, Titus, Ephesians, Colossians, and 2 Thessalonians were not written by Paul, some clarification of terminology is in order.

To begin, it might be useful to distinguish between the canonical Pauline corpus and what might be called the critical Pauline corpus. The canonical Pauline corpus (Romans, 1-2 Corinthians, Galatians, Ephesians, Philippians, Colossians, 1-2 Thessalonians, 1-2 Timothy, Titus, Philemon, Hebrews) is the product of the consensus judgment of various local churches toward the end of the fourth century. During the sixteenth century, the Council of Trent proclaimed that these fourteen books belonged to the canon of the New Testament.

The critical Pauline corpus is the result of the consensus judgment of recent and contemporary biblical scholarship. To the critical Pauline corpus belong Romans, 1-2 Corinthians, Galatians, Philippians, 1 Thessalonians, and Philemon, works whose Pauline authorship is upheld by virtually all biblical scholars. Long ago Eusebius of Caesarea used the Greek term *homologoumena* (literally, "those similarly called") as a classification for those ancient writings whose normativity was admitted by all the churches. Today, when discussion of the bible has moved from the church to the classroom, the expression Pauline *homologoumena* might appropriately be used as a category to identify those seven New Testament books whose Pauline authorship is readily admitted by contemporary New Testament scholarship.

Eusebius used the term *amphiballomena*, the disputed

works, to describe the ancient writings whose normativity and liturgical usefulness was not universally admitted within the various churches. By analogy, those New Testament books whose authorship has been seriously questioned in the academic forum might be called the Pauline *amphiballomena*. To this category belong 1-2 Timothy, Titus, Ephesians, Colossians, and 2 Thessalonians. Hebrews would hardly belong to the category since there is, today, virtually no dispute as to its non-Pauline origins. Scholars commonly recognize not only that it was not written by Paul, but also that it makes no claim to have been written by the apostle. As an anonymous writing, Hebrews is in a category all by itself within the canonical Pauline corpus.

1-2 Timothy, Titus, Ephesians, Colossians, and 2 Thessalonians constitute the New Testament's Pauline pseudepigrapha. The designation is appropriate only when a writing is judged not to have been written by Paul, even though it explicitly lays claim to Pauline authorship. Thus, properly speaking, Hebrews is not one of the Pauline pseudepigrapha. At most, the list of the New Testament's Pauline pseudepigrapha includes the six disputed works, but some scholars might have a shorter list because they might judge 2 Thessalonians and Colossians, for example, to have been written by the apostle.

According to the classic canonical order, the Pauline pseudepigrapha are Ephesians, Colossians, 2 Thessalonians, 1 Timothy, 2 Timothy, and Titus. Using the analogy of the Old Testament's deuterocanonical books, some scholars designate these six epistles as deutero-Pauline. The designation is useful provided that it is not taken to mean that the works are less than canonical. The category of deutero-Pauline simply indicates that a work is attributed to Paul in some derived fashion.

Other scholars have adopted the term "paulinist" to describe the Pauline pseudepigrapha. This neologism has the advantage of suggesting a deliberate intention to give a Pauline allure to a piece of writing. In addition, "paulinist" can be distinguished from "Pauline." In this case the use of "Pauline" can be restricted to the description of that which genuinely comes from Paul. The restricted use of "Pauline" is occasionally found in current exegetical literature. Of itself, however, "Pauline" properly designates anything that properly relates to the apostle and his epistles.

A Pastoral Problem

Each of the six pseudepigraphal works begins with the name of Paul *(Paulos)*. In the Roman Catholic and other churches which employ the common lectionary, the formula "A reading from the first letter of Paul to Timothy" (and so forth) is used to introduce liturgical readings taken from these epistles. Because there is substantial reason for calling into question the Pauline authorship of these texts, some pastors have questioned the liturgical practice which seemingly proclaims that these epistles are from Paul the apostle. Would it not be more honest, they ask, to introduce the text with a simple and noncommittal "A reading from the first letter to Timothy?"

A pastoral response to a truly pastoral question is never very simple. It must take into consideration all the dimensions of the matter at hand. There is more to truth than simply the adequation of the mind to reality. In our case a truly pastoral response must weigh not only scholarly judgments as to the authorship of a text, but also the norms and customs of liturgical practice, the traditions of the church, and the faith of the community to whom and for whom the text is being read.

The sensitive pastor is little inclined to disturb the faith of his community by dropping the mention of Paul from the liturgical introduction to the lection. He or she might well recall the tale which Augustine told about a congregation in Oea, North Africa, which walked out on the bishop during a liturgical celebration. The reason for this dramatic protest was simply that a familiar reading from the text of Jonah had been replaced by a more "accurate" translation (cf. *Ep.* 71, IV, 6; PL 33, 243). While the liturgy teaches, it can be argued quite reasonably that a modification of customary liturgical formulae is not the most appropriate way for a pastor to teach the flock.

Some might suggest that a liturgical homily might be used to instruct the congregation on a more correct understanding of the authorship of 1 Timothy, for example. In my judgment, the homily is not the proper place for such instruction. The homily and the instruction are two different modes or genres of communication. The proper place for the homily is the church with its liturgy; the proper place for instruction is the classroom with its lecture, the parish hall with its talk, or the living room with its discussion group. Occasionally, pastoral conditions warrant the abandonment of the homily because of the urgency of a needed instruction. In such cases, both pastor and flock should realize that a homily is not being preached. In its stead necessary instruction is being given.

Of course, homilies are not lacking in factual reference. Thus a pastor might subtly suggest that at various points during his discourse that 1 Timothy, for example, was not written by Paul. At the very least, the pastor should not reinforce the view that Paul the apostle was the actual author of the text. If the homily is not the place for instruction, it is certainly not the place for misinformation. Surely, there are ways of using and even of preaching about 1 Timothy without affirming Pauline authorship. As an example, although it was not a homily, one can cite Pope John Paul II's 1986 Christmas Address to the Roman Curia. The pope introduced his citation of 1 Tim 2:4-6 with the simple and quite appropriate statement, "as we read in the first letter of Timothy."

In addition to the demands of pastoral sensitivity, there are other substantial reasons for continuing to cite 1 Timothy as the first letter of Paul to Timothy. One such reason is the need for identification. No matter how one judges the issue of its authorship, one must admit that tradition has identified the text as the first epistle of Paul to Timothy. That is the name by which it is commonly known. It is the conventional sign by which the document is designated. There is more than mere respect for tradition which is at issue when 1 Timothy is cited as the first epistle of Paul to Timothy; there is also a matter of the acceptance of useful social conventions.

There is, moreover, the matter of the acceptance of the text itself. Although the pseudonymity of the text shrouds the identity of the real author, it must be acknowledged that the author of the text has presented his work as an epistle of Paul to Timothy. The two epistles to Timothy do not make any internal claim to have been written in a particular sequence, yet each of them is presented as an epistle of Paul to Timothy. Respect for the claims which the anonymous authors made for their own texts can easily lead a modern commentator to adopt as a descriptive epithet "the epistle of Paul to Timothy" and then to add an ordinal so as to distinguish one from the other.

Finally, linguistic analysis has something to offer by way of reflection on the traditional designations of the pseudepigraphal texts. Increasingly, analysts of language are stressing the distance that exists between signs and their referents. Verbal signs serve as codes which provide an opening onto reality for the reader. In a structural analysis of any given text, it is not unusual for students to see words, including proper nouns, enclosed within quotation marks in order to stress the fact that the word is but a sign. It is merely a code. From this vantage point the retention of the traditional nomenclature is easily understood. "Paul" serves as a siglum to designate the author of the text, no matter who he might have been.

Paul and Tradition

Brevard Childs has sharply criticized the application of the genre of pseudepigraphy to the pastorals. "Paul," he wrote, "is no longer the real subject of the letter, but its object. The letters are not from Paul, but about Paul (*ein Paulusbild!*)." In my judgment, Childs' criticism is not only rather severe, it is also unwarranted.

It is not quite accurate to say that the pastorals are about Paul. It is only 2 Timothy that is really about Paul; the other two pastoral epistles are about church order. The author of the pastorals did not have the creation of an image of Paul—an image which many contemporary German scholars call a *Paulusbild*—as his primary purpose. Neither did the authors of the other Pauline pseudepigrapha.

As they wrote, the pseudepigraphers certainly had an image

of Paul in mind. To a certain extent, each of their images was partially of their own creation, the product of their respective imaginations. Yet, to another extent these various images are based on the images of Paul that had been passed along by tradition. The *Paulusbild* is not a *creatio ex nihilo*; it is rather a selection from, an adaption of, and an expansion upon features of the historical and literary Paul.

On the basis of a careful study of each of the pseudepigraphal works, it is possible to sketch the image of Paul entertained and created by its respective authors. The *Paulusbild* of the Pauline pseudepigrapha is, in fact, a creation of contemporary exegetes who seek to discover the image of Paul held by each of the pseudepigraphers as he wrote. As written, the pseudepigraphal texts do not present an image of Paul so much as they reveal something of the image of Paul entertained by their authors at the time when they composed their texts. Indeed, it is only with some hesitancy that one can speak of the image of Paul. There are as many images of Paul operative in the Pauline pseudepigrapha as there are authors who have written the different texts.

If the pseudepigraphers were the beneficiaries of one or another traditional image of Paul, the image which each created served as one of the bases for his own work. Each pseudepigrapher utilized his respective images of Paul for his own literary and pastoral purposes. Common to each of the pseudepigraphers was the realization that Paul was a writer of letters and that his letters enjoyed authority within the early church(es). For them, the fact that Paul produced a correspondence was singularly important. It led to their respective choice of the epistolary genre as a means for their own communications. This trait of the Pauline profile was apparently absent from Luke's *Paulusbild*. His Acts of the Apostles does not once mention the fact that Paul wrote letters.

The pseudepigraphers shared a vision of Paul as an authority for the Hellenistic churches and that of his letters as authoritative. Each of the pseudepigraphal writings has its own way of projecting the image of Paul as an authority, but the fundamental trait is reflected in each of the texts. Each of the texts also shows that the Pauline letter was considered to be an authoritative form of communication in the communities for which they were intended.

If the production of the Pauline pseudepigrapha witnesses to the authority of the Pauline letter in the late first century A.D., it also serves to underscore the uniqueness of Paul's own letter writing. His letters are genuine personal communications. They represent a development of the Hellenistic personal letter. The pseudepigrapha, however, belong to the epistolary genre only to the extent that this is understood as a fairly broad category (as it probably should be!). Among the Pauline epistles in the New Testament it is only Paul's own writings that are truly letters in the ordinary sense of the term.

To some extent, it can also be maintained that the Pauline pseudepigrapha are the result of an emerging Pauline hagiography. The image of the Paul which they project is an image of Paul about to be placed on the pedestal of sainthood. The pseudepigraphers' Paul is one whose life and ministry were considered to be exemplary. He is a revered figure from the past who deserves to be imitated in the present, and, imitation, it is said, is a form of praise.

A Pauline School?

For each of the pseudepigraphers, Paul is decidedly a figure from the past, albeit a relatively recent past. The present study has deliberately avoided an issue traditionally raised in works of Introduction to the New Testament, namely, the issue of determining a time of composition for the various writings. The indication of a precise date for each of the books studied was not really germane to our primary purpose. However, it should be indicated, at least in passing, that not all of the pseudepigraphers stood in the same temporal relationship to the historical Paul. While it may be that some of the pseudepigraphers had personal knowledge of the apostle himself, it is quite likely that the author of the pastorals, as well as the author of Ephesians, knew about Paul only on the basis of his writings and the oral tradition which had developed in his regard.

Should we, therefore, speak about a Pauline school, as do Conzelmann, Lohse, Schenke and Giblet? Was a Pauline school the milieu in which the various pseudepigrapha were composed? Are the New Testament's Pauline pseudepigrapha products of a school in a way that is somewhat similar to some of the philosophical pseudepigrapha? Were the Pauline pseudepigrapha written to honor Paul, as many of the philosophical pseudepigrapha were written to honor esteemed teachers?

Certainly, many features of the pseudepigrapha are the result of a self-conscious study of Paul's letters. Some of the pseudepigraphers had carefully studied Paul's letters. The pseudepigraphers were certainly influenced by Paul. They had made various and conscious efforts to imitate one or another aspect of the apostle's style and thought.

To be sure, there are similarities among the pastorals and between Ephesians and Colossians, but there are also differences between these two groups and there are certainly differences which stand out when all six Pauline pseudepigrapha and Hebrews are compared among themselves. Indeed, no one of the epigones seems to have known of the work of all the others. Apart from the small sub-groups within the pseudepigrapha, their relative independence should be acknowledged. Given these circumstances, it does not seem entirely accurate to present the pseudepigraphers as belonging to a Pauline school. Although there may have been Pauline schools from which the sub-groups have come, one should not speak too readily of a Pauline school, except if one were to use the term "school" as a wide umbrella under which stands anyone who has been influenced by the apostle.

Paul and Pseudepigraphy

A reading of the pseudepigrapha with a critical eye leads to the conclusion that each of the pseudepigraphers used Paul in a somewhat distinctive way. In reflecting on the *Paulusbild*, one must be very wary of undue generalizations. Dennis MacDonald has suggested that the pastorals were written with a conscious intent on the part of their author to create an image of Paul which would replace the faulty image present in the *Acta Pauli*. Replacement of the teaching, if not of the image, of Paul is the note sounded by Lindemann and others in their interpretations of 2 Thessalonians. Even if 2 Thessalonians was not intended as a replacement for 1 Thessalonians, it is clear that 2 Thessalonians has exploited an image of Paul in an attempt to correct erroneous beliefs and practices.

By and large, however, it cannot be said that the pseudepigrapha were written in order to correct an image of Paul. Rather, they used an image of Paul in order to present teaching pertinent for a new situation. A great deal of what the historical Paul actually wrote and taught has been woven into their writings. Sometimes, this traditional material has been misinterpreted; even more often has it been reinterpreted. The Pauline pseudepigrapha represent a reinterpretation of the Pauline tradition.

It is occasionally said that the pseudepigrapha teach what Paul would have taught had he been physically present in later circumstances. However, no one really knows what Paul would have taught, said, and written had he not died when he did—not even the various pseudepigraphers. The pseudepigraphers could not read the mind of the Paul who had died several years previously, the Paul whose memory they revered and whose authority they respected. What the pseudepigrapha really represent is the actualization of the Pauline tradition, the application of the tradition in new and different circumstances.

An analogy from the civic sphere might help to clarify the matter. The Constitution of the United States, with the appended Bill of Rights, is an extant literary text. At the present time there is no way of entering into the minds of the framers of the Constitution so as to determine what they would think and write were they to be still alive in the final years of the twentieth century. It is the responsibility of the Supreme Court of the nation to interpret the Constitution of the United States in such a way that it applies to contemporary circumstances. The work of the court is essentially an actualization of the constitutional tradition. Similarly, the work of the Pauline pseudepigrapher is an actualization of the Pauline tradition.

A New Testament analogy can be drawn from the synoptic gospels. In the Christian church of the first century, the gospel of Mark enjoyed the privilege of being an authoritative literary witness to the tradition about Jesus. It was Mark's creative genius which created the gospel form (at least according to the hypothesis of Markan priority, today accepted by the vast majority of New Testament scholars). His gospel was not altogether relevant for later and different Christian communities. Matthew and Luke then reinterpreted the gospel tradition for the particular sets of circumstances within which they wrote. The authority of the gospel genre was, however, sufficiently strong that these authors adopted the Markan genre for their own work.

Because the Pauline pseudepigrapha truly represent an actualization of the Pauline tradition, they can be considered not only to provide significant witness to the importance of apostolic (in this case, Pauline) authority in the church of the first century, but also to provide a biblical witness to the importance of tradition as the process of actualization. Somewhat ironically, the questioning of the Pauline authorship of these epistles, which developed in academia and which for a time seemed to "threaten" the main line and tradition-based churches, actually provides a biblical warrant for the very notion of an ongoing and developing apostolic tradition.

Authority and Canon

Vatican Council II proclaimed that "besides the four Gospels, the canon of the New Testament also contains the Epistles of St. Paul and other apostolic writings, composed under the inspiration of the Holy Spirit" (*Dei Verbum*, 20). Our study of Hebrews, 1-2 Timothy, Titus, Ephesians, Colossians, and 2 Thessalonians should leave the reader with some ambiguity as to whether these seven writings are to be properly subsumed under the rubric of "the epistles of St. Paul" or under the rubric of the "other apostolic writings." While admitting the legitimacy of the traditional identification of them as epistles of Paul, the application of merely historical criteria would seem to indicate that the Pauline pseudepigrapha belong within the category of other apostolic writings. Indeed, they were written in an attempt to actualize the apostolic tradition.

There can be no reasonable doubt as to the canonicity of the pseudepigraphal works contained in the New Testament. Hebrews, along with 1-2 Timothy, Titus, Ephesians, Colossians, and 2 Thessalonians, was included under the rubric of the "fourteen epistles of the apostle Paul" in the canon of the New Testament proclaimed at the Council of Trent (1st Decree, 4th Session; February 4, 1546; DS 1503). In this statement, the Council of Trent was merely echoing a centuries-old tradition of the church. The oldest extant complete listing of the books of the New Testament in the East is to be found in Athanasius' Easter letter in the year 367. The bishop of Alexandria listed these books among the "fourteen epistles of Paul" (*Ep.* 39; PG 26, 1437-1438). Similarly, the Roman synod of 382 A.D. included the seven books as it listed "the epistles of Paul, in number fourteen" (DS 180).

The so-called Canon of Muratori, commonly thought to have been a Roman document of the second century, but more likely an Eastern document of the fourth century, mentions 2 Thessalonians as an additional letter written by Paul to one of his seven churches and notes that Philemon, Titus, and 1-2 Timothy "were put in writing from personal inclination and attachment, to be in honor, however, with the Catholic Church for the ordering of ecclesiastical discipline." The fragmentary text makes no mention whatsoever of Hebrews, but does mention that an epistle to the Laodiceans and an epistle to the Alexandrians were "both forged in Paul's name to suit the heresy of Marcion." Marcion himself, having omitted Hebrews and the pastorals from his collection, included only ten epistles in his *Apostolikon*, named after Paul whom he considered to be the apostle *par excellence.*

Hebrews was always a special case. Not bearing the name of Paul, it was not cited as an epistle of Paul by many of the Fathers of the Church. Eusebius, the fourth-century church historian, has summed up the situation of Hebrews fairly well in his *Ecclesiastical History*. Hebrews was especially revered in the East. Nonetheless, even in the East there was some uncertainty as to the place of Hebrews among the ecclesiastical writings. Commenting on Origen, perhaps the greatest of the Eastern Fathers of the Church, Eusebius indicates that Origen included thirteen epistles under the rubric of *homologoumena*, and that he listed Hebrews among the disputed writings. As for himself, Eusebius is quite content to consider Hebrews as one of the epistles of Paul. It is due to the influence of Jerome, who served as Pope Damasus' *peritus* for the Roman synod of 382, that Hebrews has been accepted as canonical in the Western church.

The existence of the canon is a matter of history. It is an indisputable historical fact that beginning with the end of the fourth century the various Christian churches accepted fourteen epistles attributed to Paul for use in their worship and as normative for their belief. Lists of these fourteen books are found among the decrees of various synods and councils as well as in the writings of bishops and theologians. The first ecumenical council to cite the list was the sixteenth-century Council of Trent, a gathering called together to witness to the common and traditional faith of the church toward the beginning of the Reformation.

"Canon" is derived from a Greek word meaning measuring stick. In ancient times the word "canon" was used to designate a list or a norm. The twenty-seven books of the New Testament, including the fourteen epistles of Paul, are traditionally identified as canonical, that is, they are listed and they are normative. The word "canon" was not always used as a title for the church's list of normative books. Even the Council of Trent did not use the word canon as it listed "the books that are accepted by this Synod." When, however, a list of New Testament books was cited, whether called canon or not, it always included the fourteen epistles of Paul. It is historically certain that the fourteen epistles of Paul were commonly considered to be normative for the church's faith from the fourth to the sixteenth centuries. They were an integral part of the church's New Testament.

Since the sixteenth century, the various Christian churches of the West, and of the East, have continued to consider these fourteen epistles as part of the New Testament. The churches may have disputed about the authority of various synods and councils, but they have had and continue to have no doubt that the New Testament is an essential part of the Christian heritage and that it includes Hebrews, 1-2 Timothy, Titus, Ephesians, Colossians, and 2 Thessalonians. Within Roman Catholicism, the language of "tradition" was used to speak about the Christian heritage. Thus, the Fathers of the Second Vatican Council declared: "Through the same tradition the Church's full canon of the sacred books is known" (*Dei Verbum*, 9).

The existence of a twenty-seven book New Testament is simply a fact of church history. The several Christian churches have always used these books for their worship and their belief. Since the end of the fourth century, they have done so in self-conscious fashion. The New Testament included fourteen epistles of Paul. The presumption of the churches has been that these epistles were written by Paul.

Questions as to the real identity of their authors have arisen in academic circles during an age when there has been a real separation between church and university. Nonetheless, the questions that were being raised within academic circles on the basis of historical and literary considerations were a source of no little concern for the churches.

Within Roman Catholicism, the Pontifical Biblical Commission reaffirmed the Pauline authorship of the pastorals on June 12, 1913. Just one year later, on June 24, 1914, it did the same for the epistle to the Hebrews. Commenting on these decisions in 1955, Athanasius Miller, then the secretary of the commission, stated that "the decrees of the Pontifical Biblical Commission have great significance. However, as long as these decrees propose views which are neither immediately nor mediately connected with truths of faith and morals, it goes without saying that the scholar may pursue his research with complete freedom and may utilize the results of his research.... Today we can hardly picture to ourselves the position of Catholic scholars at the turn of the century, or the dangers that threatened Catholic teaching on Scripture...."

Miller wrote about the threat to the Catholic understanding of the Scriptures. The experience of the new questions arising in the academic world was perceived as threatening. The reaction was fear. Similar fears were experienced within Protestant communities. As recently as 1974, Aart Van Roon stated that: "If the final verdict is that the work [specifically, Ephesians] is not authentic, the fact will be that although the Christian church has always invested the epistle with canonical authority, it will nevertheless have to be relegated to the periphery of the New Testament."

In fact, an academic judgment that one or another New Testament "epistle," or even seven of them, was not written by Paul does not mean that it has to be relegated to the periphery of the New Testament. Each of them has contributed to the shaping of the church as it presently exists. The scholar's verdict as to the inauthenticity of the Pauline pseudepigrapha should not lead the churches to restructure their New Testament, as if there really were a canon within the canon. The scholarly judgment about the Pauline pseudepigrapha is a judgment that concerns history. The facts of history do not call for a re-ordering of the New Testament. The facts call for a renewed understanding of the New Testament.

Essentially, the New Testament has been, and continues to be, authoritative for the churches because it provides indisputable testimony to the apostolic witness about Jesus of Nazareth and his significance for those who believe in him. Even if the Pauline pseudepigrapha do not contain the personal testimony of Paul, they do provide apostolic witness to the significance of the Lord Jesus Christ. They represent an actualization of the apostolic tradition and in this respect they resemble the gospels which also represent different actualizations of the apostolic tradition. The Pauline pseudepigrapha belong to the canon because of what they represent. What they represent is authoritative and normative for the churches.

Exegesis

Ultimately, therefore, our issue is not really whether Paul did or did not write the texts which we have studied. Since that is not the real issue, and in the absence of very clear clues as to who the author of any one of the pseudepigrapha might possibly be, the effort spent in the search for identification is effort needlessly spent in a cul-de-sac. The issue of authorship is only one among the introductory questions of textual interpretation. From the standpoint of exegesis or textual interpretation, it is even more important to know what an author represents than it is to know the name of the author.

Thus, the determination that a given New Testament text has not been written by Paul can, in no wise, be considered the last word in the interpretation of the text. The identification of the pseudepigraphal character of a New Testament text is only the first step in the interpretation of it. A necessary second step is the determination of what the text represents. Our suggestion has been that the Pauline pseudepigrapha represent so many actualizations of the Pauline tradition. Citing the case of the pastoral epistles as a post-Pauline development, Hans Conzelmann noted that Timothy and Titus symbolize the communication of the tradition from the apostle to the present. In the words of Norbert Brox, these names serve as codes for apostolic tradition.

Using this vantage point as a point of departure, the exegete can proceed to an interpretation of the texts at hand. The limited scope of the present work precludes any extended exegesis of the texts under consideration. Yet it should be noted that the exegete who begins an interpretation of Hebrews, 1-2 Timothy, Titus, Ephesians, Colossians, and 2 Thessalonians from the pseudepigraphal stance does so with a newly given freedom. There is no longer any need for him or for her to interpret these texts in the light of Paul. His or her exegesis is freed from the constraints of Paul's own thought, even when it is a matter of Paul's thought that has been reinterpreted in the text at hand. For an exegete to forego this freedom and interpret the pseudepigrapha as if they had been written by Paul or as if they represent what Paul would have said in circumstances different from his own is indeed a strange way to pay homage to the memory of Paul, the apostle of freedom.

The exercise of responsible exegetical freedom in the interpretation of the Pauline epistles not only allows the exegete to make an interpretation of each of the deutero-Pauline texts in its own right, it also determines legitimate parameters for the interpretation of Paul's own letters. The interpreter must be wary of using deutero-Pauline texts in an effort to explain Paul's own words. The pseudepigraphal hypothesis also makes it illegitimate to include material taken from the deutero-Pauline texts in a synopsis of "Pauline theology" or "Paul's understanding of the church." Cautious authors have long suggested that Ephesians, and to a somewhat lesser extent Colossians as well, should be used in summary presentations of Paul's thought only with very considered prudence. Acknowledgement of their pseudepigraphal character means that they should not be so used at all.

When the Pauline pseudepigrapha are freely interpreted, their theological differences are readily apparent. If the interpretation of any one of the pseudepigrapha as if it had really been written by the apostle himself runs a very strong risk of radically misinterpreting the text, so an interpretation of one of the pseudepigrapha in the light of another is similarly to make it subject to misinterpretation. Each of the pseudepigrapha represents a unique actualization of the apostolic tradition. As a matter of fact, although there is a decided commonality among the pastoral epistles, the real differences among these texts must not be overlooked.

The Richness of the Pauline Tradition

Negatively speaking, the present study has argued against a naive pan-Paulinism which interprets all fourteen books in the canonical Pauline corpus as if they (or at least thirteen of them) had been written by Paul himself. It has rejected the view that there is but one Pauline prism through which all thirteen or fourteen of these writings must be interpreted, as if they enjoyed some sort of stylistic and ideological homogeneity because they issued from the pen of a single author.

This final chapter has also argued against a naive historicizing view of Christianity, one which would relegate Hebrews and the Pauline pseudepigrapha to a lesser status simply because they had not been personally composed by the apostle Paul. Just as the tradition deriving from Jesus was actualized by Mark, and the Markan gospel was actualized by Matthew and Luke, so the Pauline tradition has been actualized in the Pauline pseudepigrapha. As the Matthean gospel is no less canonical, nor less authoritative, nor less significant, because it represents an actualization of the earlier witness, so the deutero-Paulines are not less significant simply because they represent a later actualization of the Pauline tradition.

Finally, the present chapter has also argued against the existence of a single Pauline school, from which one might presume that all of the New Testament's Pauline pseudepigrapha might have come. As it argued against a myopic Paulinism, so it has also argued against an overly simplistic view of the canonical deutero-Pauline texts. They must not be interpreted as if all of them came from the same milieu.

These three lines of negative argumentation have been advanced with a positive goal in mind. Their common purpose has been that Hebrews and each of the Pauline pseudepigrapha in turn should be interpreted in its own right. Each of the pseudepigrapha represents a unique appropriation and actualization of the Pauline tradition. When each text is interpreted in its own right, the rich diversity of the New Testament appears in fuller clarity.

The texts which have been studied show that christological diversity has been part of the Christian experience since its origins. There are many different ways of interpreting the abiding significance of Jesus Christ the Lord. The author of Hebrews presents the Son in a very personal and imaginative fashion. The paulinist who wrote Ephesians viewed the Christ and Lord in quite a different manner. The pseudepigrapher who wrote 2 Thessalonians had yet another appreciation of the Lord. In a word, the recognition of the non-Pauline origins of Hebrews and of the pseudepigraphal character of 1-2 Timothy, Titus, Ephesians, Colossians and 2 Thessalonians leads to an appreciation of the real diversity and great richness of New Testament christology.

Since the demands of the Christian life are to a large extent dependent upon one's views of Jesus Christ the Lord, the seven epistles which have been studied also attest to somewhat different understandings of the Christian life. A commitment in faith to Jesus Christ the Lord leads to appropriate action, but appropriate differences in action correspond to differences in appreciation of the Lord. Similarly, the exigencies of the Christian life also vary according to the demands of the times in which one lives. Thus an appreciation of the uniqueness of Hebrews and of the deutero-Pauline character of the pseudepigrapha leads to an appreciation of the real diversity of truly Christian life styles.

Paul himself was a man of history. He lived with his Christian faith from his Jewish tradition in the midst of the Hellenistic world. Those who came after him understood him in different ways, even as we do today. His legacy is not only to be found in the letters which he wrote, as if they were some sort of static historical monument, his legacy is also to be found in the tradition of which he was personally a keen interpreter and a vital mediator. The New Testament tradition views Paul in a variety of lights, each of which brings a different insight into the significance of the apostle.

As this book draws to its close, it is the rich diversity of the New Testament that most deserves to be highlighted. To be sure, the recognition that more authors are responsible for the New Testament books than was thought to have been the case in previous generations has significant bearing on the way in which the New Testament ought to be taught. The awareness that there is a greater diversity of theology in the New Testament than earlier systematic studies allowed has major implications for the way in which Christian theology is to be understood. Limitations of time and space, however, do not allow for a fuller development of the pedagogical and theological consequences of the positions that have been taken in this book.

In conclusion, therefore, let it simply be said that what the hypothesis of Pauline pseudepigraphy really does is to open up more fully the richness of the New Testament. The New Testament is like a diamond, fully appreciated only when each individual facet is properly polished and allowed to reflect the light.

A Brief Bibliography

Collins, Raymond F. "The Formation of the New Testament," in *Introduction to the New Testament*. Garden City: Doubleday, 1983, 1-40.

De Boer, Martinus C. "Images of Paul in the Post-Apostolic Period," *CBQ* 42 (1980) 359-380.

Hoffman, Thomas A. "Inspiration, Normativeness, Canonicity and the Unique Sacred Character of the Bible," *CBQ* 44 (1982) 447-469.

MacDonald, Dennis Ronald. *The Legend and the Apostle: The Battle for Paul in Story and Canon*. Philadelphia: Westminster, 1983.

Patzia, Arthur G. "The Deutero-Pauline Hypothsis: An Attempt at Clarification," *EVQ* 52 (1980) 27-42.

A Glossary of Terms

Adam Christology: A presentation of Jesus Christ developed by means of expressions and motifs associated with the Adam or the creation traditions.

Amanuensis: A Latin term meaning "a scribe"; specifically one who writes from dictation.

Antinomian: Pertaining to one or that which holds that Christians are not bound to uphold the moral or traditional law.

Apocalyptic: A term sometimes designating a literary form, sometimes a fashion of writings, and sometimes a world view. It entails a dramatic and symbolic description of the end-time events (e.g. Mark 13; Rev).

Apostolic Parousia: A literary type, identified by Robert Funk and characterized by the motif of apostolic authority and power as these are expressed in a statement of the apostle's reason for writing, his intention to send an emissary, and his desire to pay the addressees a personal visit.

Antitype: Something (someone) that is represented by a type or symbol.

Catalog of Virtues (or, Vices): A literary type, developed from Stoic usage and frequently found in the epistolary literature of the New Testament. It is characterized by a listing of virtues or vices (e.g. Gal 5:22-23; Gal 5:19-21).

Catena: A technical term borrowed from the Latin. It is used to describe a sequence of collected items, for example, the various scriptural passages grouped together in Heb 1:5-13.

Colophon: An inscription found at the end of a book or manuscript, generally offering information about its production or composition.

Conflation: The fusion of two passages into a composite, single passage.

Dei Verbum: Literally, the "Word of God." The expression serves as the title of the Second Vatican Council's *Dogmatic Constitution on Divine Revelation.*

Deutero-Pauline: An adjective used to describe works not written by the apostle Paul but nonetheless attributed to him.

Diaspora: Transliteration of the Greek *diaspora,* "dispersion." The term designates the extra-Palestinian dispersion of the Jews, which had its beginnings in the Assyrian (722 B.C.) and Babylonian (597 B.C.) deportations.

Distributive exegesis: A word by word or phrase-by-phrase interpretation of a text.

Double pseudepigraphy: The phenomenon which exists when both the purported author and the purported recipient of a work are other than the actual author and recipient of the text.

Early Catholicism: A technical term used to designate a doctrinal system characterized by a resolution of the tension between Jewish and Hellenistic Christianity, the resolution of the crisis caused by the delay of the Parousia, and the gradual institutionalization of the church.

Ecclesiology: Doctrine about, or an understanding of, the church.

Enthusiasm: The experience of extraordinary phenomena (e.g. speaking in tongues) believed to be manifestations of the Holy Spirit.

Epigone: An imitative follower, often an inferior imitator of a creative thinker.

Exegesis: 1) the science of textual interpretation; 2) the interpretation of a specific text within its original historical context.

Form criticism: A methodology of biblical exegesis which attempts to trace the origins of a pericope and otherwise seeks to understand it by means of those characteristics of its vocabulary and style (i.e., its literary form) which enable it to be categorized within a given literary type.

Fragment hypothesis: The theory that a work was composed by a compiler-editor who incorporated into his own work earlier material actually written by the one to whom his own work is attributed.

Functional (or relational) Christology: An understanding of Jesus Christ with particular reference to his role and various functions in salvation history.

Gezerah shavah **principle:** The comparison of similar expressions. One of the thirteen principles of biblical interpretation traditionally associated with the name of Rabbi Ishmael, it holds that if the same word occurs in two different scriptural passages, one passage may be used to interpret the other.

Gnosticism: A technical term without a technical definition. Derived from the Greek noun *gnōsis* meaning "knowledge," the term generally describes the highly dualistic movements of thought which were widely diffused throughout the Mediterranean Basin during the first and second centuries.

Hapax legomenon (in the plural, *hapax legomena):* A word or expression that occurs only once in a given work or body of literature (for example, Heb or the New Testament).

Henotheism: The worship of only one god, without the denial of the existence of other gods.

Household Code: A literary type characterized by a listing of the responsibilities of the various members of a household (e.g. Col 3:18-4:1).

Hymn: A unit of material, essentially separable from the literary context in which it is found, characterized by distinctive vocabulary and rhythmical cadence. As the term is used in biblical scholarship, it does not necessarily imply a composition intended for congregational singing.

Inclusion and exclusion principle (*ribbui u-mu'it*): A method of scriptural interpretation, traditionally associated with Rabbi Akiva, which proceeds from the premise that every word (and form of word) has importance. It determines the parameters of the interpretation of the text.

Lemma: An introductory phrase; typically, a passage of scripture. When a passage of scripture is cited as a lemma, the subsequent text is often a commentary on the words that have been cited.

Lexis: In rhetorical criticism, the choice of words.

Literary Type: A manner of written expression characteristic of a number of texts with a similar style, vocabulary, thought pattern, and purpose.

Lycus Valley heresy: The gnosticizing version of Christianity apparently combatted in Col. It is so called from the region in Asia Minor, where the cities of Colossae and Laodicea are located.

Marcionism: A heresy associated with Marcion, a mid-second-century Christian. Marcion believed that there is a radical incompatibility between the Christian God of Love and the Jewish God of Wrath, the New Testament and the Old. He accepted only his own version of the New Testament, that is, ten epistles of Paul and an edited version of the gospel according to Luke.

Midrash: Derived from the Hebrew *darash*, "to search," midrash literally means an exploration or an interpretation. More specifically, it designates a literary genre, namely that which consists of a literary interpretation of a biblical text.

Mimesis: In Hellenistic rhetoric, the literary device of imitating the style of a master.

Muratorian Fragment (or, **Muratorian Canon**): Fragment of a mutilated codex found in the Ambrosian Library (Milan, Italy) by L.A. Muratori in 1740. A scholarly dispute exists as to whether the original text dates from ca. 400 A.D. or ca. 200 A.D. The extant fragment contains a list of 22 books, i.e. the Apocalypse of Peter, the Shepherd of Hermas, and all the canonical New Testament books except Matt, Mark, Heb, Jas, 1-2 Pet, 3 John.

Ontological Christology: An understanding of Jesus Christ with particular reference to his nature.

Oratio perpetua (Oratio continua): In rhetoric, an extended discourse, generally characterized by periodic composition.

Orthonymous work: A composition which bears the name of its real author.

Oxymoron: A figure of speech in which contradictory or incongruous words are grouped together, for example, "genuine pseudepigraphy."

Paraenesis: Moral exhortation.

Parousia: A transliteration of the Greek term meaning "presence." In the New Testament scholarship the term is principally used of the presence of Jesus Christ as Lord or Son of Man at the close of the present era of history.

Pauline *homologoumena:* The seven letters indisputably attributed to Paul, i.e. Rom, 1-2 Cor, Gal, Phil, 1 Thess, Phlm.

Pauline reductionism: A tendency, found in some deutero-Pauline literature, to consider the apostle Paul in independence from his associates and/or in isolation as if he were the only apostle.

Paulinism: 1) Paul's theological system (even though Paul was not a systematic theologian); 2) Pauline influence in the post-apostolic period.

Performative function: In semiotics, the ability of language to accomplish something by virtue of its utterance.

Peristatic catalogue: A literary type characterized by a listing of various circumstances, for example, 2 Cor 11:23-27.

Pneumatology: Doctrine about the Spirit, or, more generally, an understanding of the Spirit.

Pseudepigraphal work: A composition attributed to someone other than the real author.

Pseudonymous work: A composition whose author is deliberately and explicitly identified by a name other than the author's real name.

Q Source: A collection of sayings attributed to Jesus, most probably compiled ca. 50 A.D., which critical scholarship generally acknowledges to be the principal source of the discourse material common to Matt and Luke.

Redaction criticism: A methodology of biblical exegesis which clarifies the thought and theological vision of an author by means of a detailed analysis of the author's editorial and compositional techniques, including the use of specialized vocabulary.

Ring construction (Latin, *inclusio*): A literary device that unifies a composition or a particular passage by (verbally) repeating at the end of the passage a theme with which it began, for example, the refrain "for theirs is the kingdom of heaven" in Matt 5:3 and 10 and the reference to sitting at the right hand (from Ps 110:1) in Heb 1:3 and 13.

Sitz-im-Leben: A German term meaning "life situation." Used as a technical term in biblical exegesis, it denotes a set of social circumstances which evoke a characteristic use of spoken and written language.

Soteriology: Doctrine related to salvation or, more generally, the understanding of salvation.

Synthesis: In rhetorical criticism, the way words are put together to form phrases, clauses, and sentences.

Tendency Criticism: A methodology of New Testament criticism, particularly associated with F.C. Baur and the Tübingen school, which seeks to identify the particular ideological bias of the works under consideration.

Theopoetics: A literary exercise of religious imagination.

Topos: A stock treatment of a topic or theme in a passage which is generally separable from its literary context.

Wisdom Christology: A presentation of Jesus Christ by means of expressions and motifs associated with divine wisdom in Jewish tradition.

Bibliography

Aland, Kurt. "The Problem of Anonymity and Pseudonymity in Christian Literature of the First Two Centuries," *JTS* 12 (1961) 39-49.

Aland, Kurt, et al., *The Authorship and Integrity of the New Testament*. Theological Collections, 4. London: SPCK, 1965.

Albertz, Martin. *Die Botschaft des Neuen Testamentes* 1/2. Zurich: Evangelischer Verlag, 1952.

Albright, William J. "Retrospect and Prospect in New Testament Archaeology," in E.J. Vardeman and J.L. Garrett, eds., *The Teacher's Yoke*. Waco, TX, Baylor University. 1964, 27-41.

Allan, John A. "The 'In Christ' Formula in Ephesians," *NTS* 5 (1958-1959) 54-62.

Allan, John A. "The 'In Christ' Formula in the Pastoral Epistles," *NTS* 10 (1963-64) 115-21.

Aletti, Jean-Noël, *Colossiens 1, 15-20: Genre et exégèse du texte. Fonction de la thématique sapientielle*. AnBib, 91. Rome: Biblical Institute Press, 1981.

Andriessen, Paul. "La communauté des 'Hébreux': était-elle tombée dans le rélanchement?" *NRT* 10 (1974) 1054-1066.

Anton, Paul. *Abhandlungen der Pastoralbriefe* (1753/1755; reference in W.G. Kümmel, *Introduction,* p. 367, n.1).

Aus, Roger D. "II Thessalonians," in Arland J. Hultgren— Roger Aus, *I-II Timothy, Titus, II Thessalonians.* Augsburg Commentary on the New Testament. Minneapolis, MN: Augsburg, 1984.

Bacon, Benjamin W. *The Making of the New Testament.* New York: Henry Holt, n.d.

Bahnsen, W. "Zum Verständnis von II Thess., II, 3-12: Ein Beitrag zu Kritik des 2ten Thessalonicherbriefes," *Jahrbuch für protestantische Theologie* 6 (1880) 681-701.

Bahr, Gordon J. "Paul and Letter Writing in the Fifth [=First] Century," *CBQ* 28 (1966) 465-477.

Bailey, John A. "Who Wrote II Thessalonians?" *NTS* 25 (1978-1979) 131-145.

Baker, N.L. "Living the Dream: Ethics in Ephesians," *SWJT* 22 (1979) 24-38.

Balchin, John F. "Colossians 1:15-20: An Early Christian Hymn? The Arguments from Style," *VE* 15 (1985) 85-94.

Balz, Horst R. "Anonymität und Pseudepigraphie im Urchristentum: Überlegung zum literarischen und theologischen Problem des urchristlichen und gemeinantiken Pseudepigraphie," *AZTK* 66 (1969) 403-436.

Bardot, D.N. (Reference in W.G. Kümmel, *Introduction,* p. 367, n. 1).

Barth, Markus. *Ephesians: Introduction, Translation and Commentary.* AB, 34-34A. Garden City, NY: Doubleday, 1974.

Barth, Markus. "Traditions in Ephesians," *NTS* 30 (1984) 3-25.

Bassler, Jouette M. "The Enigmatic Sign: 2 Thessalonians 1:5," *CBQ* 46 (1984) 496-510.

Bassler, Jouette M. "The Widow's Tale: A Fresh Look at 1 Tim 5:13-16," *JBL* 103 (1984) 23-41.

Baur, Ferdinand Christian. *Das Christenthum und die christliche Kirche der ersten drei Jahrhunderte*. Tübingen, 1853; 2nd. ed., 1860.

Baur, Ferdinand Christian. *Die sogenannten Pastoralbriefe des Apostels Paulus*. Stüttgart: Gotha, 1835.

Baur, Ferdinand Christian. *Paulus der Apostel Jesu Christi, sein Leben und Wirken, seine Briefe und seine Lehre*, 2 vols. Stüttgart: Becker & Muller, 1845; 2nd. ed., Leipzig, 1866-1867; ET: *Paul the Apostle of Jesus Christ*, 2 vols. London, 1875-1876.

Beckwith, Roger. "The Ancient Attitude to Pseudonymity," in *The Old Testament Canon of the New Testament Church: and its Background in Early Judaism*. Grand Rapids, MI: Eerdmans, 1985, 346-358.

Benoit, Pierre. "Ephésiens," *DBSup*, 7 (1961) 195-211.

Benoit, Pierre. *Les épîtres de saint Paul aux Philippiens, à Philémon, aux Colossiens, aux Ephésiens*. La Sainte Bible. Paris: Cerf, 1949.

Benoit, Pierre. "Rapports littéraires entre les épîtres aux Colossiens et aux Ephésiens," in Josef Blinzer, ed., *Neutestamentliche Aufsätze*. Regensburg: Pustet, 1963, 11-22.

Benoit, Pierre. "L'unité de l'Eglise selon l'épître aux Ephésiens," in A. Descamps, *et al.*, *Studiorum Paulinorum Congressus Internationalis Catholicus*, 1. AnBib, 17. Rome: Pontifical Biblical Institute, 1963, pp. 57-77.

Best, Ernest. *The First and Second Epistles to the Thessalonians*. HNTC. New York: Harper, 1972.

Beyer, Klaus. *Semitische Syntax im Neuen Testament.* SUNT, 1. Göttingen: Vandenhoeck und Ruprecht, 1962.

Black, David Alan. "The Peculiarities of Ephesians and the Ephesian Address," *GTJ* 2 (1981) 59-73.

Bornemann, Wilhelm. *Die Thessalonicherbriefe.* KEK, 10. 5th and 6th eds. Göttingen: Vandenhoeck und Ruprecht, 1894.

Bornkamm, Günther. "Die Höffnung im Kolosserbrief: zugleich ein Beitrag zur Frage der Echtheit des Briefes," in E. Klostermann, *et al., Studien zur Neuen Testament und zur Patristik.* TU, 77. Berlin: Akademie-Verlag, 1961, 56-64.

Bornkamm, Günther. "The Heresy of Colossians," (1948), reprinted in F.O. Francis and W.A. Meeks, *Conflict at Colossae,* 123-145.

Bornkamm, Günther. *Paulus.* Kohlhammer Urban-Taschenbucher, 119. Stüttgart: Kohlhammer, 1969; ET: *Paul.* London: Hodder and Stoughton, 1971.

Bowen, Clayton R. "The Original Form of Paul's Letter to the Colossians," *JBL* 43 (1924) 177-206.

Braun, Herbert. *An die Hebraër.* HNT, 14. Tübingen: Mohr, 1984.

Braun, Herbert. "Zur nachpaulinischen Herkunft des zweiten Thessalonicherbriefes," *ZNW* 44 (1952-1953) 152-156.

Bröker, L.O. "Die Methoden Galens in der literarischen Kritik," *Rheinisches Museum* 40 (1885) 415-438.

Brown, Raymond E. *The Churches the Apostles Left Behind.* New York: Paulist, 1984.

Brown, Raymond E., Fitzmyer, Joseph A., and Murphy, Roland E. *The Jerome Biblical Commentary.* Englewood Cliffs, NJ: Prentice Hall, 1968.

Brown, Raymond E.—Meier, John P. *Antioch and Rome: New Testament Cradles of Catholic Christianity.* New York: Paulist, 1983.

Brox, Norbert. *Die Pastoralbriefe.* RNT, 7. 4th rev. ed.: Regensburg, Pustet, 1969.

Brox, Norbert. *Falsche Verfässerangaben: zur Erklarung der frühchristlichen Pseudepigraphie.* SBS, 79. Stüttgart: KBW, 1975.

Brox, Norbert. *Pseudepigraphie in der heidnischen und jüdisch-christlichen Antike.* WdF, 484. Darmstadt: Wissenschaftliche Buchgesellschaft, 1977.

Bruce, F.F. *1 & 2 Thessalonians.* WBC, 45. Waco, TX: Word, 1982.

Bruce, F.F. *The Epistles to the Colossians, to Philemon, and to the Ephesians.* NICNT. Grand Rapids, MI: Eerdmans, 1984.

Bruce, F.F. *Paul: Apostle of the Heart Set Free.* Grand Rapids, MI: Eerdmans, 1978.

Bruce, F.F. "Recent Contributions to the Understanding of Hebrews," *ExpTim* 80 (1969) 260-264.

Buchanan, George W. *To the Hebrews: Translation, Comment and Conclusions.* AB, 36. Garden City, NY: Doubleday, 1972.

Bujard, Walter. *Stilanalytische Untersuchungen zum Kolosserbrief: ein Beitrag zur Methodik von Sprachvergleichen.* Göttingen: Vandenhoeck und Ruprecht, 1973.

Bultmann, Rudolf. *Das Urchristentum im Rahmen der antiken Religionen.* Zürich: Artemis, 1949.

Bultmann, Rudolf. *Die Geschichte der synoptischen Tradition.* Göttingen: Vandenhoeck und Ruprecht, 1921. ET: *The History of the Synoptic Tradition.* New York: Harper & Row, 1963.

Cadbury, Henry J. "The Dilemma of Ephesians," *NTS* 5 (1959) 91-102.

Cambier, Jules. "La bénédiction d'Ephésiens 1, 3-14," *ZNW* 54 (1963) 58-104.

Cambier, Jules. *Vie chrétienne en église: L'épître aux Éphésiens lue aux chrétiens d'aujourdui.* Paris: Desclée, 1966.

Cannon, George E. *The Use of Traditional Materials in Colossians.* Macon, GA: Mercer University Press, 1983.

Casey, Juliana M. "Christian Assembly in Hebrews: a Fantasy Island?" *TD* 30 (1982) 323-335.

Casey, Juliana M. *Hebrews.* NTM, 18. Wilmington, DE: Glazier, 1980.

Cerfaux, Lucien. *The Spiritual Journey of Saint Paul.* New York: Sheed & Ward, 1968.

Cerfaux, Lucien. *Le Christ dans la théologie de saint Paul.* LD, 6. Paris: Cerf, 1951. ET: *Christ in the Theology of Saint Paul.* New York: Herder and Herder, 1959.

Cerfaux, Lucien. "Les épîtres pastorales," in A. Robert—A. Feuillet, eds., *Introduction à la Bible,* 2. Tournai: Desclée, 1959, 515-530.

Charles, R.H. *The Apocrypha and Pseudepigrapha of the Old Testament,* Vol. 2: *Pseudepigrapha.* Oxford: Clarendon, 1913.

Childs, Brevard S. *The New Testament as Canon: an Introduction.* Philadelphia: Fortress, 1984.

Collins, Raymond F. "Glimpses into Some Local Churches of New Testament Times," *LTP* 42 (1986) 291-316.

Collins, Raymond F. "Ministry in the Pastoral Epistles," *Church* 3 (1987) 20-24.

Collins, Raymond F. "The Formation of the New Testament," in *Introduction to the New Testament.* Garden City, NY: Doubleday, 1983, 1-40.

Collins, Raymond F. "The Image of Paul in the Pastorals," *LTP* 31 (1975) 147-173.

Conzelmann, Hans. *Grundriss der Theologie des Neuen Testaments*. 2nd ed.: Munich, Christian Kaiser, 1968; ET: *An Outline of the Theology of the New Testament*. NTL. London: SCM, 1969.

Conzelmann, Hans. "Luke's Place in the Development of Early Christianity," in Leander E. Keck, ed., *Studies in Luke-Acts*. Nashville: Abingdon, 1966, 298-316.

Coutts, John. "The Relationship of Ephesians and Colossians," *NTS* 4 (1957-1958) 201-207.

Cross, F.L., ed. *Studies in Ephesians*. London: Mowbray, 1956.

Cullmann, Oscar. *Die Christologie des Neuen Testaments*. Tübingen: Mohr, 1957; ET: *The Christology of the New Testament*. London: SCM, 1959.

Culpepper, R. Alan. "Ethical Dualism and Church Discipline: Ephesians 4:25-5:20," *RevExp* 76 (1979) 529-539.

Culpepper, R. Alan. *The Johannine School: An Evaluation of the Johannine-school Hypothesis Based on an Investigation of the Nature of Ancient Schools*. SBLDS, 26. Missoula, MT: Scholars Press, 1975.

Dahl, Nils A. "Adresse und Proöemium des Eph," *TZ* 7 (1951) 241-264.

Dahl, Nils A. "Ephesians, Letter to the," *IDBSup* 268-269.

Dahms, John V. "The First Readers of Hebrews," *JETS* 20 (1977) 365-375.

Dalton, William J. "Pseudepigraphy in the New Testament," *Catholic Theological Review* 5 (1983) 29-35.

Dautzenberg, Gerhard. "Theologie und Seelsorge aus Paulinischer Tradition—Einführung in 2 Thess, Kol. Eph," in J. Schreiner. ed., *Gestalt und Anspruch des Neuen Testaments*. Wurzburg: Echter, 1969, 96-119.

Day, Peter, "The Practical Purpose of Second Thessalonians," *ATR* 45 (1963) 203-206.

de Boer, Martinus C. "Images of Paul in the Post-Apostolic Period," *CBQ* 42 (1980) 359-380.

de Wette, W.M.L. *Kurze Erklarung der Briefe an die Colosser, an Philemon, an die Ephesiër und Philipper.* Leipzig: Weidmann, 1841.

de Wette, W.M.L. *Kurze Erklarung der Brief an die Galater und der Briefe an die Thessalonicher.* Kurzgefasstes exegetisches Handbuch zum Neuen Testament 2/3; 3rd ed.: Leipzig, Hirzel, 1841.

de Wette: W.M.L. *Lehrbuch der historisch-kritischen Einleitung in die Bibel Alten und Neuen Testaments.* Berlin: Reimer, 1826; 4th. ed., 1841; 5th ed., 1848.

Deichgräber, Reinhard. *Gotteshymnus und Christushymnus in der frühen Christenheit.* SUNT, 5. Göttingen: Vandenhoeck und Ruprecht, 1967.

Dibelius, Martin. *An die Kolosser, Epheser, an Philemon.* HNT, 12. Tübingen: Mohr, 1913.

Dibelius, Martin. *An die Thessalonicher I-II. An die Philipper.* HNT, 11. 3rd. ed.: Tübingen: Mohr, 1937.

Dibelius, Martin. "The Isis Initiation in Apuleius and Related Initiatory Rites," (1917), reprinted in F.O. Francis and W.A. Meeks, *Conflict at Colossae,* 61-121.

Dibelius, Martin—Conzelmann, Hans. *Die Pastoralbriefe.* HNT, 13. 4th ed.: Tübingen: Mohr, 1966; ET: *The Pastoral Epistles.* Hermeneia. Philadelphia: Fortress, 1972.

Dibelius, Martin—Greeven, Heinrich. *An die Kolosser, Epheser, an Philemon.* HNT, 12. 3rd. ed.: Tübingen: Mohr, 1953.

Dodd, C.H. *Ephesians, Colossians and Philemon.* The Abingdon Commentary. Nashville: Abingdon, 1929.

Donelson, Lewis. *Pseudepigraphy and Ethical Argument in the Pastoral Epistles.* HUT, 22. Tübingen: Mohr, 1986.

Dornier, Pierre. *Les épîtres pastorales.* SB. Paris: Gabalda, 1969.

Doty, William G. "The Classification of Epistolary Literature," *CBQ* 31 (1969) 183-199.

Doty, William G. *Letters in Primitive Christianity.* GBS. Philadelphia: Fortress, 1973.

Dukes, J. "The Humanity of Jesus in Hebrews," *ThEd* 32 (1985) 38-45.

Dunn, James D.G. *The Living Word.* London: SCM, 1987.

Dunn, James D.G. *Christology in the Making: A New Testament Inquiry into the Origins of the Doctrine of the Incarnation.* London: SCM, 1980.

Efird, James M. *Christ, the Church, and the End: Studies in Colossians and Ephesians.* Valley Forge, PA: Judson, 1980.

Eichhorn, Johann Gottfried. *Einleitung in das Neue Testament,* 5 vols. Leipzig: Weidmann, 1810-1827.

Ellingworth, P. "Reading through Hebrews 1-7: Listening especially for the theme of Jesus as high priest," *EpR* 12 (1985) 80-85.

Ellingworth, P. "The Unshakeable Priesthood: Hebrews 7.24," *JSNT* 23 (1985) 125-126.

Erasmus, Desiderius. *In Epistolam ad Ephesios,* in *Desiderii Erasmi Roterodami Opera Omnia,* 6. Leiden: Vanderaa, 1705 (republished: London, Gregg, 1962), 829-860.

Estius, Guilielmus. *In omnes Pauli epistolas: item in Catholicas commentarii,* 6. New edition by Francis Sausen: Mainz, Schotti & Thielmanni, 1844.

Evans, Craig A. "The Colossian Mystics," *Bib* 63 (1982) 188-205.

Evanson, Edward. *The Dissonance of the Four Generally Received Evangelists and the Evidence of their Respec-*

tive Authenticity Examined. Ipswich, 1792; 2nd. ed., 1805.

Ewald, Heinrich. *Die Sendschriften des Apostels-Paulus.* Göttingen, 1857.

Fabris, Rinaldo. "La lettera agli Ebrei e l'Antico Testamento," *RivB* 32 (1984) 237-252.

Fee, Gordon D. *1 and 2 Timothy, Titus.* GNC. San Francisco: Harper & Row, 1984.

Fee, Gordon D. "Reflections on Church Order in the Pastoral Epistles, with Further Reflection on the Hermeneutics of *Ad Hoc* Documents," *JETS* 28 (1985) 141-151.

Fenton, J.C. "Pseudonymity in the New Testament," *Theology* 58 (1955) 51-56.

Feuillet, André. "Une triple préparation du sacerdoce du Christ dans l'Ancien Testament (Melchisédec, le Messie du Ps 110, le Serviteur d'Is 53). Introduction à la doctrine sacerdotale de l'Epître aux Hébreux," *Divinitas* 28 (1984) 103-136.

Fiore, Benjamin. *The Function of Personal Example in the Socratic and Pastoral Epistles.* AnBib, 105. Rome: Biblical Institute Press, 1986.

Fitzmyer, Joseph A. "'Now this Melchizedek...' (Heb 7:1)," *CBQ* 25 (1963) 305-321.

Francis, Fred O.—Meeks, Wayne A., eds. *Conflict at Colossae: A Problem in the Interpretation of Early Christianity Illustrated by Selected Modern Studies.* Sources for Biblical Study, 4. Rev. ed.: Missoula, MT, Scholars Press, 1975.

Friedrich, Gerhard. "Die erste Brief an die Thessalonicher," in Jürgen Becker, *et al., Die Briefe an die Galater, Epheser, Philipper, Kolosser, Thessalonicher und Philemon: überzetzt und erklart.* NTD, 8. 14th ed. Göttingen,: Vandenhoeck und Ruprecht, 1976.

Fuller, Reginald. *A Critical Introduction to the New Testament.* London: Duckworth, 1966.

Funk, Robert. "The Apostolic 'Parousia.' Form and Significance," in William R. Farmer, ed., *Christian History and Interpretation.* Cambridge: University Press, 1967, 249-268.

Gächter, Paul. *Summa introductionis in Novum Testamentum.* Innsbruck: Rauch, 1938.

Garland, D.E. "A Life Worthy of the Calling: Unity and Holiness: Ephesians 4:1-24," *RevExp* 76 (1976) 517-527.

Getty, Mary Ann. "The Primacy of Christ," *TBT* 23 (1985) 11-17.

Giblet, Jean. "L'Epître aux Ephésiens," a paper delivered during the thirty-sixth *Colloquium Biblicum Lovaniense,* August 28, 1986; to be published in a forthcoming volume of the *BETL.*

Giblin, Charles H. *The Threat to Faith: An Exegetical and Theological Re-examination of 2 Thessalonians 2.* AnBib, 31. Rome: Pontifical Biblical Institute, 1967.

Gnilka, Joachim. *Der Epheserbrief.* HTKNT, 10/2. Freiburg: Herder, 1971.

Gnilka, Joachim. *Der Kolosserbrief.* HTKNT, 10/1. Freiburg: Herder, 1980.

Goguel, Maurice. "Esquisse d'une solution nouvelle du problème de l'épître aux Ephésiens," *RHPR* 111 (1935) 254-285; 112 (1936) 73-99.

Goguel, Maurice. *Introduction au Nouveau Testament,* 4/1. BHR. Paris: Leroux, 1926.

Goodspeed, Edgar J. *The Meaning of Ephesians.* Chicago: University Press, 1933.

Graafen, J. *Die Echtheit des zweiten Briefes an die Thessalonicher.* NTAbh, 14/5. Munster: Aschendorff, 1930.

Grässer, Erich. *Der Glauber im Hebraërbrief.* MaTS, 2. Marburg: Elwert, 1965.

Grässer, Erich. "Der historische Jesus im Hebraërbrief," *ZNW* 56 (1965) 63-91.

Grassi, Joseph. "The Letter to the Ephesians," in R.E. Brown, *et al,* eds., *The Jerome Biblical Commentary,* 341-349.

Grayston, K.—Herdan, G. "The Authorship of the Pastorals in the Light of Statistical Linguistics," *NTS* 6 (1959-1960) 1-15.

Gregson, R.G. "A Solution to the Problem of the Thessalonian Epistles," *EvQ* 38 (1966) 76-80.

Grimm, Karl Ludwig Wilibald. "Die Echtheit der Brief an die Thessalonicher," *TSK* 23 (1850) 753-816.

Grotius, Hugo. *Annotationes in Novum Testamentum,* 7. 2nd. ed.: Groningen, Zuidema, 1829.

Gunther, John J. *Paul: Messenger and Exile.* Valley Forge, PA: Judson, 1972.

Guthrie, Donald. *New Testament Introduction,* 2. London: Tyndale, 1962.

Guthrie, Donald. "The Development of the Idea of Canonical Pseudepigraphy in New Testament Criticism," *VE* 1 (1962) 43-59.

Hanson, Anthony T. "The Domestication of Paul: A Study in the Development of Early Christian Theology," *BJRL* 63 (1981) 402-418.

Hanson, Anthony T. *The Pastoral Epistles.* NCB. Grand Rapids, MI: Eerdmans, 1982.

Hanson, Anthony T. *The Pastoral Letters: Commentary on the First and Second Letters to Timothy and the Letter to Titus.* CMCNEB. Cambridge: University Press, 1966.

Hanson, Paul D. *The People Called: The Growth of Community in the Bible.* San Francisco: Harper & Row, 1986.

Harnack, Adolf von. "Das Problem des zweiten Thessalonicherbriefs," *Sitzungsberichte der königlichen preussischen Akademie der Wissenschaften zu Berlin* 31 (1910) 560-578.

Harrington, Wilfrid J. *The New Testament: Record of the Fulfillment.* Rev. 2nd. ed.: New York: Alba, 1975.

Harrison, P.N. "Onesimus and Philemon," *ATR* 32 (1950) 268-294.

Harrison, P.N. *The Problem of the Pastoral Epistles.* London: Oxford University Press, 1921.

Harvill, J. "Focus on Jesus (Studies in the Letter to the Hebrews)," *ResQ* 22 (1979) 129-140.

Harvill, J. "The Humanity of Jesus in Hebrews," *ThEd* 32 (1985) 38-45.

Hasler, Victor. "Epiphanie und Christologie in den Pastoralbriefen," *TZ* 33 (1977) 193-209.

Havener, Ivan. "A Concerned Pastor," *TBT* 24 (1986) 223-227.

Héring, Jean. *L'Epître aux Hébreux.* CNT, 12. Neuchâtel: Delachaux et Niestlé, 1954.

Heyler, L.R. "Colossians 1:15-20: Pre-Pauline or Pauline?" *JETS* 26 (1983) 167-179.

Hilgenfeld, Adolf. *Historisch-kritische Einleitung in das Neue Testament.* Leipzig: Fues, 1875.

Hitchcock, F.R. Montgomery, "The Use of *graphein*," *JTS* 31 (1930) 271-275.

Hitzig, Ferdinand. *Zur Kritik paulinischer Briefe.* Leipzig: Hirzel, 1870.

Hobson, Donald. *The Authorship of Colossians* (doctoral dissertation, Claremont Graduate School and University Center, 1968).

Hoekstra, Sytze. "Vergelijking van de brieven aan de Efeziërs en de Colossers vooral uit het oogpunt van beider leerstellige inhoud," *Theologisch tijdschrift* 2 (1868) 599-652.

Hoffman, Thomas A. "Inspiration, Normativeness, Canonicity and the Unique Sacred Character of the Bible," *CBQ* 44 (1982) 447-469.

Holland, Glenn S. "Let No One Deceive You in Any Way: 2 Thessalonians as a Reformulation of the Apocalyptic Tradition," in K.H. Richards, ed., *Society of Biblical Literature 1985 Seminar Papers*. Atlanta, GA: Scholars Press, 1985, 329-341.

Holland, Glenn S. *The Tradition that You Received From Us: 2 Thessalonians in the Pauline Tradition* (Ph.D. Dissertation, University of Chicago, 1986).

Hollmann, Georg. "Die Unechtheit des zweitens Thessalonicherbriefs," *ZNW* 5 (1904) 28-38.

Holsten, Carl Johann. *Das Evangelium des Paulus*, 2. Berlin: Reimer, 1898.

Holtz, Gottfried. *Die Pastoralbriefe*. THKNT, 13. Berlin: Evangelische Verlagsanstalt, 1965.

Holtzmann, H.J. *Kritik der Epheser—und Kolosserbriefe auf Grund einer Analyse ihres Verwandtschaftsverhältnisses*. Leipzig: Engelmann, 1872.

Holtzmann, H.J. *Lehrbuch der historisch-kritischen Einleitung in das Neue Testament*. Tübingen: Mohr, 1885; 3rd. ed., 1892.

Holtzmann, H.J. *Lehrbuch der neutestamentlichen Theologie*. Freiburg: Mohr, 1897; 3rd. ed.: Tübingen, 1911.

Holtzmann, H.J. "Zum zweiten Thessalonicherbrief," *ZNW* 2 (1901) 97-108.

Hooker, M.D. and Wilson, S.G., eds. *Paul and Paulinism: Essays in Honour of C.K. Barrett.* London: SPCK, 1982.

Horbury, W. "The Aaronic Priesthood in the Epistle to the Hebrews," *JSNT* 19 (1983) 43-71.

Horton, Fred L. *The Melchizedek Tradition: A Critical Examination of the Sources to the Fifth Century A.D. and in the Epistle to the Hebrews.* SNTSMS, 30. Cambridge: University Press, 1976.

Hoskyns, Edwyn C.—Davey, Clement Noel. *The Riddle of the New Testament.* 3rd. ed.: London, Faber and Faber, 1947.

Howard, F.D. "An Introduction to Ephesians," *SWJT* 22 (1979) 7-23.

Hugedé, Norbert. *Le Sacerdoce du Fils.* Paris: Fischbacher, 1983.

Hughes, Frank W. *Second Thessalonians as a Document of Early Christian Rhetoric* (Ph.D. dissertation, Northwestern University, 1984).

Hughes, Graham. *Hebrews and Hermeneutics: The Epistle to the Hebrews as a New Testament Example of Biblical Interpretation.* SNTSMS, 36. Cambridge: University Press, 1979.

Hughes, Philip Edgcumbe. "The Doctrine of Creation in Hebrews 11:3," *BTB* 2 (1972) 64-77.

Hughes, Philip Edgcumbe. "The Christology of Hebrews," *SWJT* 28 (1985) 19-27.

Hulley, Karl K. "Principles of Textual Criticism Known to St. Jerome," *Harvard Studies in Classical Philology* 55 (1944) 104-109.

Hutaff, Margaret D. "The Epistle to the Hebrews," *TBT* 99 (1978) 1816-1824.

Jewett, Robert. *A Chronology of Paul's Life.* Philedelphia: Fortress, 1979.

Jewett, Robert. *Letter to Pilgrims: A Commentary on the Epistle to the Hebrews.* New York: Pilgrim, 1981.

Jewett, Robert. *The Thessalonian Correspondence: Pauline Rhetoric and Millenarian Piety.* Foundations and Facets: New Testament. Philadelphia: Fortress, 1986.

John Paul II, Pope. "Christmas Address to the Roman Curia," *L'Osservatore Romano.* Weekly Edition in English. 969 (January 5, 1987) 6-7.

Johnson, Luke T. *The Writings of the New Testament: An Interpretation.* Philadelphia: Fortress, 1986.

Jones, Peter Rhea. "An Alternative to the Ephesian 'Dilemma'" (paper delivered to a New Testament Colloquium held at the Southern Baptist Theological Seminary, January 9, 1969; see R.P. Martin, "An Epistle in Search," p. 302, n.2; and D.J. Rowston, "Changes," p. 122).

Jülicher, Adolf. *Einleitung in das Neue Testament.* Grundriss der theologischen Wissenschaften, 3/1. Tübingen: Mohr, 1894; ET: *Introduction to the New Testament.* London: Smith, 1904.

Karris, Robert J. "The Background and the Significance of the Polemic of the Pastoral Epistles," *JBL* 92 (1973) 549-564.

Karris, Robert J. *The Pastoral Epistles,* NTM, 17. Wilmington, DE: Glazier, 1979.

Käsemann, Ernst. "A Primitive Christian Baptismal Liturgy," (1949), reprinted in *Essays on New Testament Themes.* SBT, 41. London: SCM, 1964, pp. 149-168.

Käsemann, Ernst. *Das wandernde Gottesvolk: eine Untersuchung zum Hebraërbrief.* FRLANT, 55. Göttingen: Vandenhoeck und Ruprecht, 1939; ET: *The Wandering People of God: An Investigaton of the Letter to the Hebrews.* Minneapolis, MN: Augsburg, 1984.

Käsemann, Ernst. "Epheserbrief," *RGG,* 2 (1958) 517-520.

Kaye, B.N. "Eschatology and Ethics in 1 and 2 Thessalonians," *NovT* 17 (1975) 47-57.

Keck, Leander, "Toward the Renewal of New Testament Christology," *NTS* 32 (1986) 362-377.

Kehl, Nikolaus. *Der Christushymnus im Kolosserbrief: Eine motivgeschichtliche Untersuchung zu Kol 1,12-20.* SBM, 1. Stüttgart: KBW, 1967.

Kelly, J.N.D. *The Pastoral Epistles: I & II Timothy. Titus.* HNTC. New York: Harper and Row, 1963.

Kenny, Anthony, *A Stylometric Study of the New Testament.* Oxford: Clarendon Press, 1986.

Kern, F.H. "Über 2 Thess 2, 1-12. Nebst Andeutungen über den Ursprung des 2. Briefes an die Thessalonicher," *TZT* 2 (1839) 145-214.

Kertelege, Karl, ed. *Paulus in den neutestamentlichen Spätschriften: Zur Paulusrezeption im Neuen Testament.* QD, 89. Freiburg: Herder, 1981.

Kiley, Mark. "Melchisedek's Promotion to *archiereus* and the Translation of *ta stoixheia tēs archēs*," in K.H. Richards, ed., *Society of Biblical Literature 1986 Seminar Papers.* Atlanta: Scholars Press, 1986, 236-245.

Kiley, Mark. *Colossians as Pseudepigraphy.* The Biblical Seminar. Sheffield: JSOT, 1986.

Klappert, Berthold. *Die Eschatologie des Hebraërbriefs.* Theologische Existenz heute, 156. Munich: Kaiser, 1969.

Klöpper, Albert. *Der Brief an die Colosser, kritisch untersucht und in seinem Verhältnisse zum paulinischen Lehrbegriff exegetisch und biblisch-theologisch erortet.* Berlin, 1882.

Knox, John. *Philemon Among the Letters of Paul: A New View of its Place and Importance.* (1935), rev. ed., New York: Abingdon, 1959.

Knox, W. L. *St. Paul and the Church of the Gentiles.* Cambridge: University Press, 1939.

Koch, Klaus. "Pseudonymous Writing," *IDBSup*, 712-714.

Koester, Helmut. *Introduction to the New Testament*, 2. Philadelphia: Fortress, 1982.

Koester, Helmut. "1 Thessalonians. Experiment in Christian Writing," in E. Forrester Church and Timothy Gress, eds., *Continuity and Discontinuity in Church History.* Studies in the History of Christian Thought, 19. Leiden: Brill, 1979, 33-44.

Krentz, Edgar. "A Stone That Will Not Fit," unpublished paper presented during the 1984 meeting of the Society of Biblical Literature, Chicago, IL, December 8-11, 1984.

Krentz, Edgar. "Through a Prism: The Theology of 2 Thessalonians," unpublished paper presented for the Consulation on Pauline Theology during the 1986 meeting of the Society of Biblical Literature, Atlanta, GA, November 22-25, 1986.

Krodel, Gerhard. "2 Thessalonians," in J. Paul Sampley, et al., *Ephesians, Colossians, 2 Thessalonians, The Pastoral Epistles.* Proclamation Commentaries. Philadelphia: Fortress, 1978.

Kuhn, Karl Georg. "Der Epheserbrief im Lichte der Qumrantexte," *NTS* 7 (1960-1961) 334-346; ET: "The Epistle to the Ephesians in the Light of the Qumran Texts," in J. Murphy-O'Connor, ed., *Paul and Qumran,* 115-131.

Kümmel, Werner Georg. *Einleitung in das Neue Testament.* 17th. ed., Heidelberg: Quelle & Meyer, 1973; ET: *Introduction to the New Testament.* Nashville: Abingdon, 1984.

Kuss, Otto. *Paulus: die Rolle des apostels in der theologischen Entwicklung der Urkirche.* AuV, 5. Regensburg: Pustet, 1971.

Landerville, Dale. "Jesus, the Eternal High Priest," *TBT* 24 (1986) 217-222.

Langkammer, H. "Problemy literackie Listu do Efezjan, jego aspekty teologiczne i jego eklesjologia," *RoczTeolKan* 27 (1980) 93-102.

Laub, Franz. *1. und 2. Thessalonicherbrief.* Die Neue Echter-Bibel, 13. Wurzburg: Echter, 1985.

Lemaire, André. "Pastoral Epistles: Redaction and Theology," *BTB* 2 (1972) 25-42.

Lightfoot, J.B. "The Colossian Heresy," (1879), reprinted in F.O. Francis and W.A. Meeks, *Conflict at Colossae,* 13-59.

Lincoln, Andrew T. "Ephesians 2:8-10: A Summary of Paul's Gospel," *CBQ* 45 (1983) 617-630.

Lindemann, Andreas. *Der Kolosserbrief.* Zürcher Bibelkommentare NT, 10. Zurich: Theologischer Verlag, 1983.

Lindemann, Andreas. "Die Gemeinde von 'Kolossa:' Erwägungen zum 'Sitz im Leben' eines pseudopaulinischen Briefes," *Wort und Dienst* 16 (1981) 111-134.

Lindemann, Andreas. "Zum Abfassungszweck des Zweiten Thessalonicherbriefes," *ZNW* 68 (1977) 35-47.

Lipsius, Richard Adalbert. "Über Zweck und Veranlassung des ersten Thessalonicherbriefs," *TSK* 27 (1854) 905-934.

Loane, Marcus K. *Godliness and Contentment: Studies in the Pastoral Epistles.* Grand Rapids, MI: Baker, 1982.

Lohymeyer, Ernst. *Die Briefe an die Philipper, an die Kolosser und an Philemon.* KEK, 9. 13th. ed., Göttingen: Vandenhoeck und Ruprecht, 1964.

Lohse, Eduard. *Die Briefe an die Kolosser und an Philemon.* KEK, 14. Göttingen: Vandenhoeck und Ruprecht, 1968; ET: *Colossians and Philemon.* Hermeneia. Philadelphia: Fortress, 1971.

Longenecker, Richard N. "Ancient Amanuenses and the Pauline Epistles," in R.N. Longenecker and M.C. Tenney, eds., *New Dimensions in New Testament Study.* Grand Rapids, MI: Zondervan, 1974, 281-297.

Ludwige, Helga. *Der Verfasser des Kolosserbriefes: ein Schuler des Paulus* (doctoral dissertation, Georg-August-Universität, Göttingen, 1984).

Luther, Martin. *Die Ganze Heilige Schrifft Deudsch.* Wittemberg, 1545.

MacDonald, Dennis Ronald. *The Legend and the Apostle: The Battle for Paul in Story and Canon.* Philadelphia: Westminster, 1983.

Maloney, Elliott C. "Biblical Authorship and the Pastoral Epistles," *TBT* 24 (1986) 119-123.

Manns, Frederic. "L'hymne judéo-chrétien de 1 Tim 3, 16," *Euntes Docete* 32 (1979) 232-339; digest: Judeo-Christian Context of 1 Tim 3:16," *TD* 29 (1981) 119-122.

Manson, T.W. "The Letters to the Thessalonians," *BJRL* 35 (1952-1953) 428-447.

Manson, T.W, "The Problem of the Epistle to the Hebrews," (1949), in Matthew Black, ed., *Studies in the Epistles and Gospels.* Philadelphia: Westminster, 1962, 242-258.

Manson, William *The Epistle to the Hebrews.* London: Hodder and Stoughton, 1951.

Marshall, I. Howard. *1 and 2 Thessalonians.* NCB. Grand Rapids, MI: Eerdmans, 1983.

Marshall, I. Howard. "Pauline Theology in the Thessalonian Correspondence," in M.D. Hooker and S.G. Wilson, eds., *Paul and Paulinism,* 173-183.

Martin, Ralph P. "An Epistle in Search of a Life-Setting," *ExpTim* 79 (1968) 296-302.

Marxsen, Willi. *Der zweite Thessalonicherbrief.* Zürcher Bibelkommentare, 11/2. Zurich: Theologischer Verlag, 1982.

Marxsen, Willi. *Einleitung in das Neue Testament: eine Einführung in ihre Probleme.* Gütersloh: Mohr, 1963; ET: *Introduction to the New Testament: An Approach to its Problems.* Philadelphia: Fortress, 1968.

Masson, Charles. *L'Epître de Saint Paul aux Colossiens.* CNT, 10. Paris: Delchaux et Niestlé, 1950.

Masson, Charles. *Les deux épîtres de saint Paul aux Thessaloniciens.* CNT, 11A. Paris: Delchaux et Niestlé, 1957.

Mayerhoff, Ernst. *Der Brief an die Colosser, mit vernehmlicher Berucksichtigung der drei Pastoralbriefe kritisch geprüft.* Berlin: Mayerhoff, 1838.

McCown, Wayne. "The Hymnic Structure of Colossians 1:15-20," *EvQ* 51 (1979) 156-162.

McCullough, J.C. "Some Recent Developments in Research on the Epistle to the Hebrews," *IBS* 2 (1980) 141-165; 3 (1981) 28-45.

McCullough, J.C. "The Old Testament Quotations in Hebrews," *NTS* 26 (1979-1980) 363-379.

McDonald, H.D. *Commentary on Colossians and Philemon.* Theta Books. Waco, TX: Word, 1980.

McGehee, Michael. "Hebrews: The Letter Which is Not a Letter," *TBT* 24 (1986) 213-216.

McNeile, Alan Hugh—C.S.C. Williams. *Introduction to the Study of the New Testament.* Oxford: Clarendon, 1965.

Meade, David G. *Pseudonymity and Canon: An Investigation into the Relationship of Authorship and Authority in Jewish and Early Christian Tradition.* WUNT, 39. Tübingen: Mohr, 1986.

Mealand, David L. "The Christology of the Epistle to the Hebrews," *ModChurch* 22 (1979) 180-187.

Mees, Michael. "Die Höhepriester-Theologie des Hebraërbriefes im Vergleich mit dem Ersten Clemensbrief," *BZ* 22 (1978) 115-124.

Megivern, James J. ed. *Official Catholic Teachings: Bible Interpretation.* Wilmington, NC: Consortium, 1978.

Meier, John P. "Symmetry and Theology in the Old Testament Citations of Heb 1, 5-14." *Bib* 66 (1985) 504-533.

Merklein, Helmut. *Christus und die Kirche: die theologische Grundstruktur des Epheserbriefes nach Eph 2,11-18.* SBS, 66. Stüttgart: KBW, 1973.

Merklein, Helmut. "Paulinische Theologie in der Rezeption des Kolosser-und Epheserbriefes," in K. Kertelge, ed., *Paulus,* 25-69.

Metzger, Bruce M. "A Reconsideration of Certain Arguments against the Pauline Authorship of the Pastoral Epistles," *ExpTim* 70 (1958-1959) 91-94.

Metzger, Bruce M. "Literary Forgeries and Canonical Pseudepigrapha," *JBL* 91 (1972) 3-24.

Michaelis, Wilhelm. "Der 2. Thessalonicherbrief kein Philipperbrief," *TZ* 1 (1945) 282-285.

Michel, Otto. *Der Brief an die Hebraër.* KEK, 13. 13th. ed., Göttingen: Vandenhoeck und Ruprecht, 1975.

Miller, Athanasius. "De nova Enchiridii Biblici editione," published under the name of A. Kleinhaus, in *Antonianum* 30 (1955) 63-65.

Minear, Paul S. "An Early Christian Theopoetic?" *Semeia* 12 (1978) 201-214.

Mitton, C. Leslie. *Ephesians.* NCB. Grand Rapids, MI: Eerdmans, 1976.

Mitton, C, Leslie. *The Epistle to the Ephesians: Its Authorship, Origin and Purpose.* Oxford: Clarendon, 1951.

Moda, A. "Le lettere pastorali e la biografià di Paolo. Saggio bibliografico," *BeO* 27 (1985) 149-161.

Moffatt, James. *A Critical and Exegetical Commentary on the Epistles to the Hebrews.* ICC. Edinburgh: Clark, 1924.

Moffatt, James. *Introduction to the Literature of the New Testament.* 3rd. rev. ed.: Edinburgh, Clark, 1918.

Montagni, F. "La figura di Paolo nelle lettere ai colossesi e agli efeseni," *RivB* 34 (1986) 429-449.

Moore, A.L. *I and II Thessalonians.* NCB. London: Nelson, 1969.

Moore, Michael S. "Ephesians 2:14-16: A History of Recent Interpretation," *EvQ* 54 (1982) 163-168.

Morgan, Robert. "The Significance of 'Paulinism,'" in M.D. Hooker and S.G. Wilson, eds., *Paul and Paulinism,* 320-338.

Morgenthaler, Robert. *Statistik des neutestamentlichen Wortschätzes.* Zurich: Gotthelf, 1958.

Morris, Leon. *The First and Second Epistles to the Thessalonians.* NICNT. Grand Rapids, MI: Eerdmans, 1959.

Morris, Leon. *The First and Second Epistles to the Thessalonians: An Introduction and Commentary.* Tyndale New Testament Commentaries. Grand Rapids, MI: Eerdmans, 1984.

Morton, Andrew Q.—McLeman, James. *Christianity and the Computer Age.* New York: Harper, 1964.

Morton, Andrew Q.—Michaelson, S. *A Critical Concordance to I, II Thessalonians.* The Computer Bible, 26. Wooster, OH: Biblical Research Association, 1983.

Mott, Stephen Charles. "Greek Ethics and Christian Conversion: the Philonic Background of Titus ii 10-14 and iii 3-7," *NovT* 20 (1978) 22-48.

Moule, C.F.D. *The Epistles of Paul the Apostle to the Colossians and to Philemon.* CGNTC. Cambridge: University Press, 1968.

Moule, C.F.D. "The Problem of the Pastoral Epistles: A Reappraisal," *BJRL* 47 (1964-1965) 430-452.

Moulton, James Hope. (reference in D.J. Rowston, "Changes," p. 122).

Mullins, T.Y. "The Thanksgivings of Philemon and Colossians," *NTS* 30 (1984) 288-293.

Murphy-O'Connor, Jerome, ed. *Paul and Qumran: Studies in New Testament Exegesis.* Chicago: Priory, 1968.

Murphy-O'Connor, Jerome. "Redactional Angels in 1 Tim 3:16," *RB* 91 (1984) 178-187.

Murphy-O'Connor, Jerome. "Who Wrote Ephesians?" *TBT* 18 (1965) 1201-1209.

Mussner, Franz. "Contributions Made by Qumran to the Understanding of the Epistle to the Ephesians," in J. Murphy-O'Connor, ed., *Paul and Qumran*, 159-178.

Neyrey, Jerome H. *Christ Is Community: The Christologies of the New Testament.* GNS, 13. Wilmington, DE: Glazier, 1985.

Nickle, Keith F. *The Collection: A Study in Paul's Strategy.* SBT, 48. London: SCM, 1966.

Nielsen, Charles M. "The Status of Paul and His Letters in Colossians," *Perspectives in Religious Studies* 12 (1985) 103-122.

O'Brien, Peter T. *Colossians, Philemon.* WBC, 44. Waco, TX: Word, 1982.

O'Brien, Peter T. "Ephesians 1:1: An Unusual Introduction to a New Testament Letter," *NTS* 25 (1978-1979) 504-516.

O'Neill, J. "The Source of the Christology in Colossians," *NTS* 26 (1979-1980) 87-100.

Oberlinner, Lorenz. "Die 'Epiphaneia' des Heilswillens Gottes in Christus Jesus: Zur Grundstruktur der Christologie der Pastoralbriefe," *ZNW* 71 (1980) 192-213.

Ochel, Werner. *Die Annahme einer Bearbeitung des Kolosserbriefes im Epheserbrief in einer Analyse des Epheserbriefes untersucht* (doctoral dissertation, University of Marburg, 1934).

Osswald, Eva. *Falsche Prophetie im Alten Testament.* Samlung gemeinverständlicher Vorträge und Schriften aus dem Gebiet der Theologie und Religionsgeschichte, 237. Tübingen: Mohr, 1962.

Osswald, Eva. "Zum Problem der *Vaticinia ex eventu*," *ZAW* 75 (1963) 27-44.

Paley, William. *Horae Paulinae: or the Truth of Scripture History of St. Paul.* London: Rivington, 1922.

Parker, H.M. "Domitian and the Epistle to the Hebrews," *IlRev* 36 (1979) 31-43.

Patzia, Arthur G. *Colossians, Philemon, Ephesians.* GNC. San Francisco: Harper & Row, 1984.

Patzia, Arthur G. "The Deutero-Pauline Hypothesis: An Attempt at Clarification," *EvQ* 52 (1980) 27-42.

Pax, Elpidius. *EPIPHANEIA: Eine religionsgeschichtlicher Beitrag zur biblischen Theologie.* MuTS, I, 10. Munich: Zink, 1955.

Penny, D.N. *The Pseudo-Pauline Letters of the First Two Centuries* (Ph.D. thesis, Emory University, 1980).

Percy, Ernst. *Die Probleme der Kolosser-und Epheserbriefe.* Lund: Gleerup, 1946.

Pesch, Rudolf. *Die Entdeckung des altesten Paulus-Briefes: Paulus—neu gesehen: die Briefe an die Gemeinde der Thessalonicher.* Herderbucherei, 1167. Freiburg: Herder, 1984.

Pfammatter, Josef. *Epheserbrief. Kolosserbrief.* Die Neue Echter-Bibel 10/12: Wurzburg: Echter, 1987.

Pfleiderer, Otto. *Das Urchristentum: seine Schriften und Lehren in geschichtlichen Zusammenhang.* Berlin: Reimer, 1902; ET: *Primitive Christianity.* New York: Putnam's, 1906.

Pokorný, Petr. *Der Epheserbrief und die Gnosis: die Bedeutung des Haupt-Glieder-Gedänkens in der enstehenden Kirche.* Berlin: Evangelische Verlagsanstalt, 1965.

Polhill, J.B. "An Introduction to Ephesians," *RevExp* 76 (1979) 517-527.

Pollard, T.E. "Colossians 1. 12-20: A Reconsideration," *NTS* 27 (1980-1981) 572-575.

Prior, Michael. *Second Timothy: A Personal Letter of Paul* (Ph.D. thesis, University of London, 1985).

Quinn, Jerome. "Paul's Last Captivity," in Elizabeth A. Livingstone, ed., *Studia Biblica 1978, 3: Papers on*

Paul and Other New Testament Authors. JSNTSup, 3. Sheffield: JSOT, 1980, 289-299.

Quinn, Jerome D. "The Last Volume of Luke: The Relation of Luke-Acts to the Pastoral Epistles," in Charles H. Talbert, ed., *Perspectives on Luke-Acts.* Danville, VA: Association of Baptist Professors of Religion, 1978, 62-75.

Reese, James M. *1 and 2 Thessalonians.* NTM, 16. Wilmington, DE: Glazier, 1979.

Renan, Ernest. *Histoire des origines du Christianisme, 3: Saint Paul.* Paris: Levy, 1869.

Renner, Frumentius. *"An die Hebraër"—ein pseudepigraphischer Brief.* Münsterschwarzächer Studien, 14. Münsterschwarzach: Vier-Turme, 1970.

Rice, George E. "Apostasy as a Motif and Its Effect on the Structure of Hebrews," *AUSS* 23 (1985) 18-25.

Rigaux, Béda. *Les Epîtres aux Thessaloniciens.* EB. Paris: Gabalda, 1956.

Rigaux, Béda. *Saint Paul et ses lettres.* Paris-Bruges: Desclée de Brouwer, 1962. ET: *Letters of St. Paul: Modern Studies.* Chicago: Franciscan Herald, 1968.

Rissi, Mathias. *Die Theologie des Hebraërbriefs.* WUNT, 41. Tübingen: Mohr, 1987.

Rist, Martin. "Pseudepigraphy and the Early Christians," in D.E. Aune, ed., *Studies in New Testament and Early Christian Literature.* SupNT, 33. Leiden: Brill, 1972, 75-91.

Robinson, John A.T. *Redating the New Testament.* Philadelphia: Westminster, 1976.

Robinson, John A.T. *The Body: A Study in Pauline Theology,* SBT, 5. London: SCM, 1966.

Robinson, H. Wheeler. *Corporate Personality in Ancient Israel.* Rev. ed., Philadelphia: Fortress, 1980.

Roetzel, Calvin. *The Letters of Paul: Conversations in Context.* Rev. ed., Atlanta: John Knox, 1982.

Rogers, Patrick V. *Colossians.* NTM, 15. Wilmington, DE: Glazier, 1980.

Rogers, Patrick V. "The Pastoral Epistles as Deutero-Pauline," *ITQ* 45 (1978) 248-260.

Rogers, Patrick V. "Hopeful, in Spite of Chains: The Indominatable Spirit of Paul in the Captivity Epistles," *BTB* 12 (1982) 77-81.

Rohde, Joachim. "Pastoralbriefe und Acta Pauli," *SE,* 5; *TU,* 103. Berlin: Akademie, 1968, 303-310.

Roller, Otto. *Das Formular der paulinischen Briefe: ein Beitrag zur Lehre von antiken Briefe.* BWANT 4 F,6. Stüttgart: Kohlhammer, 1933.

Rowland, Christopher. "Apocalyptic Visions and the Exaltation of Christ in the Letter to the Colossians," *JSNT* 19 (1983) 73-83.

Rowston, Douglas J. "Changes in Biblical Interpretation Today: The Example of Ephesians," *BTB* 9 (1979) 121-125.

Russell, D.S. *The Method and Message of Jewish Apocalyptic, 200 B.C.—A.D. 100.* OTL. London: SCM, 1964.

Russell, D.S. *The Old Testament Pseudepigrapha: Patriarchs & Prophets in Early Judaism.* London: SCM, 1987.

Sabourin, Leopold. *Christology: Basic Texts in Focus.* New York: Alba, 1984.

Sahlin, Harald. "Die Beschneidung Christi, *Symbolae biblicae Upsalienses* 12 (1950) 5-22.

Sampley, J. Paul. *"And the Two Shall Become One Flesh."* *A Study of Traditions in Ephesians 5:21-33.* SNTSMS, 16. Cambridge: University Press, 1971.

Sand, Alexander. "Überlieferung und Sammlung der Paulusbriefe," in K. Kertelge, ed., *Paulus,* 11-24.

Sanders, Ed. "Literary Dependence in Colossians," *JBL* 85 (1966) 28-45.

Sanders, J.N. "The Case for Pauline Authorship," in F.L. Cross, ed., *Studies in Ephesians,* 9-20.

Sanders, Jack T. "Hymnic Elements in Ephesians 1-3," *ZNW* 56 (1965) 214-232.

Sanders, Jack T. *The New Testament Christological Hymns: Their Historical Religious Background.* SNTSMS, 15. Cambridge: University Press, 1971.

Sanders, James A. *Canon as Paradigm: From Sacred Story to Sacred Text.* Philadelphia: Fortress, 1987.

Sanders, James A. *Torah and Canon.* Philadelphia: Fortress, 1972.

Saunders, Ernest W. "The Colossian Heresy and Qumran Theology," in B.L. Daniels and M.J. Suggs, eds., *Studies in the History and Text of the New Testament.* SD. Salt Lake City, University of Utah, 1967, 133-145.

Schelkle, Karl Hermann. *Paulus-Leben-Briefe-Theologie.* Ertrage der Forschung, 152. Darmstadt: Wissenschaftliche Buchgesellschaft, 1981.

Schenk, Wolfgang. "Christus, das Geheimnis der Welt, als dogmatisches und ethisches Grundprinzip des Kolosserbriefes," *EvT* 43 (1983) 138-155.

Schenk, Wolfgang. "Zur Entstehung und zum Verständnis der Adresse des Epheserbriefes," *Theologische Versuche* 6 (1975) 73-78.

Schenke, Hans-Martin, "Das Weiterwirken des Paulus und die Pflege seines Erbes durch die Paulus-Schule," *NTS* 21 (1974-1975) 505-518.

Schenke, Hans-Martin (*et al*). *Einleitung in die Schriften des Neuen Testaments.* Gütersloh: Mohr, 1978.

Schleiermacher, Friedrich. *Über den sogenannten ersten Brief des Paulos an den Timotheos.* Berlin: Realschülbüchhandlung, 1807.

Schleiermacher, Friedrich. *Einleitung ins Neue Testament.* Edited by G. Wolde, Berlin, Reimer, 1845.

Schlier, Heinrich. *Der Brief an die Epheser: ein Kommentar.* Dusseldorf: Patmos, 1957.

Schlier, Heinrich. *Christus und die Kirche im Epheserbrief.* BHT, 6. Tübingen: Mohr, 1930.

Schmidt, Daryl. "Pauline Syntax: The Transformational Patterns of 1-2 Thess," unpublished paper presented during the 1978 meeting of the Society of Biblical Literature, New Orleans, LA, November 18-21, 1978.

Schmidt, Daryl. "The Authenticity of 2 Thessalonians: Linguistic Arguments," in Kent Harold Richards, ed., *Society of Biblical Literature 1983 Seminar Papers.* Chico, CA: Scholars Press, 1983, 289-296.

Schmidt, Johann Ernst Christian. *Historisch-kritische Einlietung in's Neue Testament.* Geissen, 1809 [=1804].

Schmidt, Johann Ernst Christian. *Vermütungen über die beiden Briefe an die Thessalonicher.* Bibliothek für Kritik und Exegese des Neuen Testaments und älteste Christengeschichte, 2/3. Hadamar, 1801.

Schmidt, Karl Ludwig. *Der Rahmen der Geschichte Jesu: literaturkritische Untersuchungen zur ältesten Jesusüberlieferung.* (1919). Reprinted: Darmstadt: Wissenschaftliche Buchgesellschaft, 1964.

Schmeidl, Paul Wilhelm. *Die Briefe an die Thessalonicher und an die Korinther.* HKNT, 2,1. Freiburg: Mohr, 1891.

Schmithals, Walther. "Die Thessalonicherbriefe als Briefkompositionen," in Erich Dinkler, ed., *Zeit und Geschichte.* Tübingen: Mohr, 1964, 295-315.

Schnackenburg, Rudolf. *Der Brief an die Epheser,* EKKNT, 10. Zurich: Benziger, 1982.

Schott, Heinrich August. *Isagoge historico-critica in libros Novi Foederis sacros.* Jena, 1830.

Schräder, Karl. *Der Apostel Paulus,* 5. Leipzig: Kollman, 1836.

Schwartz, Eduard. *Über die pseudapostolischen Kirchenordnungen.* Schriften der wissenschaftlichen Gesellschaft in Strassburg, 6. Strassburg: Trubner, 1910.

Schweizer, Eduard. *Der Brief an die Kolosser.* EKK. Zurich: Benziger, 1976.

Schweizer, Eduard. "Der zweite Thessalonicherbrief ein Philipperbrief?" *TZ* 1 (1945) 90-105.

Schweizer, Eduard. "Die Kirche als Leib Christi in den paulinischen Antilegomena," *TLZ* 86 (1961) 241-256.

Schweizer, Eduard. "The Letter to the Colossians Neither Pauline nor Postpauline?," in R.E. Hoekman, ed., *Pluralisme et oecumenisme en recherches théologiques.* BETL, 43. Louvain: Peeters, 1976, 3-16.

Scott, Ernest F. *The Epistle to the Hebrews: Its Doctrine and Significance.* Edinburgh: T & T Clark, 1922.

Scott, Robert. *The Pauline Epistles: A Critical Study.* Edinburgh, 1909.

Senior, Donald. "Letter to the Colossians," *TBT* 23 (1985) 11-17.

Sint, Josef. *Pseudonymität im Ältertum: Ihre Formen und ihre Grunde.* Commentationes Aenipontanae, 15. Innsbruck: Wagner, 1960.

Sowers, Stanley G. *The Hermeneutics of Philo and Hebrews: A Comparative Interpretation of the Old Testament in Philo-Judaeus and the Epistle to the Hebrews.* Basel Studies of Theology, 1. Zurich: EVZ Verlag, Zurich, 1965.

Speyer, Wolfgang. *Die literarische Falschung im heidnischen und christlichen Ältertum: ein Versuch ihrer Deutung.* Handbuch der Altertumswissenschaft, 1/2. Munich: Beck, 1971.

Spicq, Ceslas. "*atakteō, ataktos, ataktōs,*" in C. Spicq, *Notes de lexicographie néo-testamentaire,* 1. OBO, 22/1. Göttingen: Vandenhoeck und Ruprecht, 1978, 157-159.

Spicq, Ceslas. *L'Epître aux Hébreux.* 2 vols. EB. 3rd. ed., Paris: Gabalda, 1952-1953.

Spicq, Ceslas. *Les Epîtres Pastorales,* 2 vols. EB. Paris: Gabalda, 1969.

Spicq, Ceslas. "Les Thessaloniciens 'inquiets' étaient-ils des paresseux?, *StTh* 10 (1956) 1-13.

Spitta, Friedrich. *Zur Geschichte und Literatur des Urchristentums,* 1. Göttingen: Vandenhoeck und Ruprecht, 1893.

Stagg, F. "The Domestic Code and Final Appeal: Ephesians 5:21-6:24," *RevExp* 76 (1979) 541-552.

Steinmetz, Franz-Josef. *Protologische Heilszuversicht: Die Strukturen des soteriologischen und christlichen Denkens im Kol und Eph.* FTS, 2. Frankfurt: Knecht, 1969.

Stendahl, Krister. *The School of St. Matthew and its Use of the Old Testament.* ASNU, 20. Lund: Gleerup, 1954.

Stenger, Werner. *Der Christushymnus 1 Tim 3,16: Eine strukturanalytische Untersuchung.* Regensburger Studien zur Theologie, 6. Frankfurt-Bern: Lang, 1977.

Stowers, Stanley K. *Letter-Writing in Greco-Roman Antiquity.* Philadelphia: Westminster, 1986.

Strachan, Robert H. *The Historic Jesus in the New Testament.* London: SCM, 1931.

Strobel, August. "Schreiben des Lukas? Zum sprachlichen Problem der Pastoralbriefe," *NTS* 15 (1968-1969) 191-210.

Swain, Lionel. *The People of the Resurrection, 1: The Apostolic Letters.* GNS, 15. Wilmington, DE: Glazier, 1986.

Swetnam, James. "Jesus as *Logos* in Hebrews 4, 12-13," *Bib* 62 (1981) 214-224.

Synge, Francis C. *Philippians and Colossians.* London: SCM, 1958.

Theissen, Gerd. *Untersuchungen zum Hebraërbrief.* STANT, 2 Gütersloh: Mohr, 1969.

Thompson, G.H.P. *The Letters of Paul to the Ephesians, to the Colossians and to Philemon.* Cambridge, MA: University Press, 1967.

Thurston, Robert W. "The Relationship between the Epistles to the Thessalonians," *ExpTim* 85 (1973) 52-56.

Torrey, C.C "Authorship and Character of the so-called 'Epistle to the Hebrews,'" *JBL* 30 (1911) 137-156.

Towner, P.H. "The Present Age in the Eschatology of the Pastoral Epistles," *NTS* 32 (1986) 427-448.

Trilling, Wolfgang. *Untersuchungen zum 2. Thessalonicherbrief.* Erfürter theologische Studien, 27. Leipzig: St. Benno-Verlag, 1972.

Trilling, Wolfgang. *Der zweite Brief an die Thessalonicher.* EKK, 14. Neukirchen-Vluyn: Neukirchener Verlag, 1980.

Trummer, Peter, *Die Paulustradition der Pastoralbriefe.* BBET, 8. Frankfurt: Lang, 1978.

Ulrichsen, J.H. *"Diaphorōteron onoma* in Hebr. 1,4. Christus als Träger des Gottesnames," *StTh* 38 (1984) 65-75.

Usteri, Leonhard. *Die Entwicklung des paulinischen Lehrbegriffs.* Zurich: Orell Fussli, 1824.

Van Bruggen, Jakob. *Die geschichtliche Einordnug der Pastoralbriefe.* Monographien und Studiebücher, 305. Wuppertal: Brockhaus, 1981.

Vanhoye, Albert. *La structure littéraire de l'épître aux Hébreux* 2nd. ed., Bruges: Desclée de Brouwer, 1976.

Vanhoye, Albert. "Literarische Struktur und theologische Botschaft des Hebraërbriefes," *Studien zum Neuen Testament und seiner Umwelt,* 4 (1979) 119-147; 5 (1980) 18-49.

Vanhoye, Albert. *Situation du Christ: Hébreux 1-2.* LD, 58. Paris: Cerf, 1969.

van Manen, W.C. *De Echtheit van Paulusbrieven aan de Thessalonicenses.* Utrecht, 1865.

Van Roon, Aart. *De brief van Paulus van de Epheziërs.* De prediking van het Nieuwe Testament, 9. Nijkerk: Callenbach, 1976.

Van Roon, Aart. *Een onderzoek naar de authenticiteit van de brief aan de Epheziërs.* Delft: Melinema, 1969; ET: *The Authenticity of Ephesians.* SupNT, 39 Leiden: Brill, 1974.

Vawter, Bruce. "The Colossians Hymn and the Principle of Redaction," *CBQ* 33 (1971) 62-81.

Verner, David C. *The Household of God: The Social World of the Pastoral Epistles.* SBLDS, 71. Chico, CA: Scholars Press, 1983.

Vielhauer, Philipp. *Geschichte der urchristlichen Literatur: Einleitung in das Neue Testament, die Apokryphen und die Apostolischen Väter.* 2nd. ed., Berlin: de Gruyter, 1978.

von Campenhausen, Hans. *Aus der Frühzeit des Christentums: Studien zur Kirchengeschichte des ersten und zweiten Jahrhunderts.* Tübingen: Mohr, 1963.

von Dobschütz, Ernst. *Die Thessalonicherbriefe.* KEK, 10. 7th. ed., Göttingen: Vandenhoeck und Ruprecht, 1909.

von Soden, Hans. "Der erste Thessalonicherbrief," *TSK* 28 (1885) 263-310.

von Wiezsäker, Karl. *Das apostolische Zeitalter der christlichen Kirche,* 1. Freiburg: Mohr, 1886.

Wake, William. "The Authenticity of the Pauline Epistles," *HibJ* 47 (1948-1949) 50-55.

Weiss, Herold. "The Law in the Epistle to the Colossians," *CBQ* 34 (1972) 294-314.

Weiss, Johannes. *Das Urchristentum.* Göttingen, 1917; ET: *Earliest Christianity.* New York: Harper, 1959.

Weisse, Christian. *Philosophische Dogmatik,* 1 (1855; reference in H.J. Holtzmann, *Einleitung,* 3rd. ed., p. 265).

White, John L. *Light from Ancient Letters.* Philadelphia: Fortress, 1986.

White, John L. "Paul and the Apostolic Letter Tradition," *CBQ* 45 (1983) 433-444.

White, R.E.O. *Biblical Ethics,* 1: *The Changing Continuity of Christian Ethics.* Exeter: Paternoster, 1979.

Wild, Robert A. "The Warrior and the Prisoner: Some Reflections on Ephesians 6:10-20," *CBQ* 46 (1984) 284-298.

Wilder, Amos N. *Theopoetics: Theology and Religious Imagination.* Philadelphia: Fortress, 1976.

Williamson, Ronald. *Philo and the Epistle to the Hebrews.* ALGHJ, 4. Leiden: Brill, 1970.

Wilson, Stephen G. *Luke and the Pastoral Epistles.* London: SPCK, 1979.

Windisch, Hans. "Zur Christologie der Pastoralbriefe," *ZNW* 34 (1935) 213-238.

Woschitz, K.M. "'Erlösende Tränen.' Gedänken zu Hebr 5,7," *BLit* 56 (1983) 196-201.

Wrede, William. *Das literarische Rätsel des Hebraërbriefes.* FRLANT, 8. Göttingen: Vandenhoeck und Ruprecht, 1906.

Wrede, William. *Die Echtheit des zweiten Thessalonicherbriefs.* TU, 24/2. Leipzig: Hinrichs, 1903.

Wrzol, Josef. *Die Echtheit des zweiten Thessalonicherbriefs.* BibS(F), 19/4. Freiburg: Herder, 1916.

Yates, Roy. "'The Worship of Angels' (Col 2:18)," *ExpTim* 77 (1985) 12-15.

Zahn, Theodor, "Hebraërbrief," *RE,* 7, 492-506.

Zmijezski, Josef. "Apostolische Paradosis und Pseudepigraphie im Neuen Testament, 'Durch Erinnerung wachhalten,' (2 Petr 1,13; 3,1)," *BZ* 23 (1979) 161-171.

Index

Index of Scripture References

Gen	57		19:2	162		2 Kgs	57
1:1	192		23:26	29		6:16	39
1:2	235		26:13	167		23:2	61
1:26-27	161						
1:26	192		Num	57		Isa	61-63
2:24	164		6:24-26	22		1-39	62
3:19	235		12:7	30		2:10	228
5:21-24	65		29:7-11	29		2:19	228
6:2-4	27					2:21	228
14:17-24	32, 35, 36		Deut	57		8.17	28, 29
15	65		1:1	57, 61		8:18	28, 29
18.23	46		1:31	34		11:4	229
19:1-3	46		5:1	61		16:5	25
22:8	68		5:2-3	61		40-55	61, 62, 66
25:33-34	44		5:16	165		52:13-	
26:34	44		29:1	61		53:12	36
27:30-40	44		29:17	44		53	282
28:15	46		34	57		53:12	36
31:6	46		34:16	61		56-66	61, 62
31:8	46					59:17	165
32:36	45		Josh	57		63:16	34
						66:5	232
Exod	57		Judg	57		66:15-16	229
3:2	228						
10:16-17	39		1 Sam	57		Jer 10:11	81
19:5-6	39		15:22	161		31 33-34	39, 40
20:12	165					31:33	40
			2 Sam	57			
Lev	57		7:14	27, 34		Ezek	
4:16	33		23:1	61		14:14	65
16:2	35					28:3	65
16:12	35		1 Kgs	57			
16:29-34	29		3.5-15	64		Hos 11:1	34
18	200		11:41	63			

Jonah	247	2:1	27	5:3	270
		38:7	27	5:10	270
Mic				5:48	162
6:6-8	161	Prov 1.1	64	10	67
		3:11-12	40	10:19-20	60
Zech				12:28	67
12:10	36	Qoh 1:1	64	13	67
14:5	228	1.12	64	18	67
		1:16	64	18:15-17	235
Mal 4:1	229	2.9	64	19:9	67
		5.14	123	24-25	67
Ps 2:7	27, 32, 33,			24:4-5	229
	34	Dan 1:4	65	25:41	228
2:8	27	7:9	228	25:46	228
8	28			26:38-46	33
8:4-6	28	1 Chr	57	27:46	33
8.7	157				
21:23	50	2 Chr	57	Mark	57, 58, 59,
22.22	28, 29				60, 67,
29:1	27	Bar 6	81		254, 261,
45:7-8	27				269
45:7	27	4 Ezra		1:11	67, 159
68:9	45	14:40	65	9:7	159
68:19	157	14:50	65	10.11-12	67
89:27	27			12:36	61
95	44, 45	Ep Jer	81	13	265
95:7-11	44			13:3-6	229
95:7-8	44	1 Macc	57	13:11	60
95:11	44	11:30-37	80	15:34	33
97:7	27				
101:26	40	2 Macc	57	Luke	57, 58, 60,
102:26-					138, 270
28	27	Sir 10:34	34	1:1-4	20, 58
104:4	27			3:22	67
110	24, 28, 61,	Tob		6:36	162
	282	4:3-19	200	11:20	67
110:1	24, 25, 26,			12:11-12	60
	27, 28,	Wis	64		
	31, 34,	2:13	34	John	57, 60
	156, 195,	2:18	34	1:1-18	20, 192
	270	5:1	167	1:1-3	24
110:4	32, 34, 35,	7	64	1:1	27
	36, 40	7:7-14	64	1:14	59
110:5	26	7:25	24	1:16	59
117:6	46			1:45	59
118:6	40	Matt	57, 58, 60,	3:11	59
135:14	40		261, 269,	4.22	59
			270	4:42	59
Job 1:6	27	3:17	67	6.5	59
1:21	123	5-7	67	6.68	59

Index of Scripture References

6:69	59		151, 185,	1:1-3	188
9:4	59		187, 245,	1:1	94, 203
11:16	59		269	1:9	230
13:31	231	1-11	185	1:12	52, 140, 204
14:26	60	1:1	203		
14:22	59	1:6	21	1.13	204
16:13	60	1:7	94	2:1	146
16:30	59	1.29-31	199, 200	2:2	51
17:22	231	2:16	239	2:7	146, 185
19:35	60	4:24	185	3:4	140, 204
20:25	59	6:1-11	185	3:5	140, 204
20:28	27	6·4	185	3:6	52, 140
20:30-31	60	6:11	185	3.11	146
21:24	59	7:8	108	3:22	140, 204
		7·12	108	4:1	146
Acts	57, 58, 66,	8:12-17	124	4:6	52, 140
	69, 85,	8:32	185	4:17	20
	93, 97-	8:35-39	50	4:20	149
	98, 107,	8:38	95	5:1-5	232
	116, 134,	9:23-24	185	5:4	233
	138, 250	10:9	156	5:9-11	235
1:8	85	11:25	146	6:14	156
2:42-47	45	12-15	185	6:9	149
3:15	195	12	147	6:10	149
4:36	49	12:3	143	7	149
6:1	22	12:6	143	7:1	149
7	22	12:10	46	7:40	60
14:14	128	12:13	46	9:5	20
15:23-29	80	14:17	149	10:13	230
16:26	167	15:24	98	11:2	105, 238
18:19-		15:26	183	11:18	147
19:40	140	15:28	98	11:23	105
18:24-28	52	15:30-32	207	12	147
19:10	140	15.30	166, 239	12:28	129, 147
19:22	97	15.33	230	13:2	146
20:1-2	97	16:1-16	141	14:2	146
20:17-38	140	16:3-23	189	14:33	230
20:23	167	16:3	140	15	210
23:29	167	16·7	203	15:3-6	51
26.29	167	16:20	188, 230	15:3	105
26:31	167	16:21-23	189	15:9	146, 168
27:7-13	98	16:22	72	15:15	156
27:21	98	16:25-26	185	15:24	185
28:16-31	97	16:25	146, 239	15:50	149
28:16-17	167	16:27	103	15:51	146
				16:21	204
Rom	15, 21, 48,	1 Cor	15, 48, 84,	16:1-4	183
	51, 71,		93, 151,	16.5-9	207
	84, 93,		185, 187,	16 12	140
	96, 108,		245, 269	16:19-20	189

16:19	140	6:18	188	1:15-23	142
16:21	72, 204			1:15-16	151, 165
16:23	188	Eph	15, 84, 132-170,	1:15	160, 162, 163
2 Cor	15, 84, 93, 151, 185, 245, 269		171-174, 179, 184, 216, 236,	1:17-22	151
				1:17-19	168
				1:17	154, 159, 160
1:1	188, 203		244, 245,		
1:3-4	151		246, 251,	1:18	162
1:4-7	205		252, 254	1:19-2:10	144
1:11	166		255, 257,	1:20-23	156
1:18	230		258, 259,	1:20	142, 154
3:6	204		260, 261	1:22-23	147, 157
3:7-18	30	1-3	301	1:22	147, 158
4:3	239	1:19-20	144	1:23	159
6:4	104	1:1-2	139, 150-151	2:1-10	162, 168
6:6	199			2:1-2	168
8-9	183	1:1	93, 139, 140, 162,	2:1	156, 159
9:12	184			2:2	148, 162, 168
10:1	204		166, 168,		
10:9-10	237		169, 170, 203	2:3-7	168
11:15	204			2:3	159, 169
11:22	21	1:2	155, 160	2:5	156, 159
11:23-27	166, 270	1:3-14	144, 151, 153, 160, 168, 277	2:6	142, 154, 157
11:23	166				
12:17-18	71			2:7	154
12:20	199	1:3-4	152	2:8-10	150, 168, 170, 291
13:10	207	1:3	142, 153, 154, 155, 156, 159, 162		
13:11	230			2:8-9	160
13:14	188			2:10	147, 160, 162
Gal	15, 51, 84, 93, 96, 108, 151, 185, 245, 269	1:4	142, 153, 155, 159, 163	2:11-22	160
				2:11-18	294
				2:11	160
		1:5	155, 162, 169	2:12	155, 158
				2:13	154, 157, 168
1:1	185, 203	1:6	143, 153, 159, 162		
1:2	147			2:14-18	157, 158
1:14	238	1:7	144, 153, 157	2:14-16	170, 295
1:19	203			2:15	158
2:10	183	1:8	142	2:16	157
2:19-20	50	1:9-10	145	2:18	158
3:19	27, 30	1:9	145, 153, 155, 169	2:19-20	142
3:28	198, 202			2:19	162
5:2	204	1:10	153, 154, 155	2:20	146, 148, 168
5:19-21	199, 265				
5:21	149	1:11	153, 169	2:21	147, 158, 160
5:22-23	199, 265	1:12	153, 154, 159		
6:11	72, 74, 223			3:1-13	145
		1:13	153, 158	3:1-7	142

Index of Scripture References 315

3:1-3	169	4:21	159		149
3:1	166, 167, 204	4:22-24	144, 161	5:33	163
		4:22	142	6:1-4	165
3:2-13	144	4:24	160, 161	6.1	160
3:2-7	144	4:25-6:10	160	6:2	165
3:2	142	4:25-32	161	6:4	160
3:3	145	4:25	167	6:5-9	165
3:4	145	4:26	163	6:5	160
3:5	146, 148, 168	4:28	163	6:6	169
		4:29	163	6:7	160
3:6	145, 154	4:31	163, 199	6:8	160
3:7-8	169	4:32	154, 163	6:9	160
3:7	204	5:1	162, 163	6:10-20	165, 170, 308
3:8-13	142	5.2	157, 162, 163		
3:8	146, 162. 168			6:10	160, 165
		5:3-5	199	6:12	142, 148, 165
3:9-10	169	5:3-4	161		
3:9	145	5:3	162, 163	6:13-17	142
3:10	142	5:5	149, 161	6:14-17	165
3:11	154, 159, 160	5:6-7	163	6:18	162, 166
		5:8-10	161	6:19	145, 166, 167, 239
3:12	167	5:8	160, 161, 162		
3:14-19	168			6:20	167
3:16	158	5:9	161	6:21-22	138, 144
3:18	162	5:10	160	6:21	160, 204
3:20-21	168	5:15	161, 162	6:23-24	160
3:21	154	5:17	160, 169	6:23	160
4:1-6:24	160	5:19	160	6:24	154, 159, 160
4:1-24	170, 283	5:20	154, 158, 160		
4:1-16	147				
4:1	160, 162, 166, 167	5:21-6:24	304	Phil	15, 84, 93, 151, 178, 185, 245, 269
		5:21-33	301		
4:2	163	5:21	164		
4:4-6	158	5:22-6:9	144, 163, 164, 201		
4:5	160			1:1	188
4.7-16	157	5:22-33	149, 165	1:9	185
4:9-10	157	5:22	160	1:13-14	166
4:9	142	5:23-32	148	1.28	225
4:11	129, 148, 168	5:23	147, 148, 159	2:6-11	185
				2:8	118
4.12	157, 162	5:24	147	2.9-11	41, 232
4:13	154, 159, 162	5.25-27	142, 164	2:15	186
		5:25	147, 157, 163	2:24	207
4:15-16	144			2:25	203
4:15	147, 163	5:27	142, 147, 148, 163	2:30	184
4:16	142, 163			3:3-4	186
4:17-24	160	5.28	163, 164	3:5	21
4:17-18	160	5:29	147	3:12-14	124
4:17	162	5:31	164	3:19-20	186
4:18-19	163	5:32	145, 147,	3:19	185

3:20	148	1:14	144, 192	2:13-14	185
4:7	185	1:15-20	185, 190, 273, 274, 285, 293	2:13	186, 187, 196
4:8	199			2:14	194
4:9	230			2:15	193
4:10-19	184	1:15-17	24	2:16	197
4:18	186	1:15-16	27	2:17	196
4:21-22	189	1:15	192	2:18	181, 186, 193, 208, 308
4:23	188	1:16	192		
		1:17	192		
Col	15, 16, 84, 133-135, 138, 144, 146, 148, 151, 171-208, 236, 244, 245, 246, 252, 254, 255, 257, 259, 260, 261	1:18	147, 187, 191, 192	2:19	144, 147, 187
		1:19	192, 194	2:20	183, 195, 196, 197
		1:20	144, 191, 192, 194	2:21	197
		1:21	198	2:22	197
		1:22	186, 194	2:23	186, 197
		1:23	187, 204, 205	3:1-4:18	185
		1:24-2:5	204	3:1-5	186
		1:24-29	144	3:1-4	187, 196
1-2	185	1:24-25	205	3:1-2	199
1	206	1:24	180, 187, 195, 205, 206	3:1	187, 195, 196
1:1-2	188				
1:1	93, 189, 196, 203			3:2	185
		1:25-26	144	3:3-8	206
1:2	196	1:25	204	3:3	196
1:3-8	179	1:26-27	185, 187	3:4	187, 196
1:3	196, 197, 204, 206	1:26	146	3:5-17	199, 202
		1:27	146, 187, 196	3:5-11	197
1:4	186, 196			3:5	199, 200
1:5	178, 180, 187	1:28	196	3:7	198
		2:1-3	205	3:8	199, 200
1:6	180	2:1	189, 206	3:9-10	144
1:7-8	189	2:2-3	187	3.10	187
1:7	177, 196, 203, 204, 205	2:2	146, 196	3:11	196, 198, 202, 205
		2:5	196		
		2:6	196, 197		
1:9-20	179	2:7	147	3:12-17	199
1:9-10	187, 206	2:8	27, 181, 193, 196	3:12	199, 200
1:9	180, 185, 204			3:13	197
		2:9-15	193, 194	3:15	185, 186, 196
1:10	185, 197, 198	2:9	194		
		2:10	147, 185, 187, 194	3:16	196, 197
1:11-12	206			3:17	193, 196, 197
1.11	144	2:11-13	179, 185		
1:12-20	191, 208, 289, 298	2:11	186, 195, 196	3:18-4:1	144, 163, 201, 202, 267
1:12-13	198	2:12-13	195		
1:13	144, 191, 196	2:12	144, 187, 194, 195	3:18	197, 201, 202

Index of Scripture References

3:20	197, 201		238	5:28	188, 219
3:22-25	201	2:1-3:13	219		
3:22	197, 201	2:2	206	2 Thess	15, 16, 49,
3:23	197	2:7	203, 237,		84, 151,
3:24	187, 196,		238		209-241,
	197, 201	2:9	183, 220,		244, 245,
4:1	197		235		246, 253,
4:3	146, 166,	2:11	238		254, 255,
	196, 239	2:12	185, 222		257, 259,
4:7-9	207	2:13	219, 222		261
4:7-8	138, 144	2:14	147	1-2	216
4:7	197, 204	2:17-20	207	1:1-2:12	215, 219
4:9	135, 186	2:17-18	71	1:1-2	219
4:10-14	177, 189,	2:18	204	1:1	226, 227,
	207	2:19	228, 229		239
4:10-13	186	3:1-2	71	1:2	188, 219,
4:10	186	3:2	20, 204,		226, 227,
4:11	149, 178,		222		230, 239
	187	3:7	222	1:3-12	219, 227
4:12-13	189	3:11-13	219, 220	1:3-10	227
4:12	177, 186,	3:11	230	1:3-4	227
	196	3:13	228	1:3	220, 222
4:13	189	4:1-5:28	219	1:4-7	233
4:15-16	188, 189	4:1-5:22	219	1:4	220, 233
4:15	187, 188	4:1	222	1:5-12	212
4:16	139, 187	4:3-5	149	1:5-10	227
4:17	188, 197,	4:7	220	1:5	149, 220,
	204	4:9	22, 46		222, 224,
4:18	166, 204,	4:10	222		228, 275
	207	4:11	235	1:7	226, 227,
		4:12	164		228, 231,
1 Thess	15, 71, 72,	4:13-5:11	209		240
	84, 93,	4:13-18	221	1:8	226, 227,
	151, 209-	4:14	227, 238		228, 231,
	218, 222,	4:15	228		232, 239
	236, 245,	4:18	222	1:9	226, 227,
	253, 269	5:1-11	212, 221		228
1:1-3:10	222	5:2	229	1:10	231, 239
1:1-10	219	5:5	161	1:11-12	233
1:1	19, 20,	5:8	165	1:11	220, 239
	188, 219	5:9-10	238	1:12	222, 226,
1:2-10	219	5:11	222		227, 230,
1:2	222	5:14	220, 222		231, 232,
1:3	220	5:23-24	219		239
1:4	230	5:23	23, 228,		
1:5	60, 239		230	2:1-17	210, 211,
1:6	234	5:24	230		216
1:9	104	5:25	166, 239	2:1-16	219
1:10	51, 143,	5:26	219	2:1-12	209, 212,
	156, 195	5:27	23		213, 215,
					289

318 Index of Scripture References

2:1-E2	213	3:6-12	238		105, 117, 126
2:1	222, 226, 227, 228, 229, 232, 239, 240	3:6	220, 222, 226, 227, 231, 232, 233, 234, 235, 236, 238, 239	1:3-20	119
				1:3-6	88
				1:3	97
2:2-3	233			1:4-5	99
2:2	212, 213, 214, 221, 223, 224, 226, 227, 237			1.4	99, 105
		3:7-9	222	1:5	105, 122
		3:7	220, 234, 238	1:7	100
				1:8	108
		3:8	235	1:9-10	120, 199
2:3-12	274	3:9	234, 237, 238	1:10	124
2:3	233			1:12-17	108
2:4	104	3:10	212, 222, 233, 235, 238	1:12-16	125
2:8	112, 226, 227, 228, 229			1:12	117, 125
				1:13-16	120, 125
		3:11-12	235	1:13	125
2:12	222	3:11	220, 234	1:14	105, 116, 117, 125, 126
2:13-14	215, 220	3:12	222, 226, 227, 233, 235, 238		
2:13	219, 220, 222, 226, 227, 229			1:15	105, 117, 118, 125
		3:13	222		
2:14	226, 227, 232, 233, 239	3:14-15	233, 235, 236	1:16	117, 125
				1:17	103
		3:14	212, 236, 237	1:18	110
2:15	212, 213, 217, 222, 233, 235, 237, 238			1:19	105, 122
		3:16	219, 226, 227, 230	1:20	97, 128
				2	127
		3:17-18	215	2:2-3	122
2:16-17	220	3 17	204, 210, 212, 213, 214, 215, 217, 219, 223, 236, 237	2:2	122
2:16	219, 226, 227, 230, 232, 239			2:3	104, 117
				2:4-6	248
				2:5-6	118
2:17	222			2:5	117
3:1-18	216, 219			2:7	128, 129
3:1-5	219, 226	3:18	188, 219, 226, 231, 232	2:8-3:13	201
3:1	166, 222, 226, 227, 239			2:8	118
				2:10	110
				2:15	99, 123
3:2	212	1 Tim	15, 84, 88-131, 244, 245, 246, 247, 248, 249, 251, 252, 254, 255, 257, 259, 261	3:1-7	102
3:3	226, 227, 230			3:1	105
				3:2-7	121
3:4	222, 226, 227, 238			3:2	46, 99, 123, 126, 199
3:5	226, 227, 230, 233			3:3	46, 122, 123, 199
3:6-16	215				
3:6-15	233	1.1	104, 117, 126, 129	3:4	123
3:6-13	221, 233, 234			3:8-13	102, 121
		1:2	20, 99,	3:8	121, 122,

Index of Scripture References 319

	123, 199	6:15-16	103, 104,	2:8	126
3:9	105, 122		113, 115,	2:9	97, 98,
3:12	123		117		167
3:13	105, 117	6:15	113	2:10	117
3:14-15	126	6:17-19	123	2:11	105
3:15	126	6:18	122	2:14	113
3:16	104, 115,	6:20	99, 105,	2:17-18	128
	116, 118,		110	2:17	97
	292, 296,	6:21	105, 110	2:18	99, 105
	305			2:19	113
4:1	104, 105	2 Tim	15, 84, 88-	2:22	113
4:2	105		131, 244,	2:24	113
4:3-4	99		245, 246,	3:1-4:8	119
4:3	105		249, 251,	3:2-5	120, 199
4:6	105, 117,		252, 254,	3:2	46
	127, 204		255, 257,	3:5	122
4:7-8	122		259, 261	3:8	105
4:7	99, 105	1:1	117, 129	3:10-11	96, 125,
4:8	112	1:2	20, 117,		126
4:9	105		126	3:10	120, 123,
4:10	104, 117	1:3-18	119		126
4:14	102, 110,	1:3	122	3:11	113, 121
	128	1:5	96	3:12	117
5:1-22	201	1:6-9	124	3:14	127
5:9-16	102	1:6	110, 128	3:15	117
5:9-13	120	1:8	97, 98,	3:16-17	60, 124
5:9-10	121		114, 118,	3:16	99
5:8	105		166	3:17	122
5:10	46	1:9-10	113	4:1-8	116
5:11	117	1:9	114, 117	4:1-2	96
5:13-16	275	1:10	112, 113,	4:1	112, 113,
5:14	105		116, 117		117, 127
5:17-22	102	1:11	128, 129	4:2	126
5:21	117, 127	1:12	105	4:3-4	99
5:23	99, 122	1:13	105, 117,	4:3	124
6:1-2	123		124	4:5	120
6:2-4	124	1:14	104	4:6-22	96, 125
6:2	105	1:15-18	120	4:6-7	120
6:3	116, 117,	1:15	97	4:7	105
	122, 124	1:16-18	96, 113,	4:8	113
6:4-5	120, 199		125	4:9	120
6:5-6	122	1:16-17	97, 98	4:10-11	120
6:6-10	123	1:16	97, 113,	4:10	71, 97,
6:10	105		117		110, 123
6:11	122, 199	1:18	88, 113,	4:12	88
6:12	105, 124		117	4:13	120
6:13	117, 118	2:1	117	4:14	97, 113,
6:14	112, 113,	2:3-13	118		120
	115, 116,	2:3	117, 118	4:17	113
	117	2:7	113	4:18	103, 113

4:19	97		199, 200			28, 31, 34, 270
4:21	97	3.4-5	114			
4 22	110, 113	3:4	104, 117		1 4	26, 40, 306
		3.5-6	114			
Titus	15, 84, 88-	3:5	104		1:5-3:6	30
	131, 244,	3:6	113, 116, 117		1:5-2:4	42
	245, 246,				1:5-14	26, 30
	251, 252,	3:7	126		1:5-13	266
	254, 255,	3:8	105, 127		1:5	26, 33, 35, 39
	257, 259,	3:9	99, 100			
	261	3:10-11	128		1:6	26, 27, 41
1:1-4	94	3 12-15	96, 125		1:7	27
1·1	105, 117, 122, 129	3:12	97		1:8-9	27
		3.13	97		1:8	31, 39
1:2	103, 126	3·15	110		1:10	40
1.3	104, 117				1·13	28, 34, 270
1:4	105, 116, 117, 126	Phlm	15, 49, 84, 93, 138,		2:1-4	23, 28, 31, 43, 44
1:5-9	102, 127		151, 185,			
1:5	88, 97		189, 245, 269		2:1	23
1:6-9	121				2:3	40, 53
1:6	99	1	166, 188		2:5-4:13	42
1 7	199	5	186		2:5-3:6	30
1.8	46, 199	9	204		2:5-18	28, 31
1:9	105, 124	10	135, 169		2:5	22, 29
1·10	100	13	186		2:6-8	28
1:12	120	18-19	184		2:6	39
1.13	105, 109, 124	19	74, 204, 223		2:7	29
					2 9	28, 29, 40
1:14-15	99, 100	22	207		2.10	29, 40, 41
1:14	99	23-24	186		2:11-12	40
2:1-10	201	23	166		2:11	29, 41
2:1	105, 124	25	188		2:12	29, 50
2:2	105, 122				2:13	29
2:4	113, 123	Heb	15, 19-56, 57, 66,		2:14	29
2 8	124		213, 245		2:16	29
2:9-10	123		252, 254,		2:17	29, 31, 39, 41
2:10-14	130. 296		255, 256,			
2·10	104, 117		257, 259,		2:18	31, 40
2:11-14	118, 119		260, 261,		3:1-2	50
2:11-12	114, 124		267, 269		3:1	23, 32, 39, 40, 41, 42, 50
2:12	122					
2:13	103, 112, 113, 116, 117, 126	1-7	281			
		1	32, 36		3:3	41
		1:1-6	54		3:4	27
2:14	112	1:1-4	20, 24, 25		3:5-6	31
2:15	127	1:1-2	25, 26		3:6	25, 35, 39
3:1	95, 122	1:2	35, 39, 41		3:7-4:11	30, 32, 43, 44
3:3-7	130, 296	1:3-4	26			
3:3	120, 121,	1:3	25, 26, 27,		3:7-4:3	23

Index of Scripture References

3:7-11	44	6:20	35, 37, 38, 39, 40, 41	10:11	39, 41
3.7	32			10:12-14	34
3:12	45			10:13	25
3:13	43	7:1-10:18	24	10:16-17	39
3:14	33	7	37	10:16	40
3:15	44	7:1-2	36	10.19-39	24, 43
4:3	44	7.1	55, 282	10:19	40
4:5	44	7.2	37	10:21	41
4:7-10	45	7:3	25, 35, 37, 38, 39	10:23	42
4:7	44			10:25	43, 45
4:9	45	7:4-9	37	10:26-39	23
4:11	23	7.4	35, 36	10:26-31	23, 43, 44
4:12-13	25, 41, 305	7:5	35	10:29	25, 35, 39
		7:7	36	10:30	40, 45
4:14-6:8	42	7.9-10	37	10:31	45
4:14-5:10	32, 35	7:10	36	10:32-35	45
4:14-16	32, 43, 54	7:11	35, 41	10.32	53
4:14	25, 30, 32, 33, 35, 39, 40, 41, 42, 47, 50	7:14	38, 40	10:34	45, 46
		7:15	35, 41	11:1-12:29	42
		7:16	38	11	44
		7:17	25, 29, 41	11:1	51
		7:20-21	38	11.3	287
4:15	32, 39, 41	7:21	40, 41	11:8-12	35
4:16	50	7:22	40, 41	11:17-19	35
5	36	7:26	38, 39, 41	11:36	45
5:1	32, 39	7:27	39	11:39-40	44
5:3	29	7:28	25, 35, 38, 39	12:1-13:17	43
5:5-6	25			12:2-3	50
5:5	33, 34, 35, 39, 41	8	38	12:2	40, 41, 44, 51
		8:1-2	34		
5:6	34, 41	8:1	22, 25, 39, 41	12:3-13	45
5:7-9	54			12:4	45
5.7	33, 308	8:2	40, 41	12:5-8	40
5:8-10	33	8:3-4	53	12:5-6	40
5:8	25, 32, 33, 35, 39	8:3	39	12:14	40, 44, 46
		8:4	41	12:15-17	44
5:9-10	32	8:6	41	12:16-17	23, 43
5:9	41	8:8-11	40	12:24	40, 41
5:10	38, 39, 41	8:13	39	12:25-29	23
5:11-6:20	24, 35	9:4	39	12:26	45
5:11-6:12	43	9:5	22	13:2	46
5:11	22, 43	9:6-7	53	13:3	40, 45
5:14-6:1	45	9:7	29, 39	13:5	46, 53
6:4-8	23, 43, 44	9:11	39, 41	13:6	40
6:6	25, 35, 39	9:15	41	13:7	46, 53
6:9-10:23	42	9:25	39	13.8	39, 50
6:9	22	9:27	45	13.9	45
6:13-20	35	9:28	36, 45	13:11	39
6:13-18	38	10:1-2	53	13:12	40
6:19-20	35	10:10	40	13:13-14	45

13:13	46	1:3-5	151	3 John	84, 269
13:15	42	2:1	199		
13:16	46	2:13-3:8	201	Jude	19, 84, 85
13:17	46	4.3	199	8	199
13:19	22, 54	4:4	199	16	199
13:20-21	23	4:9	46		
13:20	40, 41			Rev	19, 210, 211, 212, 265
13:21	40	2 Pet	84, 85, 269		
13:22-25	22, 54				
13.22	22, 42	1·13	308	1:4-5	80
13:23	20, 49	2:5	128	2·1-3:22	80, 85
13:24	53, 54	3:1	308	9:20	199
				9:21	199
Jas	19, 84, 85, 269	1 John	57, 84	13:3-10	210
		2:28	196	17:8-14	210
3:17	199	3:2	196	21:8	199
				22:15	199
1 Pet	84, 85, 269	2 John	84		

Index of Names

Aeschylus, 122
Aesop, 76
Akiva, R., 268
Aland, K., 60, 85, 87, 139, 273
Albertz, M., 137, 215, 273
Albright, W.J., 74, 273
Aletti, J.-N., 273
Allan, J.A., 273
Andriessen, P., 24, 42, 44, 273
Anton, P., 88, 274
Aristeas, 81, 82
Aristotle, 163
Athanasius, 255
Augustine, 247
Aune, D.E., 87, 299
Aus, R., 216, 274

Bacon, B.W., 137, 274
Bahnsen, W., 211, 274
Bahr, G., 74, 274
Bailey, J.A., 218, 240, 274
Baker, N.L., 274
Balchin, J.F., 190, 274
Balz, H.R., 75, 76, 80, 83, 274
Bardot, D.N., 88, 274
Barrett, C.K., 287
Barth, M., 136, 159, 164, 169, 274
Basilides, 99
Bassin, 49
Bassler, J., 225, 275
Baur, F.C., 90, 133, 172, 210, 211, 271, 275
Becker, J., 283
Beckwith, R., 87, 275
Benoit, P., 137, 176, 275
Best, E., 216, 275
Beyer, K., 96, 276
Black, D.A., 169, 276
Black, M., 293
Blinzer, J., 275

Bornemann, W., 216, 276
Bornkamm, G., 136, 174, 276
Bowen, C.R., 173, 276
Braun, H., 53, 212, 276
Broker, L.O., 276
Brown, R.E., 55, 130, 137, 151, 169, 175, 276, 284
Brox, N., 78, 80, 92, 102, 117, 259, 277
Bruce, F.F., 55, 136, 152, 175, 216, 231, 234, 277
Buchanan, G.W., 24, 53, 54, 277
Bujard, W., 175, 179, 180, 277
Bultmann, R., 31, 59, 135, 174, 277
Burgess, J., 240

Cadbury, H.J., 137, 277
Caesar, Julius, 73
Cambier, J., 153, 277
Cannon, G.E., 176, 200, 207, 278
Casey, J.M., 43, 55, 278
Cerfaux, L., 91, 136, 137, 231, 278
Charles, R.H., 83, 278
Childs, B.S., 55, 175, 249, 278
Church, E.F., 290
Cicero, 71, 73, 74, 78
Clement of Alexandria, 47
Clement of Rome, 48, 52, 53, 98, 132, 199, 201
Collins, R.F., 130, 263, 278
Conzelmann, H., 86, 100, 109, 111, 119, 130, 252, 259, 279
Coutts, J., 152, 279
Crates, 119
Cross, F.L., 279
Cullmann, O., 24, 34, 279
Culpepper, R.A., 86, 169, 279
Cyprian, 81

Dahl, N.A., 152, 279
Dahms, J.V., 279

Dalton, W.J., 87, 279
Daniels, B.L., 301
Dautzenberg, G., 177, 279
Davey, C.N., 31, 287
Day, P., 213, 279
De Boer, M., 263, 280
Deichgraber, R., 24, 143, 280
Demosthenes, 76
Descamps, A., 275
de Wette, W.M.L., 90, 133, 209, 280
Dibelius, M., 100, 109, 111, 119, 130, 137, 175, 180, 215, 216, 280
Diotimus, 81
Dodd, C.H., 69, 93, 136, 280
Donelson, L., 116, 118, 119, 280
Dornier, P., 90, 91, 100, 281
Doty, W.G., 71, 152, 281
Dukes, J., 31, 281
Dunn, J.D.G., 24, 31, 87, 281

Efird, J., 138, 176, 281
Eichhorn, J.G., 89, 173, 281
Ellingworth, P., 281
Epictetus, 200
Epicurus, 81
Erasmus, 133, 141, 281
Estius, Guilielmus, 54, 281
Eusebius, 47, 48, 59, 60, 88, 98, 245, 255, 256
Evans, C.A., 190, 281
Evanson, E., 89, 133, 171, 281
Ewald, H., 172, 176, 282

Fabris, R., 52, 282
Farmer, W.R., 283
Fee, G.D., 91, 282
Fenton, J.C., 87, 282
Feuillet, A., 36, 278, 282
Fiore, B., 111, 119, 130, 282
Fitzmyer, J.A., 55, 276, 282
Francis, F.O., 181, 208, 276, 280, 282, 291
Friedrich, G., 217, 282
Fuller, R., 175, 283
Funk, R., 126, 207, 265, 283

Gachter, P., 54, 283
Gaius, 48
Galen, 76, 79, 86
Garland, D.E., 170, 283
Garrett, E.J., 273

Getty, M.A., 190, 283
Giblet, J., 86, 177, 252, 283
Giblin, C.H., 216, 283
Gnilka, J., 136, 178, 283
Goguel, M., 137, 215, 283
Goodspeed, E.J., 134, 138, 283
Graafen, J., 216, 283
Grasser, E., 44, 284
Grassi, J., 137, 284
Grayston, K., 213, 284
Gregson, R., 215, 284
Gress, T., 290
Grimm, K.L.W., 211, 284
Grotius, H., 215, 284
Gunther, J.G., 138, 284
Guthrie, D., 83, 136, 175, 284

Hanson, A.T., 91, 92, 100, 104, 130, 284
Hanson, P.D., 92, 129, 285
Harrington, W., 137, 175, 285
Harrison, P.N., 91, 174, 285
Harvill, J., 285
Hasler, V., 112, 285
Havener, I., 55, 285
Herdan, G., 213, 284
Héring, J., 52, 54, 285
Herodotus, 76
Heyler, L.R., 190, 285
Hilary, 49
Hilgenfeld, A., 173, 211, 285
Hippocrates, 76, 79
Hitchcock, F.F.M., 74, 285
Hitzig, F., 134, 173, 184, 285
Hobson, D., 174, 286
Hoekman, R.E., 303
Hoekstra, S., 134, 172, 286
Hoffman, T.A., 263, 286
Holland, G.S., 218, 240, 286
Hollmann, G., 212, 286
Holsten, C.K., 211, 286
Holtz, G., 114, 286
Holtzmann, H.J., 90, 134, 152, 173, 184, 211, 212, 286, 287, 307
Homer, 76
Hooker, M.C., 287, 293, 296
Horbury, W., 287
Horton, F.L., 55, 287
Hoskyns, E.C., 31, 287
Howard, F.D., 136, 287
Hugedé, N., 287
Hughes, F.W., 218, 287

Index of Names

Hughes, G., 39, 52, 287
Hughes, P.E., 287
Hulley, K.K., 287
Hultgren, A.J., 274
Hutaff, M D., 55, 288

Ignatius of Antioch, 101, 132
Ishmael, R., 267

Jerome, 49, 79, 81, 86, 256, 288
Jewett, R., 43, 92, 140, 216, 217, 240, 288
John Paul II, Pope, 248, 288
Johnson, L.T., 103, 167, 175, 288
Jones, P.R., 138, 288
Josephus, 53, 58, 60, 68, 76, 200
Jülicher, A., 84, 137, 288

Karris, R.J., 130, 288
Käsemann, E., 30, 135, 147, 152, 169, 191, 288, 289
Kaye, B.N., 240, 289
Keck, L.E., 153, 279, 289
Kehl, N., 289
Kelly, J.N.D., 130, 289
Kenny, A., 91, 289
Kern, F H., 209, 210, 289
Kertelege, K., 289, 294, 301
Kiley, M., 38, 175, 177, 182, 183, 184, 185, 186, 208, 289
Klappert, B., 44, 289
Kleinhaus, A., 295
Klöpper, A., 176, 290
Klostermann, E., 174, 276
Knox, J., 135, 174, 290
Knox, W.L., 135, 138, 290
Koch, K., 87, 290
Koester, H., 71, 137, 217, 290
Krentz, E., 218, 290
Krodel, G., 214, 217, 224, 236, 240, 290
Kuhn, K.G., 143, 290
Kummel, W.G., 106, 137, 143, 179, 274, 291
Kuss, O., 175, 291

Laertius, Diogenes, 81, 122
Landerville, D., 291
Langkammer, H., 137, 291
Laub, F., 217, 291
Lemaire, A., 130, 291
Lightfoot, J.B., 180, 291

Lincoln, A.T., 170, 291
Lindemann, A., 178, 189, 214, 224, 236, 252, 291
Lipsius, R.A., 210, 291
Livingstone, É.A., 299
Loane, M.K., 90, 292
Lohmeyer, E., 175, 292
Lohse, E., 176, 177, 178, 179, 185, 191, 195, 203, 205, 206, 252, 292
Longenecker, R.N., 73, 74, 87, 292
Ludwige, H., 177, 292
Luther, Martin, 19, 52, 292

MacDonald, D.R., 92, 252, 263, 292
Maloney, E.C., 92, 292
Manns, F., 115, 292
Manson, T.W., 215, 292
Manson, W., 46, 293
Marcion, 48, 89, 99, 132, 139, 255, 268
Marshall, I.H., 216, 217, 225, 293
Martin, R.P., 138, 288, 293
Marxsen, W., 152, 213, 214, 217, 218, 236, 293
Masson, C., 174, 213, 293
Mayerhoff, E., 171, 172, 174, 180, 184, 293
McCown, W., 190, 293
McCullough, J.C., 52, 56, 293
McDonald, H.D., 176, 294
McGehee, M., 56, 294
McLeman, J., 175, 296
McNeile, A.H., 137, 294
Meade, D.G., 62, 63, 64, 65, 66, 87, 90, 92, 137, 150, 294
Mealand, D.L., 24, 294
Meeks, W.A., 175, 208, 276, 280, 282, 291
Mees, M, 48, 294
Megivern, J.J., 294
Meier, J.P., 25, 55, 276, 294
Merklein, H., 147, 177, 178, 294
Metzger, B.M., 76, 79, 87, 294
Michaelis, W., 215, 295
Michaelson, S., 214, 296
Michel, O., 25, 295
Miller, A., 257, 295
Minear, P., 30, 295
Mitton, C.L., 135, 138, 295
Moda, A., 295
Moffatt, J., 31, 134, 295
Montagni, F., 295

Moore, A L., 216, 295
Moore, M.S., 170, 295
Morgan, R., 295
Morgenthaler, R., 95, 142, 295
Morris, L , 216, 296
Morton, A.Q., 174, 214, 296
Mott, S.C., 122, 130, 296
Moule, C.F.D., 91, 175, 195, 296
Moulton, J.H., 138, 296
Mullins, T.Y., 208, 296
Muratori, L.A., 269
Murphy, R.E., 276
Murphy-O'Connor, J., 115, 137, 291, 296, 297
Mussner, F., 143, 296

Nestle, E., 139
Neyrey, J.H , 158, 170, 297
Nickle, K.F., 183, 297
Nielsen, C.M., 178, 181, 297

O'Brien, P. I., 151, 170, 176, 187, 195, 297
O'Neill, J., 208, 297
Oberlinner, L., 112, 297
Ochel, W., 143, 297
Origen, 47, 48, 52, 256
Orosius, 189
Osswald, E , 83, 297

Paley, W., 133, 297
Pantaenus, 47
Papias, 59, 60
Parker, H.M., 43, 297
Patzia, A., 137, 138, 263, 298
Pax, E., 112, 298
Penny, D.N., 298
Percy, E., 175, 298
Pesch, R., 217, 298
Pfammatter, J., 137, 178, 298
Pfleiderer, O., 173, 211, 298
Philo, 22, 51, 58, 120, 200, 303, 304, 307
Plato, 78, 122
Pliny, 73
Plutarch, 71, 200
Pokorný, P., 137, 298
Polhill, J.B., 136, 298
Pollard, T.E., 208, 298
Polycarp, 132, 199, 201
Porphyry, 78
Prior, M., 91, 298

Pythagoras, 76, 78

Quinn, J.D , 91, 103, 299
Quintillian, 73

Reese, J.M., 216, 241, 299
Renan, E., 138, 299
Renner, F., 299
Rice, G.E., 42, 299
Richards, K.H., 240, 241, 286, 289, 302
Rigaux, B., 216, 231, 299
Rissi, M., 299
Rist, M., 75, 87, 92, 175, 299
Robert, A., 278
Robinson, J.A.T., 53, 96, 103, 299
Robinson, H.W., 83, 300
Roetzel, C.J., 217, 300
Rogers, P.V., 131, 138, 170, 175, 176, 300
Rohde, J., 102, 300
Roller, O., 74, 91, 300
Rowland, C., 181, 300
Rowston, D.J., 138, 170, 288, 300
Russell, D.S., 83, 300

Sabourin, L., 25, 300
Sahlin, H., 195, 300
Sampley, J P., 240, 290, 301
Sand, A., 177, 301
Sand, Georges, 75
Sanders, E.P., 185, 208, 301
Sanders, J.A., 63, 301
Sanders, J.T., 24, 301
Saunders, E W., 175, 301
Sausen, F., 281
Schelkle, K.H., 137, 301
Schenk, W., 152, 178, 301
Schenke, H.-M., 177, 217, 252, 301, 302
Schleiermacher, F., 89, 94, 138, 302
Schlier, H., 135, 136, 152, 302
Schmidt, D., 218, 241, 302
Schmidt, J.E.C , 89, 209, 302
Schmidt, K.L., 59, 302
Schmiedl, P.W., 211, 303
Schmithals, W., 215, 302
Schnackenburg, R., 137, 303
Schott, H A., 91, 303
Schräder, K., 210, 303
Schreiner, J., 279
Schwartz, E., 128, 303
Schweizer, E., 176, 178, 194, 215, 303

Index of Names   327

Scott, E.F., 31, 303
Scott, R., 216, 303
Seneca, 200
Senior, D., 176, 208, 303
Shakespeare, W., 26
Sint, J., 75, 76, 304
Socrates, 119
Sowers, S.G., 52, 304
Speyer, W., 75, 76, 304
Spicq, C., 45, 52, 114, 129, 234, 304
Spitta, F., 211, 304
Stagg, F., 304
Steinmetz, F.-J., 174, 304
Stendahl, K., 86, 304
Stenger, W., 92, 118, 305
Stowers, S.K., 87, 305
Strachan, R.H., 31, 305
Strobel, A, 91, 305
Suetonius, 79
Suggs, M.J., 301
Swain, L., 137, 170, 305
Swetnam, J., 41, 305
Synge, F., 174, 305

Tacitus, 68, 189
Talbert, C.H., 299
Tatian, 89
Tenney, M C., 87, 292
Tertullian, 49, 52, 78, 89
Theissen, G., 48, 305
Themistocles, 80
Thompson, G.H.P., 138, 305
Thucydides, 76
Thurston, R., 215, 305
Torrey, C.C., 54, 305
Towner, P.H., 131, 305
Trilling, W., 214, 217, 236, 305, 306
Trummer, P., 116, 137, 306
Twain, Mark, 75

Ulrichsen, J.H., 40, 306
Usteri, L., 133, 306

Valentinus, 99
Van Bruggen, J., 90, 306
Vanhoye, A., 51, 54, 306
van Manen, W.C., 211, 306
Van Roon, A., 136, 151, 170, 258, 306
Vardeman, E.J., 273
Vawter, B., 208, 306
Verner, D.C., 131, 307
Vielhauer, P., 217, 307
von Campenhausen, H., 92, 109, 307
von Dobschütz, E., 216, 307
von Harnack, A, 215, 285
von Soden, H., 211, 307
von Weizsäcker, K., 211, 307

Wake, W., 174, 307
Weiss, H., 208, 307
Weiss, J., 134, 174, 215, 307
Weisse, C., 173, 184, 307
White, J.L., 87, 93, 307
White, R.E.O., 131, 307
Wild, R.A., 165, 166, 170, 308
Wilder, A., 30, 308
Williams, C.S.C., 137, 294
Williamson, R., 52, 308
Wilson, S G , 91, 100, 287, 293, 296, 308
Windisch, H., 111, 308
Woschitz, K.M , 42, 308
Wrede, W., 54, 212, 216, 217, 218, 308
Wrzol, J., 216, 308

Yates, R., 181, 207, 308

Zahn, T., 52, 308
Zmijezski, J., 93, 308